Travels Through the Book of Acts

Volume 1, Acts 1–15

"In this thought-provoking book, Jim Duddleston presents a deeply personal reading of Acts 1–15 that integrates a close reading of the narrative with personal experiences from traveling the same routes the risen Lord's apostles did . . . Whether you share Duddleston's approach to Acts or his personal witness to the relevance of its narrative message for today's evangelical congregations, his reading provides a faithful example of a devotional yet critically informed commentary of one of scripture's most important narratives."

—**ROBERT W. WALL**, The Paul T. Wall Chair Emeritus of Scripture, Seattle Pacific University and Seminary

"What a captivating tour of both the text and terrain of the Book of Acts! With a playful mix of images, personal accounts, and well-studied commentary, Duddleston immerses his readers in the world of Acts, inviting us to join the apostles' journey, not only as students of the Bible but as followers of Jesus and Spirit-filled participants in God's mission."

—**CHRIS CURRIE**, Lead Pastor, Resurrection Philadelphia

"If your desire is to mine the Books of Acts for its richness but you are not an academic, journey along with Jim Duddleston as he and his companions walk through the Books of Acts and the Middle East in the footsteps of Luke and the Apostles. In a very personal and winsome manner this travelogue will open your eyes to those ancient lands as well as to the dynamic spiritual truths embedded within the Book of Acts, truths that are intended to form and transform our lives."

—**PATRICK KRAYER**, Mentor for Doctor of Global Leadership Cohort, Fuller Theological Seminary

"As the title of Jim Duddleston's book suggests, this is a beautiful invitation to become a personal traveler through the book of Acts. . . . This book is an invitation to genuinely explore two significant questions: What is the Church and its purpose? What is the gospel? The intermingling of personal travel experiences with a thoughtful study of Acts means that the reader sometimes laughs out loud while also being deeply moved by the invitation to behold what is beautiful about God's Kingdom. Duddeston successfully accomplishes this with winsome writing, good storytelling, and the understanding of the power of place to illuminate the biblical text and to evoke empathy with the historical characters in Acts."

—**Cyndi Parker**, Director of Education and Conversation, Resurrection Philadelphia

Travels Through the Book of Acts

Volume 1, Acts 1–15

Exploring the Message and World of Acts

JIM DUDDLESTON

WIPF & STOCK · Eugene, Oregon

TRAVELS THROUGH THE BOOK OF ACTS, VOLUME 1, ACTS 1–15
Exploring the Message and World of Acts

Copyright © 2025 Jim Duddleston. All rights reserved. Except for brief quotations in critical publications or reviews, no part of this book may be reproduced in any manner without prior written permission from the publisher. Write: Permissions, Wipf and Stock Publishers, 199 W. 8th Ave., Suite 3, Eugene, OR 97401.

Wipf & Stock
An Imprint of Wipf and Stock Publishers
199 W. 8th Ave., Suite 3
Eugene, OR 97401

www.wipfandstock.com

PAPERBACK ISBN: 979-8-3852-5364-7
HARDCOVER ISBN: 979-8-3852-5365-4
EBOOK ISBN: 979-8-3852-5366-1

VERSION NUMBER 09/22/25

The Scripture quotations contained herein are from the New Revised Standard Version Bible, copyright © 1989, Division of Christian Education of the National Council of Churches of Christ in the U.S.A. Used by permission. All rights reserved.

Contents

List of Topics of Special Interest | vii
List of Figures | viii
Acknowledgements | ix

Introduction | 1
1   Instructions About the Kingdom (Acts 1:1–5) | 11
2   The Ascension (Acts 1:6–11) | 15
3   Preparing for Pentecost (Acts 1:12–26) | 23
4   Pentecost (Acts 2:1–21) | 29
5   Peter Explains Pentecost (Acts 2:22–36) | 39
6   Responding to the Gospel (Acts 2:37–41) | 52
7   The Community God Created (Acts 2:42–47) | 57
8   The Crippled Beggar (Acts 3:1–10) | 65
9   Peter's Explanation of the Power (Acts 3:11–26) | 71
10 Peter and John Before the Council (Acts 4:1–22) | 76
11 A Prayer for Boldness (Acts 4:23–31) | 83
12 The Community and Their Possessions (Acts 4:32–37) | 89
13 A Deceit Detected (Acts 5:1–11) | 93
14 Extraordinary Signs (Acts 5:12–16) | 97
15 The Apostles Are Persecuted (Acts 5:17–42) | 103
16 Stephen and His Companions (Acts 6:1–7) | 108
17 Stephen Is Arrested (Acts 6:8–15) | 114
18 Stephen's Speech (Acts 7:1–53) | 121

19 The Stoning of Stephen (Acts 7:54—8:1) | 129
20 Driven from Jerusalem (Acts 8:1–4) | 136
21 Philip in Samaria (Acts 8:5–25) | 142
22 Philip and the Eunuch (Acts 8:26–40) | 153
23 Saul's Change of Direction (Acts 9:1–31) | 163
24 Peter to Lydda and Joppa (Acts 9:32–43) | 173
25 Peter and Cornelius (Acts 10:1–33) | 182
26 Gentiles Receive the Gospel (Acts 10:34—11:18) | 192
27 The Gospel Reaches Antioch Syria (Acts 11:19–30) | 203
28 Herod Is Humbled (Acts 12:1–25) | 212
29 From Antioch to Cyprus (Acts 13:1–12) | 218
30 Paul's Gospel Sermon in Antioch Pisidia (Acts 13:13–41) | 232
31 The Response in Antioch (Acts 13:42–52) | 244
32 To Iconium, Lystra, and Derbe (Acts 14:1–20) | 248
33 The Return to Antioch Syria (Acts 14:21–28) | 259
34 Debate and a Decision About the Gentiles (Acts 15:1–21) | 267
35 The Gospel and the Story of the Bible | 281

Appendix 1: The Danger of Mixing Culture with the Gospel | 295
Appendix 2: Paul, the Artisan, Working with Leather | 298
Bibliography | 301

List of Topics of Special Interest

A Focus on Jerusalem | 21
A Focus on the Presence of God | 31
A Focus on Stages of the Kingdom's Coming | 50
A Focus on the Temple Mount | 62
A Focus on the Disciples and the Temple | 74
A Focus on the Filling of the Spirit | 86
A Focus on Signs and Wonders | 100
A Focus on Saul's Home in Tarsus | 133
A Focus on Phrases for the Gospel | 147
A Focus on the Mind and Motives of Saul: Why Was He So Violent? | 161
A Focus on Saul's Silent Years | 170
A Focus on Caesarea | 178
A Focus on the Mindset of Peter and the Jerusalem Disciples | 190
A Focus on Antioch Syria | 199
A Focus on House Gatherings | 207
A Focus on Travel by Ship | 222
A Focus on Travel by Land in the Roman Empire | 227
A Focus on Antioch Pisidia | 234
A Focus on the Synagogues | 240
A Focus on Roman Religion | 255
A Focus on the Background to the Jerusalem Debate | 269

List of Figures

Figure 1: Jim and Esuga at the Airport | x
Figure 2: Chapel of the Ascension | 16
Figure 3: Temple Layout | 64
Figure 4: Map of First-Century Israel | 143
Figure 5: Travels of Peter | 174
Figure 6: Cilician Gates | 205
Figure 7: Paul's First Missionary Journey | 224
Figure 8: Shop Area in Antioch Pisidia | 237
Figure 9: Aerial View of Perga | 260

Acknowledgements

MOST OF THIS BOOK stems from years of personal study, interaction with leading commentaries on Acts, and my passion for mission. Yet a few friends have contributed to it with important insights.

Esuga Abaya was the best of all travel companions, as together we searched out the places mentioned in the early chapters of Acts. Esuga was always patient, helpful, and generous. Paul would have been grateful to have had him along in his travels.

I am grateful to Pat Krayer for pointing out the many barriers the gospel must cross in Acts and how God raises up Spirit-filled, culturally sensitive leaders to cross those barriers to communicate the gospel without unnecessary cultural baggage.

Cyndi Parker's undying passion for understanding place and travel in the biblical narrative contributed to my fascination for traveling to the places in Acts where the events occurred to see them as first-century disciples did.

Steve Taylor's emphasis on reading the Bible as an unfolding revelation of God rather than a flat, timeless treatise on theology helped me to see that in Acts, even the apostles did not yet understand the obsoletion of the Jerusalem temple when God came to dwell in his people as his temple at Pentecost.

Many thanks to my pastor, Chris Currie, for suggesting I break the book down into short chapters with engaging introductions and that I engage with struggles the reader may have with difficult passages but not avoid comments that may make them uncomfortable.

I am very thankful for Sue Baker's keen editorial skills and encouragement to get the message of this book out. Sue put her heart into her work and went way beyond her duties as an editor. Thanks again, Sue.

Observing my wife, Eeva's, skill in living and speaking the gospel with bold wisdom across cultures always inspires me. I am grateful for her as my wife and to partner with her in the gospel.

Most of all, I am thankful to God, my Father, and to my Lord Jesus Christ, who gave me a passion for studying and meditating on the Scriptures. May they be pleased with what I have written and gracious where I have misunderstood. Above all, I pray this book will inspire many to read Acts and continue its story.

Figure 1: Jim and Esuga. Source: author's personal photo.

Introduction

A FRIEND ONCE TOLD me he read Romans each time he felt the need to awaken his spirit to the living God. For me, it has always been the book of Acts, for in Acts, I read of the wind of God filling a house of prayer and sweeping out to the streets of Jerusalem. I read of small Spirit-filled communities filled with joy and praise to God. I read of Spirit-filled witness, Spirit-filled healing, and Spirit-filled teaching.

The Spirit of God is everywhere in Acts, awakening us to life with God. Therefore, biblical scholars say the age of the Spirit began at Pentecost, for that was when God came to once again dwell on earth in and among his people. God's presence through his Spirit is everywhere in Acts, and the Lord Jesus is present everywhere through the Spirit, empowering his disciples to witness, unity, and love.

The Spirit leads, falls upon, fills, and is poured out like a mighty river into hearts, giving a new intimacy, a new love, and a deeper joy in God (Rom 5:5). I have spent seven years studying and meditating on Acts, and my spirit has been kept alive to God. Acts invites us to deeper intimacy with God and to be witnesses of what we taste and see. Join me now on our personal journey through Acts, and expect the Spirit of God to lead you into deeper intimacy with God and fruitful witness of his mighty works.

Acts is the account of how God has raised Jesus from the dead and exalted him as Lord so that the nations would know him. Through the Spirit, the word of God spreads from Jerusalem to the nations. Acts ends with Paul under house arrest in Rome, still sharing the gospel. By this open-ended ending, Luke invites his readers to continue the story of Acts in their neighborhoods and across other cultures.

Acts and this book are about travel. "Paul, both in Acts and in his letters, was nothing if not a traveler." His travels in Acts alone, mostly by foot, covered at least twelve thousand miles.[1] But travel in Acts is not as predictable as driving our interstate highways in America, and we are often surprised by the people God chooses to take the gospel to new regions.

MY JOURNEY THROUGH ACTS

This book is about three journeys: an explanation of the message of Acts itself, an invitation to practice what we learn in Acts, and lastly, my travels to the places where the gospel went in Acts with my friend Esuga and later with two of my daughters, Sonja and Daniela.

Understanding the nature of travel in Israel and then into the Roman Empire helps us visualize the journeys the gospel takes us in Acts. While not every Jewish person had visited Jerusalem to worship at the temple, they could envision it from friends who had. While not everyone in the Roman Empire had traveled to Antioch, Ephesus, or Rome, most knew what life was like in the cities and what sailing or traveling the Roman roads was like to get to those places. When they read Acts, they had mental images of what they read. Once I realized this, I became preoccupied not only with traveling to the places in Acts to understand their topography and study their ruins but also with reading in-depth about what it was like to walk the Roman roads Paul walked and to sail on the ships on which he sailed. A better understanding of history, travel, and culture in Acts makes the stories come alive with new insights. At times we can read between the lines when we learn what Luke assumed his first-century readers knew.

You will notice that at times I speculate on what Peter and Paul may have been feeling and thinking. For example, God's Spirit directed Paul and Barnabas to leave Antioch for the first mission journey ever to gentiles (Acts 13:1–3). On that journey Paul was nearly stoned to death and then, with Barnabas, spent a week walking through the treacherous central mountains of Turkey, encountering bandits and raging rivers. Yet on this journey they witnessed the Spirit opening the hearts of gentiles to the gospel all along the way. When they then safely sailed along the coastline of modern Turkey back to Antioch, what do you think went through their hearts and minds (Acts 14:26)?

---

1. Keener, *Acts, Vol. 1*, 582.

READING ACTS

Acts describes how a small community of Jewish disciples from the backwater province of Israel grew until it stretched all the way to Rome. The first all-Jewish disciples are not naturally inclined to take the gospel to Samaritans and gentiles. But God, working through the risen Lord Jesus and the Spirit, keeps the gospel, ever moving outward, *overcoming religious and cultural barriers* so that the nations might know him.

The Acts of the Risen Lord or the Acts of the Spirit are more appropriate titles for Acts than the Acts of the Apostles. Through the Spirit the Lord chooses, fills, and sends his messengers. It is beautiful to observe the mystery of the three persons of the Trinity working in beautiful harmony together in Acts.

In Luke's Gospel there is continual movement forward from the beginning to the climax with the death and resurrection of Jesus at the end. But in Acts, the major event comes at the beginning, with Pentecost pushing events forward from Jerusalem to the ends of the earth, even up to our day and beyond. One reads in anticipation of where the Spirit will lead next and what he will do. This makes Acts exciting reading.

Acts is an important book in the Bible, tying it all together. It builds on what the Gospels began by showing the fulfillment of Old Testament promises in Christ. Acts brings the promises of the Old Testament to a climax with Israel's promised Messiah exalted as Lord, who then sends the Spirit to pour out the blessing of salvation on the people of God. And Acts provides the background for reading, especially Paul's letters.

Be alert especially to the continuity between Luke's Gospel and Acts. Just as Jesus received the Spirit at his baptism, enabling him to enact and proclaim the good news of God's kingdom, so the disciples receive the Spirit at Pentecost, empowering them to follow in Jesus' footsteps to live and proclaim the good news. And just as Jesus must suffer to fulfill God's purposes for him, so must the disciples suffer.

Acts is narrative literature building on the history of the Old Testament. It shows the fulfillment of God's purposes in creating humanity and in choosing Israel to make him known among the nations. It shows how all God's purposes are fulfilled in Christ.

As narrative literature, Acts is *a selective history* of the very beginnings of the early church (from AD 33–62). Because it is a selective account, it is always helpful to ask why Luke includes the events he does. A question I often ask myself when I read narrative literature in the Bible is, What is the significance of this particular story or event, and why is it recorded here? Of course, the events happened, but since Luke does not record everything that happened, we can learn what he wants to emphasize by what he records.

We can read Acts, too, with attention to what Luke *repeats* for the sake of emphasis. Notice, for example, the repetition of the disciples always being together in prayer, their generous sharing of possessions as central to being a disciple, the many signs and wonders in Acts drawing people's attention to the gospel, and the many sermons in Acts emphasizing what we are to believe, live, and share.

Notice, also, *parallels* to which Luke draws attention, not only from the life of Jesus and the disciples but also between Peter's ministry and Paul's. We are to consider the significance of the parallels.

Luke also draws our attention to important events by *the amount of space* he gives them. The day of Pentecost in Acts 2, Peter's witness to the first gentile community in Acts 10 and 11, and the Jerusalem Council in Acts 15 are the clearest examples.

We will also see how Luke uses *other literary techniques,* such as summaries after major events, contrasts between people, and climaxes to a story, to make an emphasis.

Because Luke writes history—what happened and not necessarily what and how we are to practice what happened—we have the challenge of applying Acts. For example, Luke repeats that the Spirit gave the disciples boldness to witness of Jesus. I read this as an encouragement for us to grow in speaking about Jesus. But in Israel all the Jews shared the same story and worldview. What would bold witness look like in our diverse culture?

THE TIMES

Outwardly, not much had changed in Jerusalem since Jesus had been recently crucified and raised from the dead. The same leaders of Israel who turned Jesus over to be crucified feel safe and satisfied that they have rid themselves of a messianic pretender who threatened their power over the people. But their assurance is short-lived, for the apostles (some of whom the leaders recognized) soon began to spread the news all over Jerusalem that God had raised Jesus from the dead.

The hundred-some disciples who followed Jesus from Galilee to Jerusalem have been told to stay in Jerusalem and wait for the Spirit to come upon them. So, they huddled together in a house, praying and waiting with much anticipation.

As I reflected on the magnitude of the mission Jesus gave the twelve apostles—farmers, fishermen, and tax collectors from the rural province of Galilee—to take the gospel to the ends of the earth, I asked myself how they would ever accomplish the mission. In Luke's Gospel we read how spiritually dull and self-focused they could be. And while they are saturated with the Jewish Scriptures and the teachings of Jesus, they lacked a formal education from the scholars of Jerusalem and spoke Aramaic with a thick Galilean accent.

How does the gospel cross so many cultural barriers so that three hundred years later over half the Roman Empire belonged to the Jesus movement? These questions are part of what makes the study of Acts and the years after so stimulating.

READING THIS BOOK

This book is not a verse-by-verse commentary but an in-depth explanation of the message of each passage. Though I have carefully read thousands of pages on Acts and worked hard to arrive at my own interpretation, I seek to write in a more conversational, personal style with an emphasis on the relevance of Acts today.

Each chapter begins with an introduction, often with insights from my travels to places in Acts, followed by comments on the meaning and relevance of the passage. I have included points of special interest (for example, "A Focus on Travel by Land in the Roman Empire") that illuminate the times, places, and travel in Acts.

I encourage you to first read through each passage, underlining, taking a few notes, and asking questions that come to mind before you read what I have written. This will help you to better evaluate what I say and create interest in the passage. It is even more helpful if you meet each week with a friend or two to interact on what the Lord shows you.

MY BACKGROUND AND POINT OF VIEW

As much as I have tried to interpret Acts objectively, to write what it says and not what I would like it to say, I recognize that we all come to the Bible with our personal history that can color our interpretations. My hope is that my background has not overly influenced my interpretation of Acts, but I do know it has *influenced much of what I chose to emphasize in Acts*. So, I add a word about myself so that you will better understand why I emphasize what I do.

After seminary I taught the New Testament in a seminary and a Bible college in Sweden for fifteen years before then moving back to the States to serve as a pastor of spiritual formation and missions in several large churches. Then fifteen years ago my wife and I moved to Philadelphia, near the University of Pennsylvania, to welcome students from the Middle East to live with us. We have sought to show them the love of God shown in Christ as we engage in respectful conversation with them of God's love. This, along with my twenty-two years in Sweden, has helped me think through cultural barriers we must cross in communicating the gospel.

In my middle years of ministry, when I returned from Sweden to work as an associate pastor in several churches, two crucial questions began to consume my thinking. *The first question*: What is the church and what are its purposes? I was troubled by how many churches focused so much of their time and resources on attracting people to their Sunday services. So, I studied the New Testament and read books to better understand the functions of the church.

After much study I came to believe the church is primarily *a missional community*. That is, the church at its best is a small community of believers who know and care for each other and who build each other up in Christlikeness *to together live out God's missional purposes* in the world. Instead of attracting people to services and events at the church building, the church as a missional community seeks creative ways to live and communicate the gospel in its neighborhoods.

At this time, as a missions pastor in a large attractional church, I remember attaching to the end of all emails, "Jesus left the building and I'm out looking for him to see what he is doing."

I believe we see the church as a missional community in Acts, so I emphasize this, and I hope that this book will encourage those who are leaving the organized church to find ways to gather as small communities and live as Jesus lived in the world. From Alan Hirsch, I learned that to be the church God intends, we must start with Jesus, to learn how he was in the world. Only then can we become a community on the mission he began.[2]

---

2. See Frost and Hirsch, *Shape of Things*.

The second question that consumed my thinking for several years was: *What is the gospel?* What is the message we are to believe and live by? At this time, I remember reading through Luke's Gospel and was surprised when I read why Jesus said God had sent him. He said, "I must proclaim the good news of the kingdom of God to other cities also; *for I was sent for this purpose*" (Luke 4:43).

I was sixty years old but had to admit that I did not know what Jesus meant when he proclaimed the kingdom of God as the gospel.

Because of my background I read into Jesus' proclamation of the kingdom of God that our justification is by faith or how we can know Jesus as our personal Savior. While we treasure Jesus as our personal Savior and know that we are justified before God by his death, this seemed to limit what Jesus was proclaiming, and what we later read in Acts, about the gospel.

I came to see that because we have a narrow view of the gospel, we have a narrow view of what it means to be the church. First, we must understand what one author calls "the full, robust gospel" of Jesus and the apostles and then learn how to live it as the church.

You will see that I also emphasize the gospel sermons in Acts so that we can better understand the content of the gospel and how to live it out in our troubled world. We first read of the full content of the gospel in Acts 2 when Peter preaches it on the day of Pentecost. Then there are many more gospel sermons in Acts by Peter and Paul that communicate the same message Peter first gave at Pentecost.

With time I came to believe that a limited understanding of the gospel, which leads to a limited view of the church's mission, indicates reasons for many of the problems with evangelical Christianity in America. Perhaps by reading Acts carefully, prayerfully, we, too, will see the wind of God sweeping through our neighborhoods out to the nations as it did in Acts.

Well, that's a bit about my background and how it influenced not my interpretation but what I emphasize in Acts. I hope you will read on and that the Spirit will fill you and lead you. But if you get upset now and then, please remember that I warned you about what I emphasize because of my passion for the church on a mission.

THE STRUCTURE OF ACTS

Since Luke organizes his narrative according to the geographic expansion of the gospel, it is easy to follow, but in case you find yourself lost on the journey, you can turn back here to find your way forward.

- Introduction (1:1–14)
- The Word Goes Out in Jerusalem (1:15—6:7)
- The Word Goes Out from Jerusalem (6:8—9:31)
- The Word Advances in Judea and Syria (9:32—12:25)
- The Word Goes to Cyprus and Asia Minor (13:1—16:5)
- The Word Goes to Europe (16:6—18:22)
- The Word in Ephesus: Climax of Paul's Mission as a Free Man (18:23—20:38)
- Paul's Final Journey: To Jerusalem and Rome (21:1—28:31)[3]

I write only on Acts 1–15. But what you learn in these chapters will enable you to continue with the rest of Acts. For further resources, please review the commentaries contained in the bibliography at the end of this book.

TRAVELS WITH ESUGA

For three years Esuga and I met with two other men every Friday morning at a coffee shop in central Philadelphia to talk about our lives, discuss a chapter we had read from Luke's Gospel and then Acts, and encouraged each other to live out our faith.

Esuga practiced law in Philadelphia, was newly married, and was eager to grow in his faith. When I asked him if he would like to join me to visit the places we had read about in Acts, he was ready to go—once he checked with his wife! We agreed that the purposes of our trip were to explore the places mentioned in Acts 1–15, discuss the significance of what happened at them, encourage each other in our walk with the Lord, have Esuga keep me out of trouble, and generally have a good time. I can now say with thanks that these purposes were achieved, except for the few times I got in trouble when I traveled alone without Esuga's help.

---

3. Peterson, *Acts of the Apostles*, 35–36.

INTRODUCTION

We flew out of New York with a layover in Istanbul before landing in Tel Aviv. We located a shuttle ("*sherut*") outside the Tel Aviv airport and took it from the coast into the Judean mountains to Jerusalem. We were dropped off at the Damascus Gate, the main entrance to the northern section of Old Jerusalem. Our lodging for the week was nearby in the Muslim Quarter. Leaving the shuttle, we swung our backpacks onto our backs and then placed our day packs on our chests. In less than a minute we walked through the gate and planted our feet in Old Jerusalem. At once, we heard many languages of the world as we maneuvered through the narrow, crowded streets with shopkeepers on each side welcoming us to stop and examine their wares.

Esuga led the way in search of our hostel and home for the week. As we walked the streets packed with midday shoppers, the jetlag and fatigue from travel suddenly hit me; it was hot, and my packs were heavy. A bit careless in the crowd, my backpack bumped against a middle-aged Palestinian woman who, understandably, looked at me with displeasure. I cast an apologetic look and determined to be more careful. Stay in your lane, Jim, and you'll be all right.

Ten minutes later we checked into our hostel, Ecce Homo, which means "behold the man" in Greek. The hostel is adjacent to the northwest corner of the Temple Mount, where the Antonio once stood, a Roman fortress which towered over the Temple Mount with Roman soldiers who were alert for any signs of rebellion by the Jews. From here it is thought by some that Pilate sentenced Jesus to be crucified (thus the name Ecce Homo) to then carry his cross through the streets of Jerusalem to be crucified outside the city walls. The Via Dolorosa, the way some believe Jesus carried his cross, passed the entrance to our hostel. (It is more likely, however, that Jesus was tried before Pilate at Herod's Palace, from which he then carried his cross north outside the city walls to be crucified.)

We climbed two flights of stairs to the roof of the hostel, where we had a good view of the Temple Mount. Winding our way back to our room, we found it made of white concrete walls containing ten boxes, as they were called—one for each pilgrim. I had been assigned Box 230, beside Esuga in Box 231.

Each box was a simple six-by-nine-foot cubicle with a bed and a wardrobe. A piece of plywood extended from the floor to three feet short of the ceiling, separating my box from Esuga's. In such a small, open space, I was concerned I would disturb him at night with my snoring and coughing, but as it turned out, it was he who would keep me awake with his snoring, sleeping so soundly that he refused to be wakened.

At the foot of my bed hung a polyester curtain with a jacquard finish. The curtain, not a door, separated me from any pilgrim who might sleep across the hall from me. (As it turned out, Esuga and I were the only pilgrims occupying boxes in the room for the entire week.)

In addition to the bed and wardrobe, each box had a sink, an extra blanket for cold nights, and a small shelf, where I placed my books, maps, toiletries, and coins. An end table and a lamp attached to the wall above the bunk completed our plain but clean box. I felt like a pilgrim.

Esuga's box was identical to mine, except that he kept his much tidier. While I did hang my clothes in the wardrobe, my toiletries, coins, and maps were scattered across the shelf and often spilled on the floor beside my bunk.

I carried a nasty cold with me over the Atlantic to Israel. I mention this because of how it affected much of my journey. Every night after thirty minutes of sleep, I woke up with a persistent cough and was forced to search in the dark for the cough drops scattered on the shelf beside me. After taking one, I elevated my head on the extra blanket and pillow but found no relief. Frustrated, I got up and paced the thirty-foot hallway that separated the five boxes on one side from those on the other. It was night and too cold to go out on the roof outside our room, so I paced, slept an hour, woke up to a cough, paced, and jealously listened to Esuga snore. Finally, I slept soundly around three in the morning.

Each morning we woke up to pigeons cooing on the roof above us. They were later followed by the crow of a rooster (but not three times by my count) and finally by the Muslim call to prayer from the minaret at the corner of the Temple Mount just south of us. As I was able to fall back asleep, I came to enjoy these early morning calls to wake up.

I came to love my box. It was my home for the week, my place to retreat for much needed rest after hours of trekking through Old Jerusalem in the crowds and heat each day. It was close to the events we wanted to explore. We were two in a long line of pilgrims who stayed at Ecce Homo during the past one hundred and fifty years. Esuga said it reminded him of his dorm room from boarding school in Nigeria, with its simplicity and inherent spirituality. Sometimes Esuga used cool phrases like "inherent spirituality," but I wasn't always sure what he meant and didn't ask.

Now you know our base of operations. Enjoy your treks with us in and around Old Jerusalem.

1

Instructions About the Kingdom
(Acts 1:1–5)

YEARS EARLIER, WHEN I finished writing a book on the Gospel of Luke, I noted several unresolved questions at the end of the Gospel that leave one with a sense of suspense if you do not already know what would happen. Since we know what happened after the death and resurrection of Jesus, we can tend to miss the suspense of readers who don't, and I like to read the unfolding events of the Bible with this wonder of what happens next.

As I approached writing on Acts, I tried to study it considering the unresolved questions from the gospel of Luke that I noted. A few of them were:

- Since Jesus had always been with the apostles, teaching and correcting them as they followed him on earth, who will they turn to when he is no longer with them?
- Jesus' main message in the Gospels was the coming of God's kingdom to earth. Is this what the apostles will teach, or will they have a different message?
- If God's kingdom came as Jesus announced in the Gospels, how can he rule over it if he is in heaven?
- At the end of Luke's Gospel, the apostles still, after three years with Jesus, seem so spiritually dull and occupied with positions of importance in God's kingdom. What will it take for them to be spiritually alert and selfless servants like Jesus?

We will find answers to these questions and much more in the first few chapters of Acts. Let's begin to look for them.

LOOKING FOR ANSWERS

The Day of Pentecost is the crucial event in Acts, the event that will fulfill the promises of God and empower the disciples for witness. But it would be a mistake to hurry through this first chapter of Acts, for it shows the continuity between the life and mission of Jesus and that of his disciples.

Luke begins by reminding us of his first book (the Gospel of Luke), where he wrote all that Jesus did and taught. With this he at once suggests continuity with what he will now write. The implication is that Jesus will continue with the same mission we read of in Luke's Gospel, but now in a new way. While Jesus may no longer be physically present on earth, he will be present with his disciples through the Spirit, enabling them to continue his mission of establishing God's good and just ways on earth.

Here at the outset Luke shows the continuity between his Gospel and Acts by reminding us of two related themes in his Gospel that continue in Acts—the empowering of the Spirit and the kingdom of God. God gave Jesus the Spirit at his baptism (Luke 3:21–22) to empower him to proclaim and enact the presence of his kingdom coming to earth (Luke 4:18–19). *Now just as the Spirit was poured out on Jesus, the Spirit is poured out on the disciples to do what he has done.* This means we will see many parallels in the life of Jesus and the life of his disciples, parallels which can continue even with us!

PARALLEL 1—THE KINGDOM OF GOD

First is the crucial theme of the kingdom of God. Because Jesus frequently taught about the kingdom of God and spoke of its appearance with him, it should not surprise us that Jesus continues to teach the disciples about the kingdom after his resurrection (Acts 1:3). I find it interesting that even after his resurrection, Jesus gives "instructions through the Spirit." In Acts 2 we will see how Jesus, even as the ascended Lord, works through the Spirit of God.

What was Jesus now teaching the apostles about the kingdom that he had not already taught them? He now explains to them how his death and resurrection (events that caught them by surprise) were instrumental to the coming of the kingdom as a fulfillment of the Scriptures. When the disciples proclaim the good news in Acts, they make frequent reference to how the ancient prophets foretold the death and resurrection of Jesus. Some more skeptical scholars believe the disciples scrambled frantically after Jesus' death and resurrection to find support for them from their Scriptures. But they were simply teaching what Jesus had explained to them during the forty days between his resurrection and ascension.

While there are not as many direct references to the kingdom of God in Acts as we find in Luke's Gospel, Peter will soon proclaim that when God exalted Jesus to his right hand as Lord, Jesus began his reign over God's kingdom. Thus, all we read in Acts describes the continued growth of God's kingdom.

Luke emphasizes the continued expansion of the kingdom of God in Acts by a literary tool called an inclusion. Since the kingdom of God is emphasized at the beginning of Acts (1:3–6) and at the end (Acts 28:23, 31), it is implied that everything in between is about the kingdom. The very last verses in Acts record that Paul (under house arrest in Rome for the gospel) welcomed all who visited him and for two years boldly "preached the kingdom of God and taught about the Lord Jesus Christ" (Acts 28:31).

We are left at the end of Acts not knowing what will happen to Paul and the expansion of the kingdom of God. In this way Luke invites us, his readers, to continue the work of the risen Lord Jesus to expand his kingdom on earth. The continuity between Jesus' ministry on earth with his disciples in Acts continues with us. What Jesus did through the Spirit and what he gave the disciples he now wants to do through us.

PARALLEL 2—THE HOLY SPIRIT

We read in Acts that Jesus works through us by the Spirit, the second major theme in Luke's Gospel that continues in Acts. After instructing the apostles about the kingdom of God, Jesus orders them to wait in Jerusalem for "the promise of the Father," that is, the pouring out of the Holy Spirit. The coming of the Spirit to dwell in the disciples is referred to as "the promise of the Father" and elsewhere as "the gift of God," because when the Spirit is poured out on Pentecost, the very Presence of God, with all his promises and blessings, begins to flow into the innermost being of the disciples.

God had promised a full outpouring of his Spirit upon his people in the last days. The people of God longed for the coming of God's Spirit to dwell within them, for they knew that meant the promised Messiah would rule over all the earth.

Anticipation is peaked when Jesus promises the disciples that they "will be baptized with the Holy Spirit not many days from now" (Acts 1:5). They had seen the power of God's Spirit in Jesus, but that was only the beginning of the full outpouring God promised his people in the last days. And it will begin with them in just a few days! Imagine their eager expectation of the Spirit's outpouring to soon usher in the kingdom of God beginning with them!

I realize I am getting ahead of Pentecost in Acts 2, but what I want to say now is so important it can't wait. While clearly the life, death, resurrection, and ascension of Jesus are crucial, they were the means to God's ultimate promise to come to live in and among his people with all his blessings. We needed to be cleansed through the death of the Messiah for God to dwell among us, and Jesus needed to be raised from the dead and exalted to pour out the Spirit on us.

We live now in what some scholars describe as "the Age of the Spirit." The celebration of Pentecost has become my favorite time of the year. Certainly, some have lacked and still do lack balance with life in the Spirit. Perhaps if more of us fully embraced life in the Spirit, there would be fewer extremes, and we would be more alive and fruitful in our faith.

2

The Ascension
(Acts 1:6–11)

As we begin this chapter, Esuga and I prepare to walk up to the Mount of Olives, which is close to where Jesus' ascension took place. Our Acts passage has some of Jesus' last teachings to his disciples—to not stay in Jerusalem but to move out in mission to other parts of the world. Luke then relates how Jesus ascended, followed by how his disciples were not anxious to leave Jerusalem as he wanted them to do.

Despite a difficult night's sleep, I woke up excited on the first day to walk in the footsteps of Jesus and the apostles. We would walk up the Mount of Olives five minutes east of our hostel to the general vicinity where Jesus commissioned the apostles to be his witnesses to the world before he ascended in front of their eyes to heaven. The Chapel of the Ascension on the hillside claims to mark the spot where Jesus ascended to heaven, leaving his footprints on the spot on a stone.

Few believe this is the exact spot of the ascension (or that those are his actual footprints on the stone in the chapel!), but could this be the general location of the ascension? You might feel that it doesn't really matter, and I would agree with you. But would you agree with me that it could be inspiring to find the general area to sit and contemplate?

Sleeping poorly and weak from my cold, I knew I needed a good breakfast for the grueling hike up the high ridge that overlooks Jerusalem. So, for breakfast, in order of importance, I had two cups of coffee, a hard-boiled egg on fresh pita bread, hummus on bread layered with fresh cucumbers, and then another cup of coffee. With one pocket packed with cough drops and another stuffed with tissues and ibuprofen working through my system with the caffeine, I was ready to hike up the Mount of Olives to the general area of the ascension.

Figure 2: Chapel of the Ascension
This photo by an unknown author is licensed under CC.

It was still overcast with a chill in the morning air. Esuga wore his red hoodie and Phillies hat. I had on my West Philly T-shirt and a windbreaker. Because this was Palm Sunday (the day that celebrates Jesus' descent from the Mount of Olives into Jerusalem), we soon came upon thousands of other pilgrims with whom we would join in our walk into Jerusalem.

Now I must confess my first of several oversights I made on our trip. Caught up in the excitement of walking and singing and dancing with pilgrims from around the world, I completely forgot about stopping at the general location of the ascension at the summit of the Mount of

Olives. I never told Esuga that we missed the experience of sitting by the path to contemplate Jesus' ascension to the Father's Presence. Maybe he will read this and we'll go back, but now you know not to miss it.

How do we know the summit of the Mount of Olives is where Jesus ascended to the Father? Allow me to explain. Luke writes in his Gospel that the ascension took place in the *vicinity* of Bethany (Luke 24:50). He now adds in Acts that it took place "from the hill of the Mount of Olives, a Sabbath day's walk" to Jerusalem (Acts 1:12).

A Sabbath day's walk was three fourths of a mile from Jerusalem, and this places the ascension at the summit of the Mount. Most likely Jesus and the apostles spent the night in Bethany down on the eastern slope. Jesus then led only the apostles from Bethany up to the summit to commission them and have them witness his ascension."[1]

A month later, back in Philadelphia, I began to think more about the ascension. It seemed strange to think of Jesus shooting up to heaven from the very hill we had walked down. Perhaps I have too many images in my mind of Superman lifting his hands up towards the sky and flying up. And then, where is heaven?!

Some may think that since Jesus now had a resurrected body, his departure to God was more mysterious, more spiritual. But there he stood still, fully man, with his feet firmly planted on the ground, as the apostles watched him ascend. Did it really happen this way? If it did (without leaving any footprints), I wanted to know why. Why was the ascension so earthly, so physical? To find answers, I decided to read the passage and all my commentaries on Acts more carefully. You can find them in this chapter.

A QUESTION ABOUT THE KINGDOM (ACTS 1:6–8)

Because the ancient prophets connected the pouring out of the Spirit in the last days with the coming of God's kingdom to Israel, the apostles now logically asked Jesus, "Lord, is this the time when you will restore the kingdom to Israel?" (Acts 1:6).

The disciples had expected Jesus to establish God's kingdom when he arrived in Jerusalem but instead, he was put to death (Luke 19:11). So now, they wondered, could this be the time for him to reign as their king over Israel with the nations of the world coming to Jerusalem to learn of Israel's God? The apostles "envisioned the mass return of scattered

1. Peterson, *Acts of the Apostles*, 116.

Israelites to the holy city/mount and the establishment of a glorious new Israelite kingdom governed in peace and righteousness. This scenario also projected that the gentile nations would concurrently stream to Jerusalem and acknowledge the sovereignty of Israel and her God."[2]

Based on the apostles' question, we can infer that Jesus had not taught them *the time* when he would come again to fully restore the kingdom. He had not done this, he says, because "this is a time the Father has set by his own authority" (Acts 1:7). Jesus did not know the time of his return (Mark 13:32) and would not have told the disciples if he did know, for rather than speculate on the times and wait for the nations to come *to them* in Jerusalem, they were to leave Jerusalem as witnesses to the nations. Jesus must redirect their vision and energies to the present phase of God's kingdom. Now is the time for moving out for witness, not waiting to receive.

We can also infer from the apostles' question that Jesus had not yet taught them that the promises of God's kingdom were not exclusively for them. It would not be until some ten years later that God directed the steps of Peter to a gentile in Caesarea and showed him God's plan to include gentiles as equal participants in the blessings of the kingdom originally given to Israel (Acts 11:15–18).[3]

Until then, and especially until the ministry of Paul to the gentiles, the apostles would remain in Jerusalem and teach a restoration exclusively for the Jewish people in the land of Israel, centered in Jerusalem and the temple (Acts 3:19–20). It is important not to read what we now know into the minds of the apostles at this time but to follow the unfolding story of God's revelation in Acts. There are important lessons in doing so.

Jesus now redirected the apostles' focus from a future for them in Jerusalem to their task of taking the message about him, even to the ends of the earth. He said, "But you will receive power when the Holy Spirit has come upon you; and you will be my witnesses in Jerusalem, in all Judea and Samaria, and to the ends of the earth" (Acts 1:8). "Rather than sinking their roots in Jerusalem and waiting for the world to flood *in*, Jesus' followers were to move *out* from Jerusalem, through Judea and Samaria, and ultimately 'to the ends of the earth' (Acts 1:8). The flow is centrifugal instead of centripetal; the apostles were just beginning their journey, not ending it."[4]

2. Spencer, *Journeying Through Acts*, 36.
3. See also Eph 2:11–13, 19; 3:6.
4. Spencer, *Journeying Through Acts*, 36.

Sadly, despite Jesus' command, the twelve apostles would still sink their roots in Jerusalem. Halfway through the book, some fifteen to eighteen years later, they are still in Jerusalem (Acts 15:4–6, 22–23). Because of their strong nationalistic beliefs, focusing on their salvation in the land of Israel, God must raise up other leaders to take the good news to non-Jewish people.

The apostles would be powerful witnesses of the risen Lord in Jerusalem and the land of Israel. Their power for bold witness would begin when the Holy Spirit came upon them at Pentecost. Because one purpose of Acts is to record the spread of the gospel to the nations, Acts emphasizes the role of the Spirit in leading young evangelists always outward to new regions, empowering them with miraculous acts of healing and Spirit-inspired speeches.

Jesus' words to begin in Jerusalem and then move from Judea and Samaria to the ends of the earth not only contained a *plan* (and showed the structure of Acts); they also contained a *promise*.[5] God would lead to guarantee that all peoples heard of his love.

JESUS ASCENDS TO THE FATHER (ACTS 1:9–11)

After the risen Jesus promised the apostles that they would receive power to be his witnesses, they witnessed his ascension to God with the promise that he would return.

My guess is that Jesus' being taken up into heaven (mentioned four times here) may sound strange to many of us modern readers. But the problem may be just that—we are modern readers. Due to movies and music, both secular and Christian, we tend to think of heaven as a place far away in outer space where Jesus shoots up to.[6] But the text says Jesus was lifted (implied by God) into a cloud (apparently a low-hanging one). Biblical scholars point out that the Presence of God is often represented in the Scriptures by a cloud. So, we are intended to understand that Jesus is taken up by God to his Presence.

In the Bible heaven is where God dwells, and while heaven has a location, it is not "a location within our own cosmos of space, time, and matter, situated somewhere up in the sky."[7] It is the place of God's space;

---

5. Keener, *Acts, Vol. 1*, 697.
6. Wright, *Acts for Everyone, Pt. 1*, 13.
7. Wright, *Acts for Everyone, Pt. 1*, 12.

it is God's dimension and reality where his will is done, and it is full of goodness, love, light, and glory.[8] Heaven and earth are not viewed as two separate spheres but as two related yet different interlocking dimensions.

The more important question to ask is, *What is the significance* of Jesus' ascending to the Presence of God?

Throughout his ministry on earth, Jesus often identified himself as the Son of Man spoken of in Dan 7:13–14. There we read that "one like a son of man is brought up, on the clouds of heaven to the 'Ancient of Days' and is presented before him to be given kingly power over the nations," particularly rulers described as "beasts" because of the evil and chaos they cause on earth. So, in seeing Jesus ascend to God's Presence, the disciples would have understood the prophecy of Daniel now being fulfilled in a dramatic and unexpected way.[9] The ascension is dramatic and unexpected because the apostles had expected him to physically rule on earth in Jerusalem.

This prepares us for Peter's message at Pentecost, which climaxes with Jesus exalted to the right hand of God to be made Lord (Acts 2:36). It also prepares us for the drama of Acts, as we read time and time again of the kingdoms of this world in conflict with the kingdom of God with Jesus as the true ruler of this world.

You may have noticed that the text emphasizes that the apostles "were watching, gazing up, and looking up." This repetition underscores that the apostles witnessed that the same Jesus they walked with in Galilee was now taken up before their very eyes to God's Presence. It was important that the apostles witnessed Jesus' body ascend, for in time, people would speak of his body being stolen or of only his spirit being raised to God. The resurrection and ascension of Jesus' body emphasizes that our bodies and the earth are not evil in themselves but need to be transformed, made ready to dwell with God.

The emphasis on the apostles looking up may also be another reminder that even as we wait for his return, we are to turn our attention to the mission the Lord has given us.

---

8. Wright, *Acts for Everyone*, Pt. 1, 11.
9. Wright, *Acts for Everyone*, Pt. 1, 13–14.

A FOCUS ON JERUSALEM

First-century Jerusalem was the pride and hope of Jews all over the world. Herod had rebuilt it to instill in the Jewish people a pride for their city that would impress friends and foes alike, a city that would beam grandeur and glory. He built public monuments such as a theatre, a new palace, and above all a new temple, which became the largest religious structure in the Greco-Roman world. "The grandeur of the Temple became proverbial: 'Whoever has not seen Herod's building has never seen anything beautiful.'"[10]

Herod rebuilt Jerusalem to boost his reputation but also to signal to the Jewish people and to the world that a new era had begun.[11] His message that the Jews were a great people gave them hope. The promises in the prophets of their future prominence on earth also instilled hope in them.

The four to six million Jews scattered across the Roman Empire were viewed by non-Jews as "an odd, despised people" who gathered for worship in their small synagogues (often in homes) while non-Jews worshiped in the many grand temples built to the gods of Rome. So, the hearts of the Jews living in the diaspora swelled with pride and hope when they came to Jerusalem to celebrate the Passover and Pentecost. Herod's Temple sparkled in the sun in all its splendor as the city swelled from sixty thousand to some two hundred thousand.

"Located thirty-three miles east of the Mediterranean Sea and fourteen miles west of the Dead Sea, Jerusalem was built on a hilltop ringed by higher hills."[12] Up a hill from the Temple Mount lived the leaders of Israel, the Sanhedrin, in spacious houses with a splendid view of the temple complex.

The Sanhedrin (or the Council, as it is sometimes called) consisted of seventy-one men who governed the affairs of all the Jews in the land and indirectly throughout the empire. But because they collaborated with the Romans to maintain their wealth and positions of power and excised excessive taxes at the temple for sacrifices, they were generally loathed by the people.

---

10. Murphy-O'Connor, *St. Paul's Ephesus*, 185.
11. Murphy-O'Connor, *St. Paul's Ephesus*, 184.
12. Jeffers, *Greco-Roman World*, 279.

It was these men who were responsible for putting Jesus on trial and having him put to death because of his popularity with the people. Jealousy and fear of losing power drove them to act. Now in Acts they persecuted the apostles for similar reasons. Looming over the first chapters of Acts is the question, Who are the true leaders of Israel? The Sanhedrin or the apostles appointed by Jesus?

3

Preparing for Pentecost
(Acts 1:12–26)

ONE OF OUR GOALS for our time in Jerusalem was to get a feel for the terrain and distances the apostles walked as they moved around Jerusalem. When I had read that the apostles returned "from the mount called Olivet" to "the room" in Jerusalem where they were staying (Acts 1:12, 13), we decided to try to trace their steps.

Finding the house where they stayed was important to me because it was not only the place of the Last Supper, but, more importantly for our journey through Acts, it was the place of Pentecost, the place where God first came to dwell in his people. So Esuga and I went out in search of this house.

Like the apostles after the ascension, we descended the twenty-minute steep trek down the Mount of Olives toward Jerusalem into the Kidron Valley. When you look at a map at the back of your Bible, Jerusalem may seem flat, but it is built on hills and surrounded by mountains. The steep terrain fascinated me. Walking the hills and mountains must have made for strong legs for Jesus and the disciples.

After Esuga and I came down into the Kidron Valley, we walked south through the valley, with the Temple Mount rising high above us to the west. It was mid-April, just a few weeks before the disciples would have walked there. Sunny and in the sixties, flowers bloomed throughout the valley.

A few young boys from the Palestinian village of Silwan, immediately south of the Temple Mount, joined us on our walk. One of the older boys pointed out the snapdragons, leaning forward in the gentle wind to welcome us, and the deep-red poppies, with their stronger stems stretching toward the heavens in all their brilliance to praise their Creator. He also pointed out the southeast corner of the Temple Mount's wall elevated far above us. We enjoyed their company. All was colorful, filled with life and beauty. Then the older boy asked for some coins in exchange for pointing out the flowers and temple wall to us. Disappointed that we did not oblige, the boys returned home. I guess we can't blame small boys for wanting to make some extra change.

Continuing south in the Kidron Valley we were blinded by the sun flashing against a massive sheet of white stones on the lower part of the Mount of Olives. On this slope the Jewish people have buried their dead ever since King David had captured the city three thousand years ago. On the opposite slope descending from the Temple Mount, we spotted another massive cemetery. There Muslims have buried their dead since taking the city thirteen hundred years earlier. The cemeteries were like two dead armies facing each other across the valley. If only they knew the way of peace that Jesus said he came to give when he entered Jerusalem for the last time (Luke 19:41–42).

At the southern end of the Kidron Valley there were three possible ways the apostles could have walked back to the house where they stayed in upper Jerusalem.[1] Intrigued as you have become, I'm sure you want to know their actual path. I will describe the way that Esuga and I walked, and I'm convinced it was the right way, for as we continued, my feet caught on the pavement, and I looked down to see footprints embedded on a large stone. I'm convinced they were the footprints of Peter as he walked back to the house for which we looked.

Leaving the valley, we walked up to the Temple Mount and then turned west up the hill into Old Jerusalem. With maps in our pockets and our water bottles in our hands, Esuga and I set out to find the place of Pentecost.

Because I was writing the story of Acts, of how God came to dwell in his people and empowered them for mission, I had become a bit obsessed with locating this place. Think about it. We know that God had revealed his Presence in the Jerusalem Temple for centuries. But now

---

1. Schnabel, "Topography of Jerusalem," 20.

after Pentecost he would be present on earth in a new place, in his people, the disciples of Jesus. We will read of a mighty wind from heaven and tongues of fire filling this house, causing the disciples to spill out into the streets in praise to God.

Craig Keener points out that by using the definite article, *the* room, Luke suggests the room where the apostles stayed was likely known to all the disciples.[2] It was the upper room where Jesus ate the Last Supper with the twelve (Luke 22:12); it was the same place where the Spirit fell on the disciples on Pentecost (Acts 2:2a); and it was here they met to pray for boldness so that "the place where they were meeting" was shaken by the Spirit of God (Acts 4:23, 31). This house became the meeting place, the house church for the Galilean disciples who came to Jerusalem from Galilee with Jesus.[3]

It was this house where Peter would go after being delivered from prison, "the house of Mary . . . where many had gathered and were praying" (Acts 12:12). This Mary, the mother of John Mark who will later join Paul and Barnabas on a journey, was apparently wealthy since she owned a two-story house with a courtyard and an outer gate (Acts 12:13).

I realize I have written much about the place where the apostles stayed, but my hope is that it will help you better relive their story in Acts.

Back to our trek through Jerusalem! Esuga led the way, moving quickly through the narrow, crowded streets, six feet wide when the apostles walked them.[4] Climbing the stone steps, slippery from a morning rain, we maneuvered our way through crowds of tourists shopping at the markets on each side.

I didn't want to lose Esuga in the crowd, so I kept an eye out for his red hoodie bouncing back and forth in rhythm with the swagger in his walk. I thought he looked cool with his red hoodie and cool way of walking, so for a few minutes I tried to imitate him, but I soon gave up. What was natural for him was too much work for me.

Once we left the crowded streets, I caught up with Esuga and pulled out my map to show him that we now needed to head south to the place of Pentecost. In a few minutes we arrived at the traditional site (the Cenacle) swarmed with tourists. Now I need to tell you that even if this was the general area of Pentecost, we do not know if this was the exact

---

2. Keener, *Acts, Vol. 1*, 739.
3. Barnett, *Jesus and the Rise*, 198.
4. Schnabel, "Topography of Jerusalem," 20.

location because of extensive fires which destroyed all the buildings of Jerusalem in AD 70.

Before I traveled to Jerusalem, I had anticipated having a deep spiritual experience at this location. Think about it. This is the place where God first came to dwell among his people. But I didn't have my anticipated experience. Perhaps I had become tired from our long trek, but I think it had more to do with what I will later write about—location, or place.

I experience God's Presence most deeply alone in the quiet of my mornings or praying with a few believers in our house.

THE DISCIPLES MEET TO PRAY (ACTS 1:12-14)

After the ascension, the eleven apostles walked down the Mount of Olives along the Kidron Valley to upper Jerusalem, to the room of the Last Supper, where they stayed. There they would pray and wait to receive the Spirit.

Luke begins Acts with a detailed list of the eleven apostles to prepare us for the need for someone to replace Judas. While the apostles lived in the upper floor of the house, other disciples would gather at the house and courtyard to pray and share life together. We read that "all of these [apostles] were constantly devoting themselves to prayer together with certain women, including Mary the mother of Jesus, as well as his brothers" (Acts 1:14).

While there were one hundred and twenty persons who had followed Jesus from Galilee to Jerusalem (Acts 1:15), the nucleus of the community is made up of the eleven apostles; a group of women who had also accompanied Jesus in his ministry (some of whom had been the first to see Jesus risen from the dead [Luke 24:1-10]); Mary, the mother of Jesus; and her four other sons, the brothers of Jesus.

The brothers of Jesus had not believed his claims to be a prophet and the Messiah sent by God until Jesus appeared to them after his resurrection. Special mention is made of Jesus' brother James, who would some fourteen years later become the leader of the Jesus movement when Peter was forced to flee Jerusalem (Acts 12:17). At this point James could not be a candidate to replace Judas because he was a new disciple and did not meet the requirements to be an apostle.

While we can assume the disciples ate together, rehearsed recent events, and shared experiences of their time with Jesus, Luke emphasizes that they "were constantly devoting themselves to prayer" (Acts 1:14).

This is the first of many references in Acts that emphasizes the frequency of the disciples gathering in their homes to pray. By praying often together, they preserved their unity and kept the message of Jesus alive in them.

At this time, they prayed to be ready to receive the Spirit so that they could be effective witnesses to the risen Jesus, and of course they prayed for God's guidance in replacing Judas.

MATTHIAS IS CHOSEN TO REPLACE JUDAS (ACTS 1:15–26)

Over half of Acts 1 is devoted to finding a replacement for Judas and, if I'm honest, I've often wished Luke had not given it so much space and had hurried on to the events of Pentecost. But filling the place of Judas to again have twelve apostles before Pentecost was important. Here is why.

First, Jesus had chosen exactly twelve apostles to represent the twelve tribes of Israel and thus all of Israel. The twelve apostles were viewed by the other disciples as leaders of God's new people, a renewed and restored Israel, symbolizing God's intent for all Israel.[5] They must represent "in their number the ideal of a reunited and renewed people of God, Israel in its fullness, not a remnant."[6]

The question looming over the early chapters of Acts is, Who are the true leaders of Israel? Are they the twelve apostles, chosen and trained by Jesus, or the leaders of Israel in Jerusalem, who rejected Jesus?

Second, there is the perception of the people to whom the apostles would soon proclaim Jesus as Lord. Why should they believe in Jesus when one of those he chose betrayed him? And due to guilt by association, the integrity of the eleven was in question because of their three-year friendship with Judas.[7] Thus the passage emphasizes that the betrayal of Judas was predicted in the Scriptures and did not catch Jesus by surprise. The passage also emphasizes that Jesus, who knows everyone's heart (Acts 1:24), is fully in charge and chooses the right person to replace Judas.

These are the reasons why a twelfth apostle must be chosen. But what were the requirements?

---

5. Wright, *Acts for Everyone, Pt. 1*, 17.
6. Peterson, *Acts of the Apostles*, 126.
7. Peterson, *Acts of the Apostles*, 120.

They are stated clearly. "So, one of the men who have accompanied us during all the time that the Lord went in and out among us, beginning from the baptism of John until the day when he was taken up from us—one of these must become a witness with us to his resurrection" (Acts 1:21–22). To become an apostle, a person must have accompanied Jesus from the very beginning of his ministry until the end, when he ascended to God's Presence. Most importantly of all, they must have seen Jesus after he was raised from the dead.

Why were these two criteria given?

First, an apostle must be able to confirm that the same Jesus who ministered in Galilee was crucified, raised from the dead, and exalted to God's Presence in heaven. The same Jesus that led them in Galilee will now lead them as the exalted Lord![8] In addition, the apostles will soon teach thousands of new disciples all that Jesus said and did. They could only give bold and credible teaching if they had always been with Jesus and witnessed all he said and did.

Second, the twelve apostles, who had always been with Jesus, assure a continuity of his mission and message. They would not create a new religion called Christianity. Their mission of living and proclaiming the kingdom of God continued what Jesus began. They guaranteed the historicity of Jesus' life and teachings.

The method of how Matthias was chosen, by casting lots, seems odd to us. We can assume that after much prayer and weighing of possible candidates, the list was narrowed down to the two mentioned—Justus and Matthias. Because they had prayed much, they believed the risen Lord, who knows everyone's heart, would show them which of the two he had chosen (Acts 1:24).

So, they cast lots, one way of determining God's will *in the old era before the coming of the Spirit on Pentecost*. The Lord showed them by the casting of lots that Matthias was to replace Judas. But from now on in Acts, once the Spirit came to dwell in the disciples, the Lord would direct them by the Spirit. After the choosing of Matthias, we no longer read of God revealing his will in this way.

Now with Matthias added, the symbolism of the twelve apostles as leaders of God's people, the true Israel, is complete, and he can pour out his Spirit on them fulfilling his promises to Israel.

---

8. Peterson, *Acts of the Apostles*, 127.

4

Pentecost
(Acts 2:1–21)

THE MOST PROMINENT MOVEMENT on the day of Pentecost is from heaven to earth. This causes the disciples to move out of the house into the streets for witness. Pull out your map of first-century Jerusalem and try to visualize their movement in Acts 2.

After the hundred and twenty disciples receive the Spirit, they flood out of the house into the narrow streets around them. There, hundreds of Jews, visiting Jerusalem from the nations, hear them praising God in their own languages. More people gather. There is no room in the streets for Peter to address a crowd that will swell to the thousands. They must move to a more spacious area.

The most likely option was to walk down through the streets from upper Jerusalem to a large, open plaza just south of the Temple Mount. The plaza, roughly 787 feet (240 m) by 108 feet (33 m) could easily hold twenty-four thousand people.[1]

Archeologists have also found over 164 immersion pools in the area, which would have provided plenty of places for the thousands who would be baptized (Acts 2:41). Because "the thousands of festival pilgrims in the city for Pentecost would have all immersed themselves before ascending to the Temple Mount," the baptism of three thousand was not only

---

1. Schnabel, "Topography of Jerusalem," 23.

possible, it was also not unique.[2] Later I will write of our exploration of these pools when Luke writes of three thousand baptized on this day.

But first comes the Spirit.

THE DAY GOD CAME (ACTS 2:1–4)

The day has come. The day the ancient prophets predicted. The day Israel longed for throughout the centuries. This is the day all humanity longed for without understanding what it was. This is the day God had patiently been working toward since humankind went their own way at the beginning.

This is the day of Pentecost, when God again came to dwell in and among his people. The kingdom of God now came to earth with more power, more depth, and more breadth than it had with Jesus, for now the powers of the kingdom first manifest in Jesus also lived in his disciples.

The disciples are transformed from inert spectators, looking up into heaven at the ascension, into energized prophets, looking out to the nations which have gathered as witnesses. The modest band of 120 disciples from Galilee praying in private, turned into a public affair as they poured out into the streets, and representatives from the nations of the world joined their community.[3]

While Luke's Gospel moves steadily with Jesus' journey to Jerusalem, climaxing in his death and resurrection, Acts begins with the main event of Pentecost, which causes all that follows—from Jerusalem to Rome—to be empowered by God's Spirit.

Try to imagine yourself sitting in the large open courtyard of the house where the apostles stayed. It is nine in the morning, and you sit in the crowd of 120 disciples who had followed Jesus from Galilee to Jerusalem a few months earlier. Jesus had promised that any day, the Spirit of God would be poured on you. So, you are again gathered to pray and wait with eager anticipation. Today might be the day.

Normally you would stand to pray at the temple, but now you sit. And it is good that you sit. For suddenly what sounds *like* a mighty wind comes from heaven and fills the entire house.

The Presence of God is likened to a mighty wind in the Scriptures (Exod 19:18; 2 Sam 22:16; Ezek 13:13). Now, like a mighty wind, God

---

2. Schnabel, "Topography of Jerusalem," 24.
3. Spencer, *Journeying Through Acts*, 41.

comes to live in and among his people by his Spirit! The Spirit of God is not an impersonal power but the very Presence of God dwelling in and among his people.

A FOCUS ON THE PRESENCE OF GOD

As a potter I learned the importance of first centering the clay on the wheel if I want to make a good pot. Looking down at the clay spinning around the center has led me to see all of life as a centering. I am always asking myself, Why are we here? What is *It*? What is the center of life? I don't want to miss it; I want to live life to its fullest. I have learned to see living in the Presence of God, in joyful obedience to him, as the center. From that center I live out my life.

We were created to enjoy the Presence of God deep within our being. We have a reservoir deep within us that God wants to fill with himself! From the very beginning we lived in the Presence of God, but we decided we wanted something else to fill the reservoir within us. Now, with the coming of Christ and the giving of the Spirit, God can again dwell within us. His Presence in us is described in the Bible as a river of life flowing in our innermost being.

The Presence of God in and among us is his greatest gift, and it is also our greatest gift to the world, for only as his love is alive in us can it flow from us to others. Of the utmost importance—every day keep your heart alive to the love of God.

While we will not experience his Presence continually and fully until we see his face (Rev 22:1–4), Pentecost brings a new immediacy of God's Presence when he comes to dwell in us by his Spirit. His Presence in us is a truth we can count on. We do not so much ask God to be present as we quiet ourselves and become aware of it.

How do we live in this new reality? We learn it in different ways partly depending on our personalities, so I suggest meeting with friends to learn from each other. Some go for a quiet walk. Others sing. For years I would very slowly read the Bible until I sensed God spoke to me. Often today I simply look at the trees blowing in the wind outside the window and recall a favorite verse in Romans: "Like a mighty river the Spirit has poured out the love of God into my innermost being" (Rom 5:5). So, I welcome God's fatherly love.

> We learn from the Psalms and personal experience that approaching God is not a fixed pattern. Sometimes we are too tired or too depressed to feel anything, but we can pray, "God I'm tired, confused and down. But I love you and need you and know you are with me."
>
> As a potter I have made hundreds of mugs on which I have stamped "Come to the River" at the rim. Pentecost uses the imagery of wind and fire to depict the Presence of God, but Jesus often depicts it as a steady stream of living water welling up within us. "Come and drink," he says, "for the Scriptures declare that rivers of living water will flow out from within" (John 7: 38– 39). Sip on your coffee, and be reminded of the life of God flowing deep within you.
>
> We have so much noise in our society that we need to leave our phones at home to go for a walk or retreat to a room to keep our hearts alive to God's love.
>
> As an American I realize how I have written *how we as individuals* seek God's Presence. The disciples didn't think this way, nor do large parts of our world today. *God has made us to experience his Presence together as a community.* We will soon read that the disciples met together every day in their homes to eat and pray and praise God. And they saw him in each other!

Because an important purpose of Acts is to show how God's Spirit empowers his people for witness, Luke immediately writes of how tongues that appeared *like* fire came to rest on each disciple. God revealed his Presence with fire to Moses in the burning bush (Exod 3:1–6), and by a pillar of fire he led his people in the wilderness (Exod 13:21, 22). Now it comes with what looks like tongues of fire settling on each disciple, filling them with God's Spirit, so that each one begins to speak about the powerful events God had worked through Jesus (see Acts 2:11). But they do not speak of Jesus in their native Aramaic tongue. Miraculously,they speak in the languages of the nations of the known world, where Jesus has said they would be his witnesses!

Luke emphasizes with the words "each, all, and every" that each one of the disciples becomes a witness fulfilling the promise given only to the apostles (Acts 1:8). While Luke does emphasize the powerful witness of the apostles and other great leaders in Acts, he emphasizes here that at Pentecost every disciple is filled with God's Spirit to speak effectively about Jesus. This corporate witness, in words and deeds, of the entire community is often seen as they gathered and found favor with others.

Now standing, they spilled out into the streets to speak boldly of God's powerful works through Jesus, the Messiah. *The Spirit now dwelling in them has changed everything.* Luke wants us to see "how it was that a small group of frightened, puzzled and largely uneducated men and women could so quickly become . . . a force to be reckoned with right across the known world,"[4] and he wants each one of us to see how we, too, can be a force to be reckoned with in our world. We have the same Spirit living in us.

JEWS FROM EVERY NATION (ACTS 2:5-13)

As the 120 disciples spilled out into the streets, speaking in the languages of the nations of God's love shown through Jesus, they made quite a roar. At the sound, Jews from the nations visiting Jerusalem were astonished to hear them speak—not in Aramaic but in their very own languages. They were also astonished that these were simple, rural Galileans, not religious scholars. Articulate, Spirit-gifted Galileans speaking boldly of the mighty works of God appeared to them to be a contradiction.[5] What the crowd saw and heard could not be explained rationally.

The crowd that gathered around the disciples consisted of Jewish people who had come to Jerusalem for business and stayed or had come to visit for several months to celebrate Passover and Pentecost.[6] Soon we will read that these very people took part in having Jesus crucified (Acts 2:23, 36).

Based on Peter's speech that followed, we can assume that when the disciples spoke "about God's deeds of power," they spoke of Jesus' life, death, and resurrection. Thus, all the disciples became the first to fulfill Jesus' promise to witness of him when the Spirit came upon them (Acts 1:8). The apostle Peter would soon explain their words in more detail.

Why did God choose these Jews scattered from the nations to first hear the good news about Jesus? One reason is that God would lead many of them to return to their countries to share the good news about Jesus.

---

4. Wright, *Acts for Everyone, Pt. 1*, 23.
5. Spencer, *Journeying Through Acts*, 44.
6. Papandrea, *Week in the Life of Rome*, 135.

While proclaiming the good news to gentiles is not yet part of the story of Acts, this already hints at God's desire to include all the peoples of the world in his kingdom.

Another reason may be to reveal the long-suffering love of God. These very Jews took part in handing Jesus, God's beloved Messiah, over to be crucified (Acts 2:23), yet God still loved them and was ready to forgive them! They are the first to learn they could be forgiven and participate in God's kingdom.

The crowd is both amazed and perplexed at hearing the disciples speak in their languages. Peter must explain.

THE SPIRIT AND THE KINGDOM (2:14–21)

As Peter saw both young and old, men and women, slaves and the freed, filled with God's Spirit, he knew this was what the ancient prophets promised would occur in the last days, when God's kingdom broke into the world. It was now his task, as an apostle who had been with Jesus from the beginning and witnessed his resurrection, to explain what the bewildered crowd saw and heard.

The scene changed from scattered pockets of people listening to disciples to the whole crowd gathering to listen to Peter. He continued to fulfill Jesus' promise of witness by the empowering Spirit of God; his speech, now in Aramaic, is as Spirit-inspired as when he spoke in another language. The purpose of his speech was to explain the significance of this miraculous phenomenon. The crowd asked, *"What does this mean?"*

Before Peter explained, he first dismissed the charge that the disciples were drunk! Because wine was commonly used in Roman religions to enhance prophecy, some claimed the joyful exuberance and speech in other languages was due to too much wine! Peter insisted they were not drunk. After all, it was only nine in the morning.

Peter then raised his voice, that booming voice of a fisherman he had used to call out across the stormy sea, to now call out across the stormy crowd numbering in the thousands to quiet them so he could explain the meaning of what had happened.

What does "Pentecost" mean?

It seems many have a vague understanding about the meaning of Pentecost. When I asked a group of older, more mature believers to share the meaning of Pentecost, they responded with the following:

- The point of Pentecost was to show God's power.
- It was the birth of the church.
- It enabled us to be witnesses.

The response I believe closest to what Acts 2 says is that God's Spirit was given to enable us to know *God's Presence*, to become enabled to *obey him*, and to *follow in the steps of Jesus to spread the good news of God's kingdom coming to earth*.

I confess, as a young believer and teacher I tended to skim over Peter's sermon on Pentecost and his other sermons in Acts. They didn't seem to teach justification by faith, the gospel I had been taught. And Peter's sermons seemed so bound by the Jewish audience he addressed two thousand years ago.

In addition, I asked myself how Peter could claim "the last days" began at Pentecost. And why did he devote so much time speaking of King David? What does all that have to do with the gospel of justification by faith?

I wanted answers to my questions. If Peter was preaching the gospel at Pentecost and in his other sermons, I had not been teaching it accurately, or at least as fully for much of my life. So, I decided to set aside any previous understanding of the gospel and learn from what Peter preached. I'm embarrassed to say how many weeks I studied Acts 2 and poured over many commentaries on it before I began to understand it. That's the challenge of seeing things one way your whole life then realizing you might be wrong and trying to rebuild a more accurate understanding.

What follows is how I have come to understand both the meaning of Pentecost and *the message of the gospel we are to believe and live.* I ask you to patiently read these pages. Understanding Acts 2 will enable you to better understand the rest of Acts.

THE MEANING OF PENTECOST

As I carefully read Acts 2 time and again, I found *four major, interrelated events* that together form the meaning of Pentecost:

1. The Spirit of God is poured out on the disciples (2:1–3).
2. Peter explains that this is evidence that God has fulfilled his kingdom promises to Israel (2:14–21).

3. Peter then teaches that Jesus, Israel's Messiah, has been raised from the dead (2:22–32).

4. Finally, as a climax he proclaims that God has made Jesus Lord (2:33–36).

It is this last event, the enthronement of Jesus as Lord over God's kingdom, that is foundational to understanding Acts and the gospel. It also explains the other three events. Jesus could not be reigning as Lord if God had not raised him from the dead. And, of course, you can't have a kingdom without a king to rule over it. Finally, now that Jesus has been made Lord, he can pour out the Spirit of God, which signals the arrival of God's kingdom on earth.

Craig Keener puts it this way: "If Jesus is already enthroned at the Father's right hand, then he has begun his messianic reign, and hence 'the messianic age has begun, and the messianic blessings have been given.'"[7] The messianic blessings have come because Jesus has poured out the Spirit.

The Jewish people knew from their Scriptures that when God poured out his Spirit on his people, the promised kingdom would come to earth. What the Jewish disciples of Jesus saw so clearly, we often miss. *When God poured out his Spirit on the day of Pentecost, his kingdom with all its promises and blessings was received by his people.*

Did the disciples receive power to witness when the Spirit came? Yes. Did they receive spiritual gifts? Yes. But these and other points all fall under the one major reality that God has made Jesus Lord over his kingdom to pour out the blessings of the kingdom.

With this summary introduction we can now better understand Peter's message.

He began by quoting Joel 2:28–32 to explain to the crowd what they were seeing and hearing. He said, "This is what was spoken through the prophet Joel, 'In the last days it will be, God declares, that I will pour out my Spirit upon all flesh, and your sons and daughters shall prophesy'" (Acts 2:16–17).

Luke has condensed Peter's words, which can be read in a few minutes (Acts 2:40). So, it is likely that he quoted other prophets who linked the pouring out of the Spirit to the coming of the kingdom of God in the last days. For example, Isaiah spoke of the blessings of peace, quietness, and confidence for the people of God when "the Spirit is poured upon" the people of God "from on high" (Isa 32:15–20).

---

7. Keener, *Acts*, Vol. 1, 956.

The New Covenant that God promised to make with his people emphasizes the new life the Spirit gives. God said, "I will put my Spirit in you and move you to follow my decrees and be careful to keep my laws" (Ezek 36:27). See also Jer 31, 33, and 34. In Ezekiel's famous vision of the valley of dry bones that God brings to life, God says, "I will put my Spirit in you, and you will live" (Ezek 37:14). At that time the people of God will be cleansed of their sin and live in unity under one King, the promised descendant of King David. God will dwell with his people, and the nations will come to know that God is with them (Ezek 37:21–28).

In short, from these and other prophecies the people of Israel expected that when the Spirit was poured out upon them, they would:

- Be cleansed and forgiven of all their shame and misdeeds,
- Be liberated from the oppression of sin and evil,
- Live in unity as a people,
- Experience God's peace,
- Be able to fully obey God by the Spirit in them,
- Be able to teach one another the ways of God, and especially
- Have God come to dwell in and among them.

It is important to know the promises of the prophets so that we can understand what the disciples eagerly expected and received at Pentecost. Many of these promises are alluded to in the summary at the end of Acts 2 describing the common life of the community of Jesus. But as mentioned, because Luke writes to emphasize how the Spirit filled the apostles to be witnesses of the risen Jesus, the new life of the Spirit in all its dimensions is not recorded. Yet Luke's readers, who were gathered in small house churches all over the empire, knew of it.

The point of Pentecost then is that the promised kingdom of God with all its blessings (or his promised salvation) now comes to earth. The coming of God's kingdom was *promised* by the ancient prophets; *proclaimed and manifest* in the life of Jesus; *fulfilled* when Jesus became Lord and poured out the Spirit on the day of Pentecost (Acts 2:33); and will finally *permeate all creation* when Jesus returns (Acts 3:20–21).

Peter quotes Joel's prophesy because it highlights what the crowd sees and hears. They see God's Spirit upon all of God's people, not just a select group of prophets and kings, as in the Old Testament. They see both men and women, young and old, servants and freed men, speaking of God's powerful works through Jesus. The old boundaries are being erased. Now, like "an unprecedented deluge,"[8] the Spirit came upon each disciple regardless of gender, age, or class. This is a sign to the Jewish crowd that the kingdom of God has come for them.

It can be difficult to understand how "portents in the heaven above and signs on the earth below" are fulfilled at Pentecost. Joel speaks of "signs and wonders" occurring "before the coming of the Lord's great and glorious day" (Acts 2:19–20), and Peter will soon speak of "wonders and signs" that God did through Jesus (Acts 2:22). Then Luke will often write of the many signs and wonders done by the apostles (Acts 2:43). Thus, the disciples may have interpreted the signs and wonders done by Jesus, and now by the apostles, as a partial fulfillment of Joel's prophesy. Yet "wonders in the heaven above" and "blood and fire and billows of smoke" seem to imply more cosmic, universal signs (Acts 2:19a, 20b). Jesus had described the time before his second coming with similar language (Luke 21:25–27). So perhaps we are to expect cosmic, universal signs at the very end of the age before Jesus returns and God's kingdom permeates all creation.[9]

Peter concluded his quote from Joel with the words "then everyone who calls on the name of the Lord shall be saved" (Acts 2:21). Joel speaks of a new deliverance, the time of salvation when the Spirit is given. In Joel's prophecy, as in all the prophets, it is the Lord God, creator of heaven and earth, who pours out the Spirit in the last days. And it is on his name everyone is to call for salvation. Watch how Peter will apply these promises to the risen Lord Jesus.

---

8. Peterson, *Acts of the Apostles*, 141.
9. Peterson, *Acts of the Apostles*, 143; Spencer, *Journeying Through Acts*, 46.

5

Peter Explains Pentecost
(Acts 2:22–36)

Now I THINK THAT I might get myself in trouble. Actually, I know I will get myself in trouble with some of you. But that's all right. For what I will write now and in the rest of this chapter is the most important part of Acts. I am referring to the content of the gospel we are to believe, live, and share. In short, I believe many of us have only been taught one part of the full gospel proclaimed by Peter at Pentecost and in the other gospel sermons in Acts, and I suggest that not understanding the full gospel has too often resulted in weak living and a weak witness to the world. There. I said it. Let me explain.

I grew up with a John 3:16 version of the gospel, which taught that God sent Jesus into the world to die for our sins so that we could gain eternal life by belief in him. True. But is that all there is?

Then I went to seminary and learned the doctrine of justification by faith from the book of Romans. This explanation of the gospel gave more substance to John 3:16. I learned that God would impart the righteousness of Christ to me by trusting his sacrifice on the cross for me. Again, true. But is this the whole gospel?

This understanding of the gospel was so deeply embedded in me that it became the lens through which I read the Bible. I read it into the teaching of Jesus and then Paul.

My biggest problem was with Peter's and Paul's gospel sermons in Acts. When I read them, I couldn't find the gospel! For example, why didn't Peter proclaim the simple gospel to the thousands who listened at Pentecost? "People of Israel, your sins have separated you from your holy God, but he loves you and sent Jesus to die in your place as your Savior. Believe in him and you will receive eternal life." Why didn't Peter say that? Instead, he quotes at length from the prophet Joel and then goes on and on about David and the resurrection of Jesus.

So, for years I at best skimmed the sermons in Acts because I could not find in them the gospel I had been taught. Our Christian traditions can be so deeply ingrained is us that we are afraid to question them and study the Bible to see if they are true.

By now you are aware that by a more careful study of the gospel sermons in Acts, I have come to understand that while there was truth to the gospel I had been taught, it was partial truth and therefore incorrect. It was I who needed to be corrected, not Peter.

So, I ask you to read Peter's sermons carefully and learn the gospel from him. *I believe that by a better understanding of the full, robust gospel the apostles proclaimed in Acts, we as followers of Jesus can live more full, robust lives and strengthen our witness to the world.*

GOSPEL PROCLAMATION IN ACTS

The gospel Peter proclaims emphasizes how *Jesus fulfilled the promises given to Israel*. This was evident by Peter quoting Joel's prophecy of the Spirit poured out, as promised in the last days. What I want to do now is to go through Peter's proclamation on Pentecost as an example of what he and, later, Paul preached as the gospel.

Peter's sermon in Acts 2:14–39 is the first of eight gospel sermons in Acts (see also, for Peter, Acts 3:12–26; 4:8–12; 10:34–43; and 11:4–18; for Paul, Acts 13:16–41; 14:15–17; 17:22–31; and for Stephen, Acts 7:2–53). These are not teaching sermons. They are gospel proclamations.

We have then eight detailed gospel sermons in Acts. If we take the authority of the Scriptures seriously, we will want to learn the gospel proclaimed by the apostles in them and rethink the one with which we may be familiar. We may also want to reflect on the consequences of a more limited understanding of the gospel for ourselves and our witness to the world.

The following six truths about Jesus are all part of the gospel. It is these six truths making up the gospel that are meant throughout Acts when we read, for example, that the apostles spoke the word of the Lord or proclaimed the good news of the kingdom of God. While the death, resurrection, and exaltation of Jesus as Lord are most central, there are three other important truths that occur in most of the other gospel messages. I follow Peter's message in Acts 2 with occasional references to some of the other messages in Acts.

1. The Gospel Begins with the Spirit-Empowered Life of Jesus

You that are Israelites, listen to what I have to say: Jesus of Nazareth, a man attested to you by God with deeds of power, wonders, and signs that God did through him among you, as you yourselves know . . .

(ACTS 2:22)

. . . how God anointed Jesus of Nazareth with the Holy Spirit and with power; how he went about doing good and healing all who were oppressed by the devil, for God was with him.

(ACTS 10:38)

The story of Jesus' bringing salvation to the world does not begin the day he died but with his Spirit-saturated life. Sadly, some of our ancient confessions move straight from the virgin birth of Jesus to his death, as though his life was not part of the gospel. But the Gospels affirm that God gave Jesus his Spirit at his baptism to enact and proclaim the arrival of his kingdom. Notice—Peter says the man Jesus from Nazareth was attested by God by the miracles that God did (by his Spirit) through him. Jesus revealed in his life, ministry, and teachings the nature of God's good and just kingdom bursting into the world to restore it.

Because Jesus embodied the very life and will of God, it is important for us to saturate ourselves with his life and teachings. His life is to become our life. Imitating his life gives visible expression to confessing him as our Lord.

Why is the Spirit-empowered life an important part of the gospel? Because Jesus is the gospel! Everything he said and did is a revelation of God and what we are to become. While it is wrong to limit the gospel to the life and teachings of Jesus, it is also wrong to limit the gospel to his death for our sins. I have often talked with secular friends who are attracted to the life and teachings of Jesus! The beauty of his life can be a good way to begin people on their journey to God.

2. Jesus the Messiah Was Crucified According to God's Plan (Acts 3:13–15, 18; 4:11; 10:27–39)

> ... this man, handed over to you according to the definite plan and foreknowledge of God, crucified and killed by the hands of those outside the law.
>
> (ACTS 2:23)

Peter then teaches that the death of Jesus was part of God's plan. While Peter's listeners were part of the crowd who cried out for Jesus to be crucified, Jesus was handed over to them "according to the definite plan and foreknowledge of God" (Acts 2:23). They only did what God permitted them to do to fulfill his purposes through Jesus.

Their rejection of Jesus did not defeat the plan of God but rather accomplished it. Peter likely said more about the meaning of Jesus' death. Luke assumes his readers have read his Gospel, where he stresses Jesus' journey to Jerusalem to die in our place and deliver us from sin. Because of the emphasis on the death of Jesus in the Gospels, Acts stresses the resurrection and reign of Jesus as Lord.

The death of Jesus is central to the gospel because it is the basis for our forgiveness and freedom from the tyranny of sin over us. We rejoice that we have peace with God through our Lord Jesus Christ. The death of the Messiah is crucial because the people of God must first be cleansed before God comes to dwell in them through his Spirit.

3. God Has Raised Jesus from the Dead (Acts 2:25–29; 3:15; 5:30–31; 10:40–41; 13:30–37)

> But God raised him up, having freed him from death, because it was impossible for him to be held in its power. For David says concerning him, "I saw the Lord always before me, for he is at my right hand so that I will not be shaken."
>
> (ACTS 2:24–25)

> You know the message he sent to the people of Israel, preaching peace by Jesus Christ—He is Lord of all.
>
> (ACTS 10:36)

It can be easy to get lost in Peter's many references to David in Acts 2:24–32, but his point is clear: *because Jesus was the Messiah, it was impossible for him to remain dead, for the Messiah, as a descendent of David, must reign over God's eternal kingdom.*

Peter quotes from a psalm of King David to support this point (Ps 16:8–11). His purpose is to show how Jesus' resurrection testifies to his being the Messiah,[1] for the Messiah must be raised from the dead if he is to reign forever over God's kingdom.

Peter points out that Ps 16 cannot refer to the reign of King David when it says, "God's Holy One cannot be abandoned to death," for his listeners all knew that David's bones remained in his tomb here in Jerusalem not far from where they now stand. David must have been referring to one of his descendants, the Messiah, who would reign on God's eternal throne. In short, "Peter's point is that only through *resurrection* from the dead could a son of David rule forever over God's people."[2]

The resurrection of Jesus is central to the gospel message, for without it we would not believe he was the Messiah. Any faith we might have in him would be futile. If he is dead, what hope do we have after death? Further, because Jesus could endure his sufferings by looking forward to the joy awaiting him after the resurrection, so can we. His life becomes the pattern for our lives. We live cruciform lives with an eye to reigning with him.

Luke stresses the resurrection of Jesus in Acts because it is the sign that the age to come has already begun. The resurrection of the body for the Jews was the beginning of the age to come. By the resurrection of Jesus, God's new creation has already come upon us. Jesus is "the first fruit" of all the righteous who will be raised to reign with him. Thus, the resurrection of Jesus along with the pouring out of the Spirit were clear signs for the Jews that God's eternal kingdom had come, if not yet in its fullness.

Peter's speech now reaches its climax as he stresses that God raised Jesus from the dead to make him Lord over his kingdom. Acts repeatedly stresses the resurrection of Jesus not only to vindicate Jesus and validate his message but also to emphasize what Jesus has been raised *to*. *In Acts the resurrection of Jesus becomes a code word for his exaltation. The Messiah was raised to reign as Lord.*

---

1. Peterson, *Acts of the Apostles*, 147.
2. Peterson, *Acts of the Apostles*, 149.

4. The Day Jesus Became Lord and Messiah (Acts 2:33–36; 4:12; 5:31; 7:55–56; 9:10,15; 10:36)

This Jesus God raised up, and of that all of us are witnesses. Being therefore exalted at the right hand of God, and having received from the Father the promise of the Holy Spirit, He has poured out this that you both see and hear. For David did not ascend into the heavens . . . Therefore, let the entire house of Israel know with certainty that God has made him both Lord and Messiah, this Jesus whom you crucified.

(Acts 2:32–33a, 36)

Because God promised King David that one of his descendants would reign over his kingdom, the enthronement of Jesus as Lord at God's right hand is the fulfillment of this promise to David.

I believe we need to give Pentecost and the enthronement of Jesus at his ascension some of the attention we give to Christmas and Easter.

Imagine the reception of Jesus by the Father and all the hosts of heaven as he is exalted at the right hand of God to be made Lord. Imagine the celebration that burst forth. We don't often think about this, but it happened. If a great company of heavenly hosts celebrated Jesus' birth, how much more would all of heaven have exploded in praise and honor to the Lamb who had died and now reigns as God's King? Revelation 5 describes the praise to Jesus, the Lamb of God, that continues day and night. So, imagine. Rejoice with the heavenly hosts that Jesus is exalted.

Acts often refers to Jesus' exalted position as "at the right hand of God," but what is the full significance of this? In the Jewish Scriptures the right hand of God is "a position of power and authority and the place from which blessings and deliverance come for God's people."[3] For most Jews, "no person is able to sit permanently in God's Presence. God's glory and person are too unique to allow this."[4] But now the apostles proclaim that Jesus, the Man from Nazareth, sits and reigns forever at God's right hand. This means that *as Lord* Jesus now takes the position of power and authority over God's kingdom, and *as Messiah* he rescues and blesses his disciples.

Peter makes this point as a climax to his message: all are to "know with certainty that God has made him (Jesus) both Lord and Messiah."

---

3. Thompson, *Acts of the Risen Lord*, 51.
4. Bock, *Acts*, 134.

Puzzling. Wasn't Jesus already addressed as Lord and Messiah by his disciples in the Gospels? In what way could God have now made him Lord and Messiah?

Before addressing these questions, I want to emphasize that Jesus did not become a new person when he was raised from the dead and exalted to God's right hand. There is only one Jesus, not "an early Jesus and a heavenly Jesus." The one Jesus, now with a transformed, resurrected body, is at the right hand of God. This and similar verses in the New Testament do not refer to a change in the *being of Jesus (ontology)* but to *a change of status or position.*

Now for the crucial question. How could Jesus have been made, or appointed, Lord and Messiah? For years I had a static view of Jesus. He was eternally the same—never to change. But Peter says Jesus was made both Lord and Messiah when he was exalted to God's right hand.

To be made Messiah means that the blessings Jesus bestowed on his disciples while on earth are now poured out more fully as Jesus works through the Spirit dwelling in each of them.

That *Jesus was made Lord* when exalted to God's right hand is central to New Testament teaching. For example, Paul writes that because Jesus took the nature of a servant, humbled himself, and became obedient to death on a cross: "God exalted him to the highest place and gave him the name that is above every name . . . that every tongue confess Jesus Christ as Lord" (Phil 2:5–11). (See also Rom 1:3–4; Eph 1:19–22; and 1 Cor 15:24–28.)

Jesus is addressed as both Lord and Messiah in the Gospels. The power and authority Jesus received by the Spirit at his baptism hinted at his lordship, and his compassionate acts of healing and rescuing the lost revealed he is the Messiah. But what began while on earth, he fully entered into at his exaltation.

As one scholar comments on Acts 2:26, "Jesus did not in any full sense assume the roles of Lord and Messiah over all until after the resurrection and ascension. It was not that Jesus became *someone* different from whom he was before, but that he entered a new stage in his career or assumed new roles after the ascension. Only as an exalted one could Jesus take on the tasks overall and be the universal Messiah."[5]

"Jesus is Lord" becomes the primary identity of Jesus after his exaltation. "Lord" is the most frequently used title for Jesus in Acts (104

---

5. Witherington, *Acts of the Apostles*, 149.

times), and Paul most often writes of Jesus as "the Lord Jesus Christ," that is, Jesus who is Lord and Messiah.

"The messianic, lordly, and kingly confession of Jesus is not incidental to the Bible. It is the point of the Bible, and the gospel is the good news that Jesus is that Messiah, that Lord, and that King. We are his subjects. The question over and over in the Bible is: 'Who is the rightful Lord of this cosmic Temple?'"[6]

Confessing Jesus as our Lord means we worship him, honor him, and seek to build our lives on his example and teachings (for Luke this would have meant what he wrote about Jesus in his Gospel). While we rejoice in our salvation and daily call out to Jesus for help and healing, we are called to make his life our life. We show Jesus to the world.

Confessing Jesus as Lord means we reject allegiance to any other claims for our lives, building our lives on the false stories our culture offers. Some of those stories are:

- Individualism—the story that "I" am the center of the universe
- Consumerism—the story that I am what I own
- Nationalism—the story that my nation is God's nation
- Moral relativism—the story that we can't know what is universally good
- Postmodern tribalism—the story that all that matters is what my community believes.
- Salvation by therapy—the story that I can only come to my full human potential through inner exploration.[7]

5. As Exalted Lord, Jesus Gives the Promised Spirit (Acts 1:8; 2:14–18, 33, 38–39; 10:44–47)

Being therefore exalted at the right hand of God, and having received from the Father the promise of the Holy Spirit, He has poured out this that you both see and hear.

(ACTS 2:33)

---

6. McKnight, *King Jesus Gospel*, 141.
7. Wilkens and Stanford, *Hidden Worldviews*, cited in McKnight, *King Jesus*, 157.

And as I began to speak, the Holy Spirit fell upon them just as it had upon us at the beginning.

(ACTS 11:15)

As readers we have been waiting for Peter to connect Jesus' ascension and the pouring out of the Spirit. Peter now gives us the answer. God has given his exalted Lord the Spirit to send to the disciples.

Pentecost is about the Spirit, and it is about the Lord who gives the Spirit. Moreover, Jesus comes to dwell in and work through his disciples by the Spirit to expand the kingdom of God on earth. Jesus does not leave the disciples alone. He is still present with them. In fact, he is more present and active and alive now than when he walked the roads of Galilee, for he has become a life-giving Spirit (1 Cor 15:45), everywhere present and always at work in Acts and in our world.

The first task Jesus received at his enthronement was to pour out the Spirit. Joel's prophecy says that *God* would pour out the Spirit in the last days (Acts 2:17, 18). But now we read that Jesus receives "from the Father the promise of the Holy Spirit" to give to the disciples. This got me to thinking.

We know God gave Jesus his Spirit at his baptism to carry out his kingdom mission. I have a friend who likes to quote from John, where we read that "God gives the Spirit without measure" to Jesus (John 3:34). And Paul later writes that "God was pleased to have all his fullness dwell in him" (Col 1:19), that is, "all the fullness of the Deity. . ." (Col 2:9). I understand the fullness of God coming to dwell in Jesus to have happened at his baptism. But I suggest the giving of the Spirit at Jesus' baptism pales in comparison to what he now receives from the Father. For what he receives and pours out now brings to fulfillment all the unending blessings and promises of God for his people. Like a mighty river after a storm, the love, the blessings, and the very Presence of God come upon and deeply within the disciples.

Paul later writes that at his resurrection, Jesus "became a life-giving Spirit" (1 Cor 15:45). "By virtue of his resurrection and exaltation he has become a 'life-giving Spirit,' the fountainhead of the people of God in the new age."[8] As the risen Lord, Jesus shares fully in the life of God and pours out the life of God on all his followers. A new power, a resurrection

---

8. Ladd, *Theology of the New Testament*, 422.

power, a resurrection life, a Spirit-saturated power, was unleashed in the universe by Jesus.

Do we see what we have access to? We can live like Jesus. We can be used by him to bear fruit for God's kingdom. Just as Spirit, power, and kingdom growth are linked in Jesus' life, so now in ours. We receive the Spirit to continue his mission of building God's kingdom on earth. His mission is our mission. In Acts, Luke will show time and time again how the disciples imitate the life of their Lord because he is at work in them by his Spirit.

6. God Will Send Jesus Back to Judge All People.

He commanded us to preach to the people and to testify that he is the one ordained by God as judge of the living and the dead.

(ACTS 10:42)

Because he has fixed a day on which he will have the world judged in righteousness by a man whom he has appointed, and of this he has given assurance to all by raising him from the dead.

(ACTS 17:31)

The apostles emphasize in their proclamation the new life God desires to give. Yet they also announce (normally at the end of their message when it has been rejected) that Jesus will return as Judge to justly punish all who have opposed and rejected God's gracious offer. The Gospels speak more often than Acts of Jesus' second coming to separate the righteous from the unrighteous.

The timing and manner of speaking to a friend or neighbor of this is important. Perhaps because of images of people burning endlessly in flames of hell, the final judgment is rarely taught, at least in all the churches I have attended in the past thirty years.

But there are different interpretations of the nature of the last judgment. I have settled on the view that the New Testament teaches eternal immortality; eternal life is a gift to those who embrace the Gospel. The Bible teaches that God alone inherently possesses immortality (1 Tim 6:16) and that he graciously gives it to all who seek it through the Gospel (Rom 2:6–10, etc.).

Humans were not created by God with an immortal, eternal soul. That is what Plato taught.[9]

I believe almost everyone longs for justice. Think about how you feel when you read of sexual abuse or tens of thousands being misplaced, suffering, and dying because an autocrat wants more power and land. We all long for a world where death, darkness, division, hatred, oppression, and abuse are banished forever so that only light, love, goodness, and beauty permeate God's creation.

SPEAKING THE GOSPEL

Peter's main point then is that *Jesus has been enthroned as Lord. In his capacity as Lord, Jesus has sent the Spirit, pouring out all the blessings of the age to come, and empowers the disciples as his witnesses to continue his mission of restoring our dark and damaged world according to God's good and just ways.*

But the six events in the life of Jesus reviewed above, taken together, make up the good news about Jesus. They show how God's plan for humanity and the *promises God gave to the people of Israel* are now *fulfilled in Jesus* (Acts 2:16–17, 24–31, 39; 3:18, 24–25; 10:27). When Peter and Paul address their fellow Jews, they rehearse their common history to show how *the promises and roles* given to them have been fulfilled in Jesus the Messiah. Yet, when Paul speaks to non-Jews, he omits the history of Israel (not known to them) and connects with their common humanity as part of God's creation (Acts 14:15–17; 17:24–29). Then instead of speaking of Jesus as the Messiah, a concept unknown to them, he proclaims him as Lord.

Because most people today are not aware of the promises given to Israel in the Bible, it is important to connect the gospel to the larger

---

9. Human beings can perish, be destroyed, and thus, cease to exist. Those who have willfully rejected God's mercy and persisted in evil will stand before Jesus and be fairly judged for how they have lived. How that will look and for how long they will suffer punishment will vary. But in time, since they have not gained immortality by the gospel, they, in the words of the Bible, will perish, be destroyed, and thus, cease to exist. You may not agree with this interpretation and that's fine, but I encourage you to study and settle on a view and include it in your gospel understanding. For with compassion people need to be warned.

The idea that every human being has an immortal soul that cannot die was taught by Plato, then following him, Socrates and other Greek philosophers. Their view influenced how Christian thinkers later read the Bible until it became the dominant view in the church, largely through the influence of Augustine. (See Fudge and Peterson, *Two Views of Hell*.)

context of our common humanity and our tasks as image-bearers of God. The message about Jesus is not a new religion. It is the fulfillment of God's design for humanity from the very beginning.

The apostles stress the gospel is a story worked out by God with *a beginning* with creation and then the call of Israel; *a middle* with promises to David of a descendent who will rule over an eternal kingdom; *and a completion with Jesus,* who now rules as Lord over God's kingdom.[10]

A FOCUS ON STAGES OF THE KINGDOM'S COMING

It confused me as a young believer to read in the Gospels where Jesus said the kingdom of God had arrived and then later teach that it would come at the end time. Then adding to my confusion, I read something by a respected scholar that the kingdom of God came at Pentecost! That I could not understand. And if the kingdom of God came at Pentecost, why does Peter shortly after command the Jewish people to turn to God so that the kingdom will come for them (Acts 3:19–21)?

In case you haven't sorted this out, let me try.

There is a crucial connection between the Holy Spirit and the coming of the kingdom. As already emphasized, the prophets said that the kingdom of God would come to earth when the Spirit is poured out on God's people.

The Spirit was first poured on Jesus at his baptism. The life and powers of God's kingdom were present in Jesus for all to see. This is what Jesus meant when he said the kingdom of God was here. It was present for all to see in Jesus' person and ministry. But what about us?

The Spirit with the life and powers of the kingdom cannot live in us until our rebellion has been dealt with. This is where the death of Christ fits into the coming of the kingdom. We must be cleansed by Christ's death to receive God's Spirit and life, as well as blessings of the kingdom. This happened at Pentecost. There could not have been a Pentecost until our rebellion had been dealt with.

Jesus first receives the Spirit with kingdom powers and authority, and then after cleansing us by his death for us, he pours the Spirit and the life of the kingdom on the disciples. Judgment and blessings

---

10. McKnight, *King Jesus Gospel*, 131.

first come to Jesus, the second Adam and the firstborn of a new humanity, then to us.

This means that by the Spirit, the future kingdom of God has already come upon us so that we experience its blessings. The love, joy, and peace we experience in community now is of the same kind that we will experience fully in the future.

6

Responding to the Gospel
(Acts 2:37–41)

ONE DAY ESUGA AND I explored the ruins immediately south of the Temple Mount. I mentioned earlier that Peter may have spoken there on Pentecost and that the three thousand who believed were likely baptized in the many pools there. The Jews immersed themselves in them before entering the temple. This practice is called *mikvah*.

Archeologists have located over 164 pools, so my interest was high as we walked the length of the southern wall, finding pool after pool used for the purification of all who entered the temple. Some had been built below houses and other, much larger ones in separate buildings.

As always, Esuga was patient with me as I took picture after picture of the pools and carefully digested the signs explaining their function. Fresh water was required in each pool for the purification to be proper. One set of steps led down to the pool for a complete immersion of the body, and another set of steps led back up. The worshiper was then ready to enter the Temple Mount and pray.

When I returned home from our travels, I began to think more about the Jewish ritual of mikvah. What was its purpose? Was every Jew who entered the temple required to do it? Would the Jewish disciples, now baptized into Christ, continue to immerse themselves in these pools every day when they entered the temple? Wouldn't they raise suspicion if they walked around the lines for mikvah and went straight into the temple?

Since my baptism as a very young boy had meant little to me, I have always toyed with the idea of going to a lake to immerse myself in the water—again and again and again. If the apostles were baptized and then immersed themselves day after day before entering the temple, why couldn't I do it again now and then?

So, I met with a scholar steeped in Jewish practices at this time. She confirmed my hunch that all Jews were required to do mikvah before entering the temple and that the Jewish disciples would continue to do so. When I asked her to explain the significance of the practice, she explained it this way. "Immersion in the pools was not for cleansing of sins as we might think, but more acknowledging one's weakened humanity before standing before God in the Temple."[1]

I would like to believe that the disciples had added more meaning to their daily immersions. Perhaps they thanked the Lord for cleansing them deeply within by his death on the cross and rejoiced in their new identity in belonging to Christ.

Since my visit to Israel, I have learned that many Christians remember their baptism by making the sign of the cross over them with water. Then a Muslim friend shared that whenever it rains, she goes out to stand in the rain and lifts her hands to God, asking him to wash away all her anxiety, fears, and misdeeds.

I think you see where I've been heading. The first disciples in Jerusalem immersed themselves daily in water before entering the temple. Many in the Christian tradition remember their baptism regularly with water. And then I learn that some Muslims find it meaningful to go out into the rain and lift their hands to God for spiritual refreshment. And here I sit with my baptism as a boy wanting more water.

Don't worry. I have no plans to start a new denomination called the Church of Heavenly Rain, but I don't see any harm in immersing myself in a lake or river now and then or standing out in the rain with my hands lifted high to God, thanking him for cleansing me and asking him to wash away my anxieties, fears, and failures. Why not try it? Just don't start a new denomination.

---

1. Personal conversation with Cyndi Parker, Aug. 12, 2021.

GIVE ALLEGIANCE TO JESUS

The exaltation of Jesus as Israel's Messiah and Lord (Acts 2:26) calls for a response. Recall that Peter is speaking to fellow Jews who not only knew their Scriptures but also knew about Jesus. They knew about his claims to be the Messiah and sadly responded by taking part in his crucifixion six weeks earlier (Acts 2:23), but now they have witnessed the extraordinary events of Pentecost and listened to Peter explain that God has raised Jesus from the dead. It is true. He is the Messiah; he has been made Lord over God's kingdom and has poured out the Spirit for them to receive. They are filled with remorse for their part in having Jesus put to death.

They ask Peter and the other apostles, "Brothers, what should we do?" In short, Peter answers that they must acknowledge their wrongdoings, turn from their self-oriented life to the self-offering way of the Messiah (that is, "repent"), and be baptized in the name of Jesus, confessing him as their Lord.

When Jesus was asked in the Gospels how to inherit the kingdom of God, he answered that a person must turn in repentance to God, love him above all else, and follow Jesus as a disciple by practicing his teachings, centered on love for others.[2] But now, because of what God has accomplished through the death, resurrection, and exaltation of Jesus, one must turn to God through Jesus, that is, in his name.

While repentance—a genuine sorrow for how one has lived and a commitment to live a new way—is toward God in the ancient prophets, now a person must repent in light of God sending Jesus. Repentance now means "a radical reorientation of life with respect to Jesus."[3] This means we give our full allegiance to Jesus as our Lord and become obedient to his teachings and example.

Joining a new religious group in the Roman Empire did not require a change of behavior. A person simply changed one's previous rituals and religious experience for another.[4] In contrast, the prophets of Israel called upon the people of Israel to change their ways and demanded a reorientation of life,[5] often expressed by mercy and justice for the poor. Now the reorientation of life is more specifically to the life of Jesus, who embodied the depths of God's mercy and justice for all.

2. Duddleston, *Why Jesus the Messiah*, 143–47.
3. Peterson, *Acts of the Apostles*, 154.
4. Keener, *Acts, Vol. 1*, 972.
5. Peterson, *Acts of the Apostles*.

In reading Acts we can tend to forget that Luke assumes we know and believe all he has written about Jesus in his Gospel. Those Peter addresses knew they must devote themselves to what the apostles taught them about Jesus. So, we are to saturate ourselves with the Gospels to make Jesus' life our life. Above all, driven by love and obedience to God, Jesus denied himself and poured out his life for the good of others—even his enemies and especially the poor and downcast.

This new and fuller meaning of repentance in light of Jesus becomes even clearer when we read that we are to be baptized "in the name of Jesus Christ." The name of Jesus represents his identity, who he is. At baptism (which in Acts occurred soon after one believed), a person confessed his allegiance to Jesus as Lord—believing God has made him Lord and believing in all he did and taught.[6]

Other Jews were being baptized here in Jerusalem. How was one to know how the disciples differed from other Jewish sects? It was by putting the name of Jesus as Lord on their lips at their baptism. "People being baptized 'in his name' designated whose followers they would be."[7]

THE PROMISE OF GOD

Peter promises both the forgiveness of sins and the gift of the Spirit to those who confess Jesus as Lord. Peter's hearers had committed the hideous sin of taking part in crucifying Jesus. But God's mercy knows no bounds. They can now be fully cleansed and forgiven. Because our sin alienates us from God, the forgiveness of sins is our greatest need and thus God's greatest gift.

The indwelling of the Spirit is called the promise of God (Acts 1:4; 2:33, 39; etc.) because *all the promises of God become a reality when the Spirit comes to dwell within us.* These promises include the new covenant promises: cleansing from sin and shame, freedom from fear, living in unity, the power to obey God, and above all, knowing God, experiencing his peace and Presence (Jer 31:33–34). The summary of the disciples' life together at the end of this chapter (Acts 2:42–47) provides a glimpse of the new life they experienced together as God's new community.

It is often overlooked that when the gospel is proclaimed in Acts, people were promised that they would receive the Spirit when they

6. Peterson, *Acts of the Apostles.*
7. Keener, *Acts, Vol. 1,* 983.

believed. Thus, they *expected* to receive God's Spirit when they believed and were *conscious of receiving him and the blessings he gave.* Their experiences may have varied, but all were told that God's Spirit would come to dwell within them. They believed this and rejoiced in it.

Not promising people that they would receive the Spirit when they believe may be one reason for the lack of power and enthusiasm in the lives of many Christians. Perhaps we would have more dynamic, joyful, effective communities of Jesus followers if we followed this pattern of sharing the gospel in Acts.

Before Luke writes a summary of the kind of community the Spirit creates, we read that on this very day, the day of Pentecost, which began at 9:00 a.m. with 120 disciples from Galilee praying privately in the house where they met now ends with three thousand devout Jews from the nations publicly joining their community.

This is a remarkable result. Some even believe Luke may have exaggerated the number. He likely rounded it off (a normal practice at the time), in that Jerusalem swelled to nearly two hundred thousand during Jewish festivals. Since these new disciples already knew both the Scriptures and about the life and death of Jesus, the numbers are realistic. When Paul later took the gospel to the gentiles, the response is much smaller and had to slowly grow as a mustard seed until it penetrated the Roman Empire.

7

The Community God Created
(Acts 2:42–47)

I MENTIONED EARLIER THAT I am a potter. The first thing I teach new potters is that to make quality ceramic pieces, they must first center the clay well. I've spent many years centering clay on my wheel. Sometimes when making a large shallow bowl, I like to slow down the wheel, put my fingers inside, and watch the concentric circles form as I move them toward the center. Then I will sit for a few minutes looking at the center of the bowl as it slowly turns on the wheel. And I think, that's the kind of person I want to be. Always moving toward the Center.

I'm often thinking about what's in the Center. What is there? What are we to be moving toward? I don't want to miss it, with all the distractions of life. I guess you could say that I am passionate about living, living fully as a human being for all it's worth. We have been reading about the Center in Acts 2. It is the living, loving God coming to live in us and with us.

What strikes me about the following summary of the early Jesus movement is that the disciples met daily together to live in the Center—the Presence and power of God—and their lives together attracted those around them to come and see. Notice some of the descriptions of their life together: awe, signs showing God's Presence, eating together daily with glad and generous hearts, praising God, and taking care of all those who had need. This is what God has created us for. This is the Center. Isn't this what we all want?

As written, it is better to speak of moving toward the Center than living in the Center. Someday we will live fully, forever in the Center, but in this life, we easily get distracted and must keep moving back. Staying close to the Center is best done in a small community of believers. This is what we learn in the following summary. We see the life in others, we taste the life in others, and we enjoy our life with God together.

My wife, Eeva, and I often invite people over for meals or coffee, and when we do, Eeva always asks if we can pray together before they leave. The Spirit leading us in prayer for each other and the needs of others always ties our time together.

As we live like these first followers of Jesus, our neighbors will notice, and some will be attracted and want to learn. For even if they are not conscious of it, they, too, long for the Center, and God longs to bring them there.

LUKE'S FIRST SUMMARY—LIVING AS A NEW COMMUNITY

The narrative shifts from a description of specific events on the day of Pentecost to a summary of the days in the new community God has created.[1] *We now see God's intention for sending Jesus and why he gave the Spirit. It was for this kind of life together.* This is a picture of the kind of world God has been working toward. He seeks to remake our shattered, broken world of relationships into vibrant communities: alive to him, rejoicing in him, always together, always caring for each other's needs.

This is the first of similar summaries in Acts (see, for example, Acts 4:32–37 and 5:12–16) which function to show us the effects of the Spirit working in his disciples. The summaries show how the disciples, filled with the Spirit and living by the teachings of Jesus, modeled the ideal community.[2] This first portrait of the community of disciples after Pentecost suggests "the gift of the Spirit brought about a community which realized the highest aspirations of human longing: unity, peace, joy and the praise of God."[3]

Luke will not gloss over the weaknesses of the disciples, but he writes so that his readers will be fully devoted to the Lord and create

---

1. Peterson, *Acts of the Apostles*, 158.
2. Keener, *Acts, Vol. 1*, 991.
3. Johnson, *Acts of the Apostles*, 62, quoted in Peterson, *Acts of the Apostles*, 158.

similar communities in their homes and neighborhoods throughout the Roman Empire. We, too, are challenged to devote ourselves to this life if we are to live in the Center, thrive as human beings together, and live as an attractional life-changing force in the world.

Luke begins with what we would call a theme sentence. He writes, "They devoted themselves to the apostles' teaching and fellowship, to the breaking of bread and the prayers" (Acts 2:42). These four areas summarize what we read in verses 44–47 and are repeated throughout Acts.[4] I will use them to frame my comments. But first I draw attention to the important word translated as "devoted." It indicates the disciples were "continually occupied, diligent in practicing" the life summarized here.[5] They made it their aim to practice this way of life together.

Devoted to the Apostles' Teaching

We read first that the disciples devoted themselves daily (Acts 2:46) to the apostles' teaching. They were taught by all the apostles, not just Peter. The teaching likely took place just east of the temple proper in the open, shaded area of Solomon's Portico (Acts 5:12) overlooking the Mount of Olives.

Since it was common for Jewish leaders to teach in the temple courts, and since the temple platform which covered thirty-five acres could hold up to 200,000 people,[6] groups of 250 disciples, each gathering around an apostle, would not in itself have attracted too much attention. More important than where they met is what the apostles taught.

We recall that to be an apostle, a person must have been with Jesus from the beginning of his ministry to his ascension (Acts 1:21–22). Since it was the common practice of a disciple to memorize the teachings and events of his rabbi's life, the apostles could now teach about Jesus to the thousands of new disciples in Jerusalem.

Because they met in homes scattered across Jerusalem in the evenings, I suggest they discussed what they had learned from the apostles at the temple in their small gatherings in their homes. In this way, the life of Jesus became more personal and formed their individual communities.

Right in the middle of the summary we read two verses stressing how the disciples practiced Jesus' teaching about the generous use of one's

---

4. Blenkinsopp et al., *New Interpreter's Bible*, 71.
5. Peterson, *Acts of the Apostles*, 160.
6. Keener, *Acts, Vol. 1*, 997, 1103.

possessions to provide for the poor. Nearly "15% of typical urban populations in antiquity were 'expendables,' those for whom the rest of society had no use, such as beggars, widows without families, and orphans."[7] In the countryside roughly 80–85% of the empire lived in abject poverty.[8]

Surrounded by such poverty, their confession of Jesus as Lord meant obeying his teaching to not make money their god but to use their possessions to care for the needy. We will soon read of one of society's expendable beggars, who is not only healed by Peter but is provided for by the community of disciples (Acts 3:1–10).

Later in Acts we read that it is the apostles who oversee the needs of the poor in their fellowship (Acts 4:35, 37). In some way they were connected and organized so that all were cared for. As needs arose, those who had more means would sell their property (or parts of it) and give the proceeds to the apostles to be distributed.

In this and following summaries, Luke highlights the example of the disciples' use of their possessions to provide for the needy among them. But this was not a primitive form of communism. The selling of possessions, while common, was voluntary and meant to meet immediate known needs.

Many disciples kept their homes not only to house and feed others but to host the churches that gathered in them. With more than three thousand disciples in Jerusalem and few houses large enough to accommodate even fifty people (and the average home accommodating only ten to twelve),[9] many homes were needed to maintain their small, vibrant gatherings.

In the immediate centuries that followed, the disciples continued to share their resources in common. "Tertullian remarks wittily that Christians readily shared everything in common except their wives—the one thing, he complains, pagans were most willing to share."[10]

The Greeks wrote of a utopian society in which everyone's needs were provided for but viewed it as an ideal in the distant future. Luke wants us to see that the Jesus community, alive to God's Spirit, not only fulfilled the teaching of Jesus but also the ideals of Greek utopianism.[11]

---

7. Keener, *Acts, Vol. 1*, 997, 1012.
8. Keener, *Acts, Vol. 1*, 997, 1013.
9. Keener, *Acts, Vol. 1*, 997, 1030.
10. Peterson, *Acts of the Apostles*, 160.
11. Keener, *Acts, Vol. 1*, 1013.

Devoted to the Fellowship

We then read that the disciples devoted themselves to fellowship. The word translated "fellowship" signifies something much deeper than simply meeting together. The Greek word (*koinonia*) normally means "to share with someone in something above and beyond the relationship itself." The word also expresses partnership, "the sort of harmony created by shared purpose and working together."[12] As we have just read, this partnership included the sharing of goods as one concrete expression of fellowship.

Above all they shared their lives together. *The something above and beyond their relationship was the Spirit of God in them and holding them together.* The Spirit was the glue uniting them, enlivening their prayers and the words of Jesus.

It is one thing to meet for a Bible study and a meal and yet another thing to gather alive to God's Presence so that we meet "with glad and generous hearts," aware of Someone above and beyond us among us. This is Spirit-led fellowship.

Our relationships with friends and spouses can become strained when we place unrealistic expectations on them to fulfill our deepest longings. God has created us for community but a community where he is at the center, satisfying our deepest longings.

Devoted to the Breaking of Bread

To break bread was a Jewish expression for beginning an ordinary meal. In the following verses we read that they broke bread together every day in their homes "with glad and generous hearts, praising God and having the goodwill of all the people" (Acts 2:46–47).

Their gatherings were not as formal as "going to church" for many today. Gathering in the warmth and familiarity of homes invited interaction. Just as we meet with friends to talk about our day over a meal, so would they. Have you heard from your family in Galilee recently? Did you hear John teach at the temple today? Have you witnessed any miracles by the apostles lately? Tell us again about your experience on the Day of Pentecost. Do you have enough food and clothing for the cold

---

12. Keener, *Acts, Vol. 1*, 1002.

weather coming? In this way they knew each other's needs and found ways to meet them.

Of course, they would discuss what they had learned about Jesus from the apostles at the temple that day and how they could practice it. And as part of their meal, they remembered the Lord's life and death for them, that is, they celebrated the Lord's Supper. But there is nothing that suggests that their gatherings were formal, structured services led by an apostle.

They gathered as *an open community* both at the temple and, it seems, in their homes, inviting relatives, friends, and neighbors to join them. For we read in the context of their eating together that they "found favor with all the people" (Acts 2:47).

By living as an open community, they were an attractional force in the world, a collective witness to all around them. Observing their way of life, hearing their stories, seeing the power at work among them, and seeing how they cared for each other, they made a positive impression on the people.

Devoted to Prayer

Finally, and most importantly, they were devoted to prayer. This would have included the set times of prayer at the temple each day and the more personal and spontaneous prayers in their homes in the evenings.

After reading through Acts with some friends several years ago, I came away with one major takeaway that I remember to this day: the disciples in Acts were always together and always praying.

> ### A FOCUS ON THE TEMPLE MOUNT
>
> Since most of the events in the last six chapters of Luke's Gospel and the first seven chapters of Acts take place on and around the Temple Mount, Esuga and I spent nearly a week exploring the area. Becoming familiar with the Temple Mount will help you to better picture the events we now read of in Acts.
>
> It is important to distinguish between the Temple Mount and the temple proper built prominently in its center for sacrifices and prayer. The Temple Mount itself was a gigantic, ornately paved area surrounded by covered colonnades.

I was most impressed with its vast size, which Herod had doubled from Solomon's. Its dimensions still today are the same as in the first century with a length of 512 yards (470 m) and width of 345 yards (315 m). I remember running 100-yard sprints the length of a football field in high school. So, running five football fields speaks to me of its size. The Temple Mount would enclose roughly thirty-five football fields!

Learning that over three hundred thousand Muslims gathered on the Temple Mount for prayer during Ramadan[13] also helped me to visualize its vast size. With two hundred thousand Jews worshiping there during Pentecost, the disciples gathered there for teaching would not have stood out.

Elaborate porticos were built along all the walls of the Temple Mount. Herod built his most magnificent secular edifice ever, the Royal Porch (or Royal Stoa), along the entire 345-yard length of the southern end as a center for public meetings and commercial activity. All the porticos were public places where people could gather, sheltered from the heat and rain.

We read that the disciples gathered daily at Solomon's Portico, which ran the entire 500 yards along the east side with a view to the Mount of Olives (Acts 5:12). Here and there all along Solomon's Portico the disciples in the thousands gathered in groups to be taught or healed by an apostle. Here they would meet as friends, pray together, and likely speak to those who noticed their new way of life and perhaps even witnessed one of them healed.

Solomon's Colonnade is an important part of the story we are now about to read. After the healing of the lame beggar at the gate called Beautiful, just west of Solomon's Portico, Peter speaks to the crowd that gathers there.

At the northwest corner of the Temple Mount, Herod built a fortress, the Antonia, towering over the temple to station Roman soldiers and remind the Jews that the Romans occupied their land and that they were always watched. But when we read that the apostles are arrested and placed in prison in the early part of Acts, they are detained by Jewish authorities and put in their jails. It is not until much later in Acts that the Antonia is mentioned, when Roman troops arrest Paul in the temple and take him there (Acts 21:31–37).

---

13. Beitzel, *Lexham Geographic Commentary*, 117.

Elevated at the highest point in the center of the Temple Mount was the temple proper, with its own courtyards surrounded by its own fortification wall. The façade of the temple itself was covered with gold plates and the upper part built with pure white marble, so that on a clear day the brilliance of the temple could be marveled at from far away as pilgrims approached the city.

The Jewish people believed that God revealed his Presence in a unique way in the temple, making it the meeting place on earth between heaven and earth. It was for them a sign that God had chosen them as his people and that one day the nations would stream to Jerusalem to worship at their temple.[14]

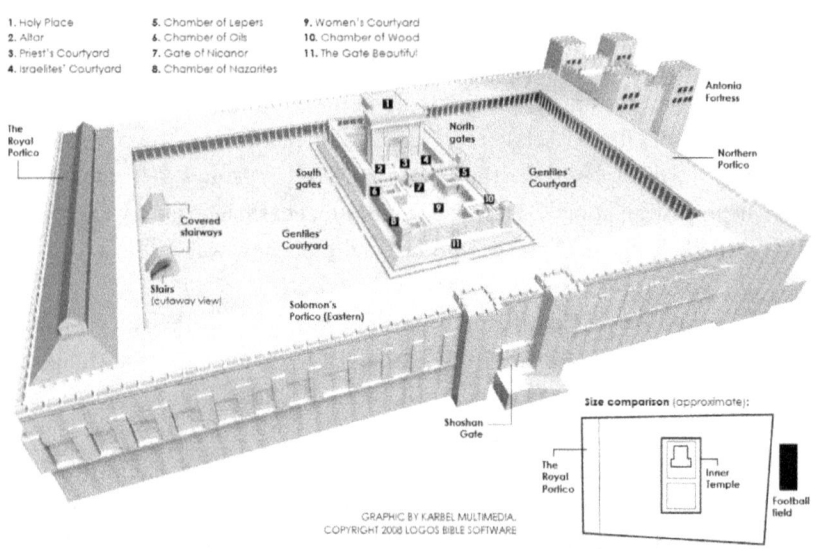

Figure 3: Temple Layout. Used with permission

14. Duddleston, *Jesus the Messiah*, 181–82.

8

The Crippled Beggar
(Acts 3:1–10)

PETER AND JOHN NOW go to the temple to pray, as they and all the other disciples did daily. I wanted to get a feel for how Peter and John made their way from the house where they stayed to the temple. So, after a good breakfast, Esuga and I went out to retrace their steps. He confidently led the way through the narrow, crowded streets of Old Jerusalem, and I followed behind with an eye on his red hoodie.

The distance from the house where the apostles stayed to the Temple Mount was roughly half a mile. But since the trek took us (as it took them) through busy streets, the walk was about twenty minutes. Walter Wangerin brilliantly describes a walk through the crowded city. I quote him at length to imagine your walk with Peter and James.

> [The streets were] surrounded by the rush and pressure of many people. On either side of the streets . . . were shops and merchants, traders, and craftsmen both making and selling their wares: woolen goods, carpets, and blankets. Jewelers sat under whitewashed roofs. Flax traders hung their products on smooth wood railings; bakers sold bread as fast as it came from the back of the shop; sandal makers on their stools called to tailors on theirs. Jerusalem was thriving: wines, oils, fruits, flour milled from barley, cheeses, eggs, and the chicken itself. People were sweeping the great stones of the pavement. Butchers had a street all to themselves. Weavers worked in the southwest portion of the city. Tanners and curriers were required to set their

workshops where the smell could not offend either the pilgrims or the priest.[1]

By placing their wares out in the streets in front of their shops, merchants made passage difficult. Moving quickly to the temple in time for prayer, people bumped into each other and hurried on. They maneuvered around goats and sheep bleating on their way to the temple for sacrifice. There was the stench of body odor, animal dung, and the animals sacrificed at the temple.[2]

I can imagine passing the shops selling freshly baked bread and spices, inhaling, and holding my breath as I hurry on to breathe in more baked goods and spices.

Earlier I mentioned the large plaza south of the Temple Mount where Peter may have spoken on Pentecost. This was also the most common way to enter the Temple Mount—through the Double and Triple Gates, also called the Hulda Gates.[3] So, after their immersing themselves in one of the many pools there, Peter and John climbed the steps to enter the Temple Mount through the Triple Gate.

Passing through this gate, they entered "an underground passage decorated with carved stone and stucco."[4] After walking through this passage under the Temple Mount, they would have climbed another set of stairs, stepping onto the Temple Mount with the temple proper in full view before them.

With the gates blocked up, now hot and tired, Esuga and I sat on the steps that Peter and James climbed, and we sipped on our water. I noticed the steps alternated between a broad one and a short one. I sought an explanation from a tour guide walking by. She explained that the broad step forced you to break your stride, slow down, and remember that you were about to stand before God in the temple. In addition, after visiting the temple, the steps were a good place to sit and reflect on your experience and enjoy the scenery over the southern mountains as you waited for friends to debate the Torah or to discuss the teachings of Jesus that you learned that day.[5]

---

1. Wangerin, *Book of God*, 4178.
2. Personal conversation with Cyndi Parker, Aug. 12, 2021.
3. Magness, *Holy Land*, 16.
4. Magness, *Holy Land*, 17.
5. Magness, *Holy Land*, 16.

THE POWER STRUGGLE

As more and more people around the temple responded to the apostles' teaching, hostility mounted from the leaders of Israel, who as guardians of the temple had high stakes in controlling its functions. Just as their power, prestige, and wealth were threatened when the people flocked to hear Jesus speak at the temple, so now they are threatened as the people flock to hear the apostles teach that God has raised Jesus from the dead.

Since Pentecost, the disciples had begun to live in the new reality of the Spirit working through them. As a result, "many wonders and signs were being done by the apostles" (Acts 2:43).

Acts 3–5 record a power struggle between kingdoms—the kingdom of God, with Jesus as Lord working through his chosen apostles, and unbelieving Israel, led by the Sanhedrin. The apostles' frequent miracles of restoration, compassion for the poor, and proclamation of Jesus as Israel's Lord who rules over believing Israel implies that they are the true leaders of Israel, not the authorities who resist them.

The healing of the crippled beggar at the temple (the only healing miracle recorded in detail until the end of chapter nine) became widely known throughout Jerusalem (Acts 4:16). This miracle, and especially Peter's explanation of how it happened, led to the arrest of Peter and John. The very leaders of Israel who had recently conspired to have Jesus put to death now threaten the apostles, forbidding them from speaking of Jesus.

The healing of the crippled beggar at the temple leads to a series of cause-and-effect events in Acts 3 and 4. Follow him as he is placed by the gate to ask for alms (Acts 3:2), then healed and leaping with joy, as he enters the temple praising God (Acts 3:8). After this he clings to Peter and John as Peter explains to the gathered crowd how he was healed (Acts 3:11). Then he is taken with Peter and John by the temple police; he stands beside them while they are interrogated by the Sanhedrin (Acts 4:14); and finally he joins Peter and John when they return to the disciples to pray, and he is filled with the Spirit with all the others when the house where they prayed was shaken (Acts 4:23). We can imagine his being loved and cared for by the Jesus community, returning to the temple with them each day to share how Jesus had changed his life.

THE HEALING OF THE LAME BEGGAR

We begin with some kindhearted men who again that day, as they had every day, carry the lame beggar and gently place him down at an entrance of the temple by the gate called Beautiful. This gate, the largest of all the temple gates, was covered with bronze that shone like gold when the sun rose from the east over the Mount of Olives and played with its brilliance. The frail, lame beggar with his crippled body looks pathetic on the ground beside the gate called Beautiful, but he knows this is a strategic location to sit and beg as crowds prone toward charity pass him when they pour into the temple to pray. Now, over forty years old and lame from birth (Acts 4:22), he has no choice but to beg.[6]

He was a familiar sight to the tens of thousands who frequented the temple every day. While some were prone to show him charity, "the dominant ethos" among the rich leaders of the temple was disdain. His needs seemed endless. He was one of those expendables for whom the rest of society had no use.[7] But the new true leaders of God's people look upon him with compassion, just as their Lord had looked upon the marginalized of society.

As the lame beggar is placed on the hot pavement by the gate, just as he had been placed ten thousand times on ten thousand days, he thinks this day will be like all other days—one more day to beg for some loose change to buy fragments of bread and a few olives to stay alive. But alive for what? What kind of life is this? His despair is deep, but today it will end.

As Peter and John approach the gate among the crowds, the lame man looks up to see what seem like two kindhearted young men and hopes for a handout. "Can you spare some change, kind sirs?" Peter stops, sensing the Spirit of the Lord stirring his heart, a stirring he has learned to discern. He and John look with compassion at the poor beggar, just as their Lord had looked upon the marginalized. The beggar's legs don't work, but he has learned to use his eyes. He fixes them on Peter and John in hope of receiving some coins.

They had none. Any money they had taken with them from Galilee has been placed in a common fund to be distributed to the poor among them (Acts 2:44–45). But Peter knew of the gifts poured out at Pentecost upon his people. He knew the risen Lord Jesus could raise this man to his feet, enabling him to work with dignity, and until the man could provide

---

6. Keener, *Acts, Vol. 2*, 1059.
7. Keener, *Acts, Vol. 2*, 1061.

for himself, Peter knew the community of believers would take care of him. But much, much more than this, he knew the beggar could be filled with God's Spirit, experience God's love and peace, and find a home in the new community formed by Jesus.

So, Peter looks at him and says, "I have no silver or gold, but what I have I give you; in the name of Jesus Christ of Nazareth, stand up and walk" (Acts 3:6). He then reaches down with that powerful fisherman's forearm, formed from years of pulling nets full of fish from the sea, and grabs the man's right hand and raises him to his feet. Immediately, those feet, ankles, and legs, useless for forty long years, are immediately made strong.

The man who had never walked a day in his life, the man who had always been picked up and placed down through the goodwill of others, that man, like a newborn fawn, now stands to his feet, runs, leaps, and praises God with all his might. For the first time in his life, he enters the temple proper, still leaping and praising God.

Jewish traditions prohibited the crippled from entering the temple. The crippled were widely stereotyped throughout Israelite society "as 'dead dogs': that is, pathetic, impotent, despicable creatures."[8]

But Isaiah had prophesized of the day when God would come to visit his people. "Then the lame will leap like a deer . . . and gladness and joy will overtake them, sorrow and sighing will flee away" (Isa 35:6, 10). That day had come. God came to his people at Pentecost and now to this lame man through the power of the risen Lord Jesus.

THE POWER TO HEAL

Peter is quick to point out that it was not by his power or piety that the man was healed. He was healed because God had exalted his servant Jesus to his right hand (Acts 3:13). Peter and John had only acted in faith in the name of Jesus (Acts 3:16). To have faith in "the name of Jesus" means to believe and live in light of *his present power and authority as Lord over God's kingdom*. It is not a magical formula, acted upon by an endless repetition of the word Jesus. It means to trust in the person of Jesus to act.

When God made Jesus Lord, he gave him "all power in heaven and on earth" (Matt 28:18) to continue the mission he had on earth of establishing God's good and merciful kingdom. Jesus is not absent on earth, "trapped within a fixed spatio-temporal system" in heaven. He has not

---

8. Spencer, *Journeying Through Acts*, 55.

left the disciples alone to serve God as best they can muster. As exalted Lord through the Spirit, Jesus remains an active friend, guide, and healer "channeling God's life-giving energy (cf. Acts 3:15) to the poor and lame just as he did before his departure."[9]

I like to say that the disciples *knew who Jesus was, where he was, and what that could mean for them.* And that made all the difference! They knew that he reigned as Lord at the right hand of God and wanted to lead and empower his people to continue his work on earth. We, too, must know *this Jesus, the exalted life-giving Jesus,* and his desire to lead and empower us to do his will, if we are to live out our faith with boldness and hope.

As the beggar once lame now enters the temple, "walking and leaping and praising God" (Acts 3:9), all the people recognize him as the beggar who had sat year after year at the Beautiful Gate and are filled with wonder. Just as at Pentecost, the scene is set for an explanation, a witness Peter will give.

---

9. Peterson, *Acts of the Apostles*, 177.

9

Peter's Explanation of the Power
(Acts 3:11–26)

I WANTED TO VISIT the Temple Mount with Esuga so we could visualize the movements of the lame beggar and Peter. Since the southern gates to the Temple Mount are blocked up, the following day, about three in the afternoon, we entered through the only gate open to non-Muslims at the southwest corner of the Temple Mount. We walked up a ramp along the Western Wall, peered down at the praying, passed through security, and stepped out onto the Temple Mount.

When the Romans destroyed Jerusalem in AD 70, they not only leveled the temple proper but all the colonnades and every other building. While the perimeter of the Temple Mount remains the same, nothing was left standing on it, so when Esuga and I began to explore it, we had to imagine what it would have looked like. The many reconstructions of the Temple Mount we carried helped us.

When we stepped out on the Temple Mount we saw directly before us the El Aqsa Mosque covering part of where the Royal Porch once stood. We walked over to the mosque, asked a guide if we could enter, and when not allowed, peaked through a window. Since I had visited famous mosques in Istanbul and attended many mosques for prayers in the United States, I thought of asking him why we could not enter, but since tracing the events of Acts was our goal, we thanked him and pushed on.

We walked over to the extreme southeast corner to take in the vastness of the structure stretching far north and pictured the two hundred thousand Jews gathered there for Passover. We peered south through an opening in the wall down at the plaza where Peter likely preached on Pentecost and at the many pools where the disciples were baptized.

I wanted to show Esuga the area where the lame beggar sat at the Beautiful Gate and was healed. We walked straight north up a sharp incline until we came to a series of steps that led up to the Dome of the Rock (an Islamic shrine built in 691–92 CE). Most scholars believe that it was built where the temple proper once stood on the highest point of the mountain.

The Gate called Beautiful (Acts 3:2) where the lame beggar was healed was at the eastern entrance to the temple itself looking out over the Mount of Olives. We walked to the general location where he once sat. From there it was easy to imagine him jumping and praising God as he joined Peter and John entering the temple itself before the growing crowds forced them to retreat to the shade of Solomon's Colonnade a few hundred feet east of them. Here Peter and John explained to the crowd how the man had been healed.

We made the short walk from where the temple would have stood down to where Solomon's Portico would have been. Solomon's Colonnade had a roof to provide "shade from the sun and shelter from the rain; it served as a meeting point and was used for political, religious, and commercial activities."[1] The colonnade was 49 feet (15 m) wide and extended the entire 1433 feet (437 m) of the eastern wall. With a height of 41 feet (12.5 m), Solomon's Portico became the gathering place for the disciples to meet each other each day in addition to their evening house gatherings.[2]

Since it was no longer standing, we found shade under an olive tree. We put up the three-legged stools we carried with us, finished sandwiches we had saved from breakfast, and tried to take in the events of Acts 3 and 4. There were some Muslim men sitting near us under olive trees, some reading from the Quran and others discussing the day's events. I would like to have talked with them, but it would have been forced.

When we finished our sandwiches, we read from the Bible and prayed a short time. And then it hit me. All along this entire wall, stretching out to five American football fields, thousands of our brothers and

---

1. Schnabel, "Topography of Jerusalem," 25.
2. Schnabel, "Topography of Jerusalem," 25.

sisters once gathered to be healed and learn the Way of Jesus. I was glad I was there.

I have always found spiritual renewal in reading Acts, seeing the Spirit of God leading and filling the believers. But again, I confess I have tended to skim over the sermons. Not many of us like to read sermons, even if they are by Peter or Paul. Their sermons are so steeped in Israel's history, so filled with Israel's covenants and patriarchs and promises, that they seem far removed from our lives today. But, as mentioned earlier, we need to read them carefully to understand the gospel message.

The scene changes from the lame man leaping into the temple with Peter and John to now clinging to them (not yet knowing it is Jesus he will cling to all his life) in Solomon's Portico. Astonished, the people came running to them to learn how the crippled beggar now stood beside them.

Peter repeats the more central parts of the gospel from his Pentecost speech and adds important new truths about who Jesus is. Rather than comment on what we have already learned from Acts 2, I will focus on the new points.

As we read Peter's gospel sermon, it is important to remember that *God has progressively revealed his purposes in the Bible. We do not have a flat Bible where what we now know was understood by everyone in every time.* This is especially seen here, when Peter proclaims salvation only for Israel. It is not until later (Acts 10–11) that Peter and the other apostles learn of God's plan to include gentiles as equal recipients in the salvation he promised to Israel.

WHO IS JESUS—IN PETER'S SERMON

What more do we learn about Jesus, the heart of the good news in this speech?

- The speech begins and ends with an emphasis on Jesus as *God's Servant* (Acts 3:13, 26). The background to Jesus as the servant of God is found in Isaiah, where we read that God's chosen servant will first suffer for our waywardness and only then be exalted (Isa 52:13—53:12). His example is the pattern for his followers. They, too, must endure persecution as they follow Jesus and only then will be glorified to reign with him.

- Peter also says the people of Israel rejected Jesus, *"the Holy and Righteous One"* (Acts 3:14). Jesus was without sin, innocent of any wrongdoing. Yet the people of Israel preferred to have the murderer Barabbas released instead of Jesus, the Righteous One.

- This contrast between Jesus and the people is also seen when Peter says they *"killed the Author of Life"* (Acts 3:15). Jesus came to offer the people of Israel life, God's new life, an eternal life. An expression of this life of restoration and peace is prefigured in the wholeness of the disabled beggar who stood before them.[3]

- Finally, Peter identifies Jesus as *the prophet like Moses* whom God promised to raise up to bring about a new deliverance from bondage and oppression (Acts 3:22, 23). As Moses led the people of Israel out of their bondage in Egypt to freedom in the promised land, so now by his death and resurrection Jesus breaks the bondage and oppression of evil in us to lead us into true spiritual freedom (Acts 3:20).

When Moses predicted the prophet like him, who would come after him, he said, "You must listen to whatever he tells you." Adding that those who do not listen to him "will be utterly rooted out of the people" (Acts 3:22–23).

The people of Israel have not listened to Jesus and are in grave danger. But God's mercy is so great that he will forgive their ignorance in putting Jesus to death if they turn to him for forgiveness. Peter charges Israel to turn to God "so that times of refreshing may come from the Presence of the Lord, and that he may send the Messiah" appointed for them. Peter says that if they turn to God, he may send Jesus back, bringing about the time of universal restoration, that is, the final complete fulfillment of the kingdom of God promised for them (Acts 3:20,21).

Again, we do not have a flat revelation in the Bible. Peter does not yet know that Israel will largely continue to reject Jesus as their Messiah and that gentiles will become part of the people of God. Peter and all the disciples in Jerusalem seem to anticipate that Jesus would soon return to rule over a repentant and restored Israel.

A FOCUS ON THE DISCIPLES AND THE TEMPLE

While the disciples met daily in their houses, they also continued to meet at the temple. Since we are not Jews living at their time with our minds filled with the Old Testament promises for Israel, and since

---

3. Keener, *Acts, Vol. 2*, 1097.

we know that the Spirit lives in us, making us the Temple of God, we can tend to overlook the significance the temple had for these first Jewish believers.

The temple has significance for the disciples not only in the following accounts, but even some twenty-five years later when many thousands of Jewish disciples were still zealous for the temple (see Acts 21:20–28). Why? Hadn't they read Paul's letters and learned that they were the Temple of God?

And why are all the apostles still in Jerusalem twenty-six years later, when Jesus had said they were to be his witnesses to the nations (Acts 15:4)? What kept all twelve apostles in Jerusalem seemingly active at the temple? Some believe that because the apostles knew that they now constituted the Temple of God, and that Jesus had predicted the temple's destruction, that they only met at the temple because of its large open spaces. I side with those who believe that the apostles (and most of the disciples in Jerusalem) had theological reasons for remaining in Jerusalem, active at the temple.

In brief, I think the evidence supports that the apostles believed, as the true chosen leaders of God's new Israel (rather than the present unbelieving, corrupt leaders), that they would one day oversee temple worship. This was based on their belief that the Jewish Scriptures spoke of a renewal of temple worship in the end times. "These expectations support the plausibility of the earliest Jesus movement sharing some contemporaries' expectations that Jerusalem and the temple would play a central part in God's end-time plan."[4] They may have believed that if all Israel repented (Acts 3:19–21), God would not destroy the temple, or if he did, he would rebuild it.

I say all this because it is important to our understanding of history in Acts. It not only shows why the apostles were so slow to leave Jerusalem as witnesses to the nations but also explains the conflicts that emerge between Paul and the more temple-bound, Torah-centered Jewish believers in Jerusalem.

---

4. Keener, *Acts, Vol. 2*, 1097.

10

Peter and John Before the Council
(Acts 4:1–22)

ON THE SAME DAY Esuga and I explored where Peter and John entered the Temple Mount through the southern gates, we walked among the first-century remains of the street at the southwest corner. There we spotted a huge pile of stones cast down from the upper walls of the Temple Mount by Roman soldiers two millennia earlier. This pile of stones in the middle of the street caught my attention because Jesus had predicted they would be thrown down (Luke 21:5–6).

These stones sit at the end of what was once the largest street in Jerusalem, running the entire length of the Temple Mount's Western Wall. "The street was forty-one feet (12.5m) wide and was paved with impressive stones, some five feet (1.5m) wide and eight inches (20cm) thick."[1] The street was filled with shops for pilgrims to exchange money, buy sacrifices for temple offerings, and purchase food.

Most important for our story, here on this street next to the city's gymnasium once stood the building where the Sanhedrin met to interrogate Jesus and now to question Peter and John.[2] The remains of its magnificent hall have been found here. The hall of the Sanhedrin, its central meeting place, "measured 46 x 84 feet (14 x 25.5 m) with a height of 19.6 feet (6 m); it had a monumental double doorway set in the eastern side."[3]

---

1. Schnabel, "Topography of Jerusalem," 30.
2. Schnabel, "Topography of Jerusalem," 28.
3. Schnabel, "Topography of Jerusalem," 20.

THE ARREST

We can envision someone tipping off the temple police that Peter and John were teaching a large crowd that Jesus was raised from the dead. The police rush to arrest them and lead them, along with the now healed crippled beggar walking boldly beside them, across the Temple Mount through yet more crowds gathered for business. Witnessing the arrest of the apostles in plain sight of thousands of people with whom they were popular explains why the Sanhedrin cannot punish them at this time (Acts 4:16, 21).

They are then forcibly led down a lengthy staircase (the stairs of Robinson's Arch) to where even more people entering the temple and shopping on the street below witness their arrest. The three are then led through a monumental double doorway of the Sanhedrin building and put in a holding jail until the Sanhedrin met in the morning. Can you place yourself with them in jail all night? What would you experience?

In the morning all seventy-one members of the Sanhedrin gather in full force, sitting in a half-circle as was their custom, so that they could see each other. Before them stood two scribes, one to write what was said in favor of Peter and John and one to write what was said against them. In front of the two scribes sat "three rows of students who could participate in a non-capital trial" such as this.[4] Young Saul was likely one of them.

Peter and John now stand to be interrogated by the seventy-one men whose "sphere of authority extended over the spiritual, political, and legal matters of all Jews."[5] Remember the young fishermen from Galilee who are the leaders Jesus chose and trained to lead believing Israel. In the center sat the high priest, president of the Sanhedrin. His luxurious, spacious house overlooked the temple in Upper Jerusalem, a few minutes' walk up the hill, close to where the apostles stayed.

I began commenting on the huge pile of stones Esuga and I came across when walking among the ruins near the Temple Mount. When I returned home, I took up drawing. I was so impressed with the pile of stones thrown down by the Romans that I was inspired to draw them. As I worked on the drawing, I began to ask myself if any of them smashed the Sanhedrin building, which we know was there. I would have to ask an archeologist to be sure, but I think the smaller ones came quite close.

---

4. Twelftree, "Sanhedrin," 731.
5. Twelftree, "Sanhedrin," 731.

I began to think of the significance of all this. This was where the power-hungry, luxury-living politicians and religious leaders met, the leaders threatened by and jealous of Jesus who were mainly responsible for putting him to death. And now, threatened and jealous of the apostles, they persecuted them.

Did God want to say something by where these stones landed? I often look at my drawing of the temple stones piled up where the Sanhedrin met and think of the fate of all the power-hungry oppressors today and through the centuries.

The once-crippled beggar stands beside Peter and John as straight and as strong as a pillar in the temple. Peter and John explain the power of the risen Lord Jesus to a swelling crowd in the thousands gathered around them in the shade of Solomon's Portico. They proclaim that "in Jesus there is the resurrection of the dead," that is, because Jesus has been raised from the dead, he, as the author of life, will raise his disciples to join him when the kingdom of God reaches its final fulfillment at the end of time. Around five thousand embrace their message.

All this annoys the guardians of the temple very much. When the captain of the temple, who along with a group of priests and Sadducees was responsible for maintaining order in the temple, learns of the thousands gathered around Peter and John at Solomon's Portico and investigates what is being said, they arrest them. The young Galileans are teaching that Jesus, whom they put to death, has been raised to life by God. Even more, they teach the people that they, too, will be raised and join Jesus in his kingdom if they turn to God and confess Jesus as Lord. This not only makes them guilty before Israel's God for brutally rejecting their Messiah but also teaches a radical new way to be part of God's kingdom. This new teaching threatens their lucrative positions and power over Israel.

So, they arrest Peter and John, putting them in a holding jail for the night with plans to bring them before the entire Council in the morning. Perhaps a night in jail as they anticipate standing before all the leaders of their nation for interrogation might be enough to intimidate these bold young Galileans.

The next morning all seventy of Israel's rulers gather in full force, in all their pomp and presumed authority, to place Peter and John before them. Can you see their confident display of power and authority as leaders of Israel and caretakers of the temple? What you won't see is Peter and John, leaders of the true Israel, trembling before them and denying their Lord to escape harm. Peter had done this once. Never again.

The once-lame man, now in the Temple of God, has also been arrested and stands with Peter and John (Acts 4:14). The man who had not stood a single day in his long forty years on earth (Acts 4:22) now stands fully restored and full of life beside two leaders of this new and growing Jewish sect. He stands as a living witness to God's powerful deeds through Jesus. The members of the Council stare at him in disbelief. They recognize him as the lame beggar who daily asked for alms at the Gate called Beautiful. Most of them had ignored him as they passed him by.

Then the High Priest looks at Peter and John and asks, "By what power or by what name did you do this?" (Acts 4:8). After Peter responds, the risen Lord Jesus, who has demonstrated his power to heal, fills Peter with his Spirit to witness boldly of him.

Using imagery from Ps 118:22, which likens the building of a strong structure of stones to the building of a spiritually strong people, Peter says that they, who are to be the builders of God's people, have rejected Jesus, the cornerstone chosen by God. He is the One through whom God is building people for his kingdom.

Jesus is God's chosen cornerstone. "There is salvation in no one else, for there is no other name under heaven given among men by which we must be saved" (Acts 4:12). That is, salvation in its fullest sense is found only in the crucified, risen Lord Jesus. Many can feel uncomfortable or downright angry at this exclusive claim, but before we take up the question of exclusivity, let's try to understand what is meant. It is helpful to understand before we react.

QUESTION OF EXCLUSIVITY

What is meant by salvation in Christ alone? Some tend to limit it to salvation from God's final judgment. While that is an important part of salvation, the meaning is much richer and more extensive. As one scholar says, "Salvation here as elsewhere has spiritual, physical, and social dimensions, as the very presence of the healed man in this Sanhedrin session demonstrates."[6] When Peter speaks of salvation in the immediate context, he refers to how the risen Lord Jesus has restored the lame

---

6. Witherington, *Acts of the Apostles*, 194.

beggar, a hopeless, despised outcast in society. Salvation thus includes deliverance from *physical and emotional* ailments.

But the way the man clings to Peter and John (Acts 4:11) may illustrate that he now belongs to God's new community, where he can live with dignity and be provided for until he is able to find work. This is the *social* aspect of salvation: no longer alone but belonging, cared for in God's family.

Most important of all, the man leaps in praise to God. He has experienced the power of the risen Lord. He has heard Peter teach the good news and has believed it. God's love, joy, and peace have flooded his heart so that he leaps for joy and praises God. This is the *spiritual* aspect of salvation.

So, in saying that salvation is found in no one else other than Jesus, Peter is simply saying that no one else can give such a full restoration. God has chosen Jesus to be the one person through whom broken lives are restored and the world is remade. *He alone is at God's right hand with the power, love, and authority to restore broken lives.*

It seems to me that whether we recognize it or not, we are all in need of restoration: perhaps from sickness or mental stress, from the fear of death, from loneliness and meaninglessness, from pride and self-centeredness, or from the destructive forces of evil in and around us. While others may speak helpfully on spiritual matters, only Jesus has died to reconcile us to God, and only he has the limitless love and power to restore our broken lives.

These were bold words for a young fisherman from rural Galilee to speak to the collective leadership of the nation of Israel. For they knew salvation was the one all-encompassing word in the Scriptures depicting the hope of Israel when God would come to deliver his people at the end of the ages. Peter says this salvation has come. And they have missed it. For they have rejected the Messiah, sent by God to save. How will they respond?

RESPONSE OF THE SANHEDRIN

At first, they are taken back, amazed at the boldness of these uneducated (that is, lacking formal training as rabbis) and ordinary men (that is, not members of one of their political/religious parties).[7] But then some of

---

7. Witherington, *Acts of the Apostles*, 195. While the apostles were not formally trained scribes from Jerusalem, as devote Jewish boys they had memorized the Torah and more importantly spent three years with Jesus, observing all he did and memorizing

them recognize Peter as one of the disciples of Jesus. He was the one who had caved into his fears and cowardly abandoned Jesus when one of their young female servants recognized him that dreadful night Jesus was arrested.

But now he does not flee in fear for his life. Instead, he stands confidently before the very men who conspired to have his Jesus crucified. Now he speaks with such *boldness* you would think he speaks to children in the streets. There is no hesitation, no appealing to religious authorities for what he says. His authority comes from being an eyewitness of the risen Lord Jesus, filled with his Spirit.

While the Council is amazed at the boldness of Peter and John, they know they must stop them from speaking about Jesus. With the once-lame beggar standing beside them, they cannot deny a significant miracle has taken place. But not for a minute will they attribute it to Jesus.

Proclaiming that Jesus is alive must be stopped. For if that were true, it would threaten their authority as caretakers of the temple and interpreters of the Torah. If that were true, then they were wrong to reject Jesus and were guilty of orchestrating the most unimaginable crime—aiding pagan Rome, Israel's enemy, to crucify their Messiah. And if it were true that Jesus was the Messiah now reigning at God's right hand, then they would have to humble themselves to be taught by Peter and the other apostles Jesus has chosen to lead believing Israel. Everything would change—their power and their prestige. This they will not risk for a moment. They will do whatever it takes to keep control, just as many leaders through the ages have done. So, they order the apostles to quit teaching the people about Jesus. They may continue to do good deeds (Acts 4:9), but they are not to talk about Jesus.

Peter responds, "We cannot keep from speaking about what we have seen and heard" (Acts 4:20). They are witnesses of the new reality on earth through Jesus. The leaders would like to have tied them to a post and beaten them with a whip thirty-nine times, but now they cannot. Jerusalem is filled with praise and the good news of how God worked through them to heal the lame beggar. Riots must be avoided, or Roman soldiers will be sent out challenging their ability to govern the people. So, they threaten them again and release them.

In contrast to the people, the leaders of Israel remained ignorant, unrepentant, and unqualified to lead God's people. But Jesus has

---

all he taught. They were not ignorant, untaught leaders.

prepared the Twelve to shepherd them. The deep division we read of now will continue to widen. The battle lines are drawn, but we know God's Spirit-empowered leaders will prevail.[8]

---

8. Wall, "Acts of the Apostles," 95.

11

A Prayer for Boldness
(Acts 4:23–31)

AFTER PETER, JOHN, AND the now-healed, formerly lame beggar are released by the Sanhedrin, they walk up through the city to the house where the apostles stayed to report on their arrest and pray.

The major movement now is between heaven and earth. For the Holy Spirit shakes the house where the disciples pray and so fills them all that they speak about Jesus with boldness, the very thing the Sanhedrin just ordered Peter and John not to do!

It is this bold witness that caught my attention in this passage. The believers ask God for boldness to keep speaking about Jesus (Acts 4:29), and he answers their prayer, filling them with the Holy Spirit so that they do so (Acts 4: 31).

But what will bold witness look like in our time and place?

BOLDNESS—THEN AND NOW

We can read this and think, if we are to be bold for Jesus, we would spill out into the streets with megaphones or gospel tracts or knock on our neighbor's doors. This wouldn't work where I live, and as much as I would like to speak about Jesus to everyone I meet, I have lived long enough to know that Spirit-given wisdom must accompany Spirit-given boldness.

Now I know that God wants us to talk about Jesus and that the Holy Spirit gives boldness to do so. Much of Acts is filled with this

Spirit-empowered, bold witness, but sensitivity to the culture in which we live will determine how our boldness is expressed. It may be a passing comment in quietness and confidence to a neighbor that God has helped you through a hard time.

It is important to remember that the bold witness in this first part of Acts is by Jews speaking to Jews. The disciples were speaking to other Jews, for whom conversation about God and debate about the Scriptures was as common as our conversation about the weather. The boldness the disciples prayed for is not to talk about spiritual matters, for that was part of their everyday life, but they prayed for the boldness to speak about Jesus, crucified and raised from the dead.

I so want to talk about the risen Lord Jesus to everyone I meet. I live in a part of Philadelphia filled with coffee shops and people walking the streets, and I've developed an ability to greet almost everyone I meet, hoping for an opportunity to say something about Jesus. But I've found that the more I pray for wisdom, the more I can say with a confident boldness only what is helpful for the occasion.

Our pastor gave us excellent advice for conversing with our neighbors. Instead of approaching them with our theology as objects of witness, he encouraged us to *talk with them as fellow human beings about our losses and longings in life.* We have found that in doing this, conversations will in time lead to our life with God.

The chain of events that began with the healing of the lame beggar continues. The result of the Council's attempt to silence Peter and John leads to prayer by the entire community to continue speaking boldly about the Lord.

RESPONSE OF PRAYER

Peter, John, and the healed beggar go directly to their community of friends in the house where they met (Acts 4:31) and report the order to not speak about Jesus. *The disciples immediately respond with prayer.* United in spirit and in purpose, they pray for continued boldness to speak about Jesus despite threats from their nation's leaders.

Luke summarizes what was a much longer time of prayer to encourage other disciples who may be intimidated to keep silent about Jesus. We, too, may sense a spiritual resistance when we speak about Jesus, even when done with love and respect. We may sense there is a battle going on so that when we speak "about Jesus, about his cross, about his resurrection, about the new life which can break chains and set people free, there seems to be power around the place" which does its best to silent us.[1]

The disciple's prayer begins by recognizing that their God is the Sovereign Lord over all. For he has created the heavens and the earth and everything in them. This includes the very leaders of their nation who now seek to intimidate them! Seen in God's Presence, mindful of his mighty power, their threats seem small.

Then the disciples remember what Jesus had taught them. The rulers of the earth would gather "against the Lord and against his Messiah" (Acts 4:26). The psalm speaks of the time (which has now begun) when God would install his King, the Messiah, to rule over the nations of the earth. But instead of acknowledging the Messiah's rule, the rulers of the nations (that is, the gentiles) would gather in fruitless rebellion to oppose God's appointed King.

This is what Pilate and Herod, gentile rulers in Israel, had done when they took part in putting Jesus to death. But while Ps 2 only speaks of gentile rulers opposing God's anointed King, surprisingly the people of Israel and their leaders had aligned themselves with them to have Jesus, their Messiah, crucified. Sadly, by joining ranks with the gentiles, the Jewish leaders of Israel "cease to be the Lord's people and can be ranked with unbelieving Gentiles."[2] But as we have seen, Jesus has appointed and trained the apostles as leaders of believing Israel.

FOLLOWING THE SUFFERING SERVANT

The disciples now realize that they will experience the same opposition from the rulers of this world as their Lord Jesus. But just as Jesus fulfilled God's plan through suffering, they know that they will see God's kingdom grow through their suffering.

This is alluded to with the repetition of "servant" in the passage, for the Messiah would be God's suffering Servant. God's servant King David (Acts 4:25) foreshadows his "holy servant Jesus" (Acts 4:27, 30), whom the disciples imitate as servants (Acts 4:29). This underscores their unity with Jesus, the "suffering servant" of Isa 53, in their call to suffer as servants of God to accomplish his kingdom purposes.

1. Wright, *Acts for Everyone, Pt. 1*, 71.
2. Peterson, *Acts of the Apostles*, 200.

As they pray for boldness to keep on speaking about Jesus, undeterred by possible suffering, they also pray that God will stretch out his mighty hand (as he did at the exodus) to perform signs and wonders through the name of Jesus. Signs and wonders catch the attention of the people to then be explained by proclaiming Jesus as the source.

This is a common pattern in Acts for causing the kingdom of God to spread. While it is true that there is power in the spoken word about Christ crucified, *Acts challenges us to pray for Jesus to show others he is alive and at work among us in ways that cannot be attributed to coincidence.* While most of us will not see the intensity of miracles we read of at this time, we can pray for the Lord to act specifically, demonstrating that he is alive and at work among us.

Finally, and quite dramatically, we read that when they had finished praying, God answered their prayer. As a mighty wind and tongues of fire filled this same house on Pentecost *while they prayed, so now as they pray* the Spirit causes it to shake as an unusual manifestation of God's powerful Presence among them.

This was not another Pentecost, for they had already received the promised Spirit. But it was like Pentecost in that it was a special work of the Spirit, causing the disciples to be filled with the Holy Spirit to speak boldly about Jesus. They first speak about Jesus to each other in the house and then spilling out into the streets as at Pentecost to those nearby.

We learn from this passage that *the Jesus movement*, filled with God's Spirit and united in love and prayer, *proves to be a more powerful force on earth than the political and religious authorities that would silence them.*[3] The leaders of this world threaten and plot in vain to silence the people of God.

A FOCUS ON THE FILLING OF THE SPIRIT

The Holy Spirit so permeates the life and mission of the disciples in Acts that we could title Acts "The Acts of the Risen Lord Through the Spirit." The Spirit's Presence—causing praise to God, unity among the disciples, signs and wonders, and empowering for witness—is often stated and always assumed. While the Spirit worked in remarkable

---

3. Spencer, *Journeying Through Acts*, 65.

ways through the apostles and other leaders, the life of the Spirit in all the disciples was witnessed by everyone.[4]

We read Acts and so want this life. Yet the work of the Spirit can be confusing for some, even frightening. This need not be. We can turn to Acts again and again, with its invitation for the Spirit to sweep through our lives and pray that it may be so. In overcoming my own confusion about the work of the Spirit, I have found it helpful to distinguish three expressions of the Spirit's work in Acts.

1. First, there is a rich variety of phrases used to describe receiving the Spirit when we first believe. We *receive* the Spirit as a gift; we are *baptized* with the Spirit; he *comes upon us, falls upon us, fills us,* and my favorite (because of its image of rivers of living water flowing through our innermost being), the Spirit is *poured out* on us. Many of these phrases can be found when the Spirit falls upon Cornelius and his household (Acts 10:44–47; 11:15–16). What do they suggest to you? Recall that when the gospel was proclaimed in Acts, listeners were promised they would receive the Spirit and often were vividly aware of it.

2. The Spirit *filling us* when we first believe can be confusing because we read of Peter, Stephen, Paul, and all the disciples being filled again and again. But this expression of the Spirit's work refers to *his special empowerment to speak and act for the Lord at our moment of need.*

    Examples of this are when Peter, filled with the Spirit, spoke with boldness (Acts 4:8) and later when all the disciples gathered for prayer and "were all filled with the Holy Spirit and spoke the word of God with boldness" (Acts 4:31). While these examples may appear more dramatic, not all were.

    Because we are often in need of God's power and wisdom, we can often be filled with his Spirit. I often experience this when talking with someone about the Lord, or when I need power to love someone—nothing dramatic, just a sense that the Spirit enlivens my words and works in my heart to love. Often, I have not realized the quiet, steady filling of the Spirit until later.

---

4. Marshall, *Acts of the Apostles*, 79.

> 3. There is one final way the Spirit's work is expressed in Acts. Stephen and his companions, and then later Barnabas, were said to be "full of the Spirit" (Acts 6:3, 5, 10; 11:24). This suggests that they had so emptied themselves, and lived so close to God, that *the Spirit's work in them became characteristic of their lives.* We read that Barnabas "was a good man, full of the Holy Spirit and strong in faith" (Acts 11:24 NLT).

We will now read that from his good heart Barnabas generously gave of his wealth to help the poor among the disciples. Spiritual renewal is often accompanied by releasing our hold on our possessions.

We most often recognize this steady work of the Spirit in those who have walked longer in full submission with the Lord. We see a consistency in their character.

Luke does not depict these early disciples as extraordinary persons beyond our reach. He intends for us to see that we, too, can live Spirit-filled lives. The summary of the Spirit-filled community at Pentecost implies this (Acts 2:42–47).

12

The Community and Their Possessions
(Acts 4:32–37)

I WAS ONCE ON staff at a church where the pastor claimed during a building campaign that Jesus spoke more about money than he did of his second coming. That may be true. I haven't counted. But what the pastor failed to mention was how Jesus teaches us to use our money. I had read the Gospels enough to know that Jesus frequently taught we are to use our money not to build our grand sanctuaries but to aid the poor among us.

I realize we live in different times, and buildings can have a useful function. I also believe that those who lead a church should receive a fair salary. Then there is the fact that we pay taxes which go to help the needy in our society. So, I don't have any clear-cut answers, but still, I feel uncomfortable. I remember an elder at a church where I served who told me that since a nearby church was active in helping the poor, our church should focus on discipling its members to follow Jesus' commands. But Jesus commanded us to liberally use our money to help the poor.

All this makes me feel uneasy, because I know I do not give as liberally as Jesus teaches. But his compassion for the poor keeps challenging me, and I try to keep obeying him. If we don't feel challenged when reading the Bible, that means we must have already become perfect, and we know that isn't true. I do.

This passage and ones like it teach that the early church placed the highest priority on caring for the needy among them or, as Jesus said, loving our neighbor with the use of our money.

Now I will write what can make us even more uneasy.

I am concerned that *many who identify themselves as Christians place a higher priority on their personal freedom than on the welfare of others*. I highly value the freedom of living in a Western nation, and I am not a socialist. But the words of this passage, "no one claimed *private* . . ." jump off the page at me. The kingdom of God is about setting aside our freedoms for the common good. The welfare of others trumps freedom in God's kingdom.

LUKE'S SECOND SUMMARY—CARE FOR THE NEEDY

This is Luke's second summary of the life of the first disciples and emphasizes, even more than the first (Acts 2:43–47), how the Jesus community cared for the needy among them. The summary also functions as an introduction to Barnabas (Acts 4:36–37) and the following story of Ananias and Sapphira (Acts 5:1–11). Barnabas illustrates generosity in giving, while Ananias and Sapphira, in contrast, illustrate greed and deceit.

Right in the middle of describing the sharing of possessions, Luke writes that the apostles continue to witness of their risen Lord with power, and "great grace was upon them all." The nuanced meaning of grace here refers to God's "favor and presence which rests upon the community, and which is somehow tangibly present."[1] As they provided for each other's needs, they tangibly demonstrated God's Presence among them! The text implies that as the apostles taught the people about the self-giving life of Jesus, they were motivated to live as he lived and taught. They give freely, joyfully, not out of obligation. The same Spirit that shook the house when they prayed shakes their pocketbooks to provide for the poor.

Gentile readers of Acts knew that friendship in Greco-Roman culture "involved reciprocity between those who were basically social equals."[2] One only gave to a select circle of friends and gave expecting favors in return. But the disciples, who find their identity as a family with God as their Father, care for all the needy among them without any thought of expecting anything in return. By this Luke suggests that the Jesus community, formed by Jesus' teachings and enlivened by his Spirit, realizes the best ideals of community.[3]

---

1. Peterson, *Acts of the Apostles*, 205.
2. Witherington, *Acts of the Apostles*, 205.
3. Peterson, *Acts of the Apostles*, 204.

The disciples related to one another more as a family created by God than a circle of friends who helped each other advance in society, ignoring others. It was not only miracles that caught the attention of the people but also this new way of relating that made the first disciples such an attractive, life-changing force in society. It is because of the corporate identity of the disciples that I most often refer to them as a community, family, or Jesus community rather than the church. While "church" means assembly, that is not what the word connotes for modern readers.

Richard Hays points out that God has created the church as a countercultural community to embody an alternative order in the world by obeying the teachings of Jesus.[4] While we obviously obey Jesus as individuals, the point of this and other passages is how we as a visible body of believers give witness to the world as we reject greed and the delusion that our life consists of our abundance of possessions (Luke 12:13–15).

The question we are to ask as churches is: How do our economic practices give corporate testimony to the world by rejecting materialism as our god and liberally caring for the poor among us? "To ask that question in a serious and sustained way will require of us not only imaginative reflection but also costly change."[5] Our defenses and evasion strategies for not obeying Jesus' teachings about money, wealth, and possessions are so deeply entrenched in us that it is very difficult to hear and obey Jesus' teachings on the matter.[6] But we must, for our own sake and for our witness to the world.[7]

As we interact with others, the gospel teaches us to check our hearts and motives to make sure we do not relate with them to get something from them.

BARNABAS IS INTRODUCED

Luke concludes his summary of the generous giving of the Jesus community with the positive example of Barnabas. Luke also uses Barnabas's example to introduce him as a key character in Acts who will later reappear

---

4. Hays, *Moral Vision*, 196.
5. Hays, *Moral Vision*, 468.
6. Stassen and Gushee, *Kingdom Ethics*, 414.
7. Hays, *Moral Vision*, 313. Richard Hays has identified four areas spotlighted at the heart of Christian discipleship in the New Testament: (1) the renunciation of violence, (2) the sharing of possessions, (3) the overcoming of ethnic divisions, and (4) the unity of men and women in Christ.

as a companion and encouragement to Paul (who has not yet appeared in the story).

Barnabas, growing up in Cyprus among gentiles, will be an important bridge between the Jerusalem leaders and Paul, from his travels with Paul to proclaim Jesus on Cyprus and then in the central part of modern Turkey (see Acts 13:1–14:28). Barnabas, whose name can mean "son of encouragement and son of exhortation,"[8] will both encourage Paul in his mission to the gentiles and, along with Paul, exhort gentile disciples to remain true to Jesus.

But at this point he is portrayed as an example of the best ideals of the new people created by God's Spirit. Before Barnabas becomes a prominent teacher and missionary, he is described as sacrificially caring for the poor. He sells property (possibly from Cyprus) and brings the money from the sale to the apostles, who are responsible for distributing it to needy disciples.

---

8. Witherington, *Acts of the Apostles*, 209.

13

A Deceit Detected
(Acts 5:1–11)

BECAUSE ESUGA AND I did not need to travel for the story of Ananias and Sapphira and I struggled with how to introduce it, I asked my wife, Eeva, for help. I asked for her first impression when she read the account. She responded at once that it comes across as very harsh, but then, she added, once you read it again carefully, it seems less harsh.

This story is about the lying and deceit of a couple in the Jesus community and God's quick response by taking their lives. I hope as you read my comments, the story will seem less harsh to you.

To be honest, after much study and reflection, my biggest struggle with this story is not that it happened but that it seems to happen so seldom today. I don't mean that I wish that every believer who deceives other believers would suddenly die under God's judgment, but I don't understand how many who claim to be Christians have lived in deceit, abusing both women and church finances, and seemingly gotten away with it.

I know they will not ultimately get away with it, but I don't understand why God doesn't do an Ananias and Sapphira-type judgment with such people now to maintain the holiness of his people and his reputation in the world. Perhaps you and your friends can come up with an answer.

THREATS FROM WITHIN THE JESUS COMMUNITY

The Jesus community has responded successfully to threats *from without* that seek to silence them, but now sinister forces work *within* the community, seeking to taint their good reputation so that no one will listen to their message about Jesus.

A man named Ananias and his wife Sapphira are not as forthright as Barnabas when they sell some of their property. The story of this couple is told in two parts, one for each of them, and each part ends with the same refrain, emphasizing the sense of dread that came upon all who heard of their fate (Acts 5:5, 11). We are to feel the same sense of dread.

I think most of us find this a difficult story to read. But I believe a better understanding of both the events of the story and the context of the times will make it easier to read and show its important message for us.

First, the context of the times. We recently read of such united, powerful prayer by the disciples that the house where they met shook when they were filled with the Holy Spirit. We read that all of them "were of one heart and soul," giving to the needs of others without thoughts of personal gain. Then, after this story, we will read of signs and wonders done through the apostles and through all the disciples meeting together. Their lives are such that "the people held them in high esteem" (Acts 5:12–13). This leads to great numbers believing and joining their community (Acts 5:14–16).

This is a crucial time when the Spirit of God is at work in unusual ways in this young fellowship of believers. *Deceit can infect the entire community and grow like yeast, ruining their reputation and witness among the people. What is at stake is the very well-being and growth of the community where the Spirit is at work.*

Three times we read that Ananias and Sapphira lied, not to the apostles but to the Spirit of God (Acts 5:3, 4, 9). "Luke sees this story not just as being about human greed and duplicitous actions but as an invasion of the community of the Spirit by the powers of darkness, by means of Ananias."[1]

But how do we understand the story itself? We learn at the outset that Ananias and Sapphira, a couple of considerable wealth,[2] are united in their plan to deceive the rest of the disciples. They had the wrong kind

---

1. Witherington, *Acts of the Apostles*, 215.
2. Keener, *Acts, Vol. 2*, 1185.

of togetherness.³ Again, their unity of selfish deceit contrasts sharply with the other disciples, who were of one heart and soul, open and honest in their handling of their possessions (Acts 4:32).

It is important to note that the couple was under no obligation to sell any of their property. The motives at work in their hearts is not clear. Perhaps they wanted to impress the apostles and enhance their reputation and position in the community without any real financial sacrifice.

What is clear is that Satan filled their hearts with deception. In contrast, the rest of the believers, whose hearts the Spirit filled (Acts 4:31—5:35), live open, sacrificial lives, contributing to the unity and reputation of the community. Ananias and Sapphira's deceit threatens to break down the unity of the fellowship, but due to the strong leadership of Peter and the other apostles, Satan fails in his attempt.

While Peter shows prophetic insight that enables him to see into the hearts of Ananias and Sapphira, their sudden deaths are not the result of a prophetic pronouncement of judgment by him. It is possible that their sudden deaths were due to heart attacks caused by the shock of being exposed in their deception as they stand before the apostles.⁴

Just as Satan entered the heart of Judas by using deception and the lure of money so that he would betray Jesus, causing the apostles to scatter, so now he seeks again to get a foothold within the Jesus community by planting seeds of deception. Left unchecked, the virus would spread, and the purity, power, reputation, and witness of the community would be seriously weakened. Satan had failed in his attempt to intimidate the disciples from speaking about Jesus (Acts 4:17, 18, 29–31), so now he seeks to taint their reputation so that no one would listen to them.

We may struggle when reading of God's judgment of the couple. We may think the crime doesn't seem to fit the punishment. Perhaps this will help. Since there is no suggestion in the story that Ananias and Sapphira were not true believers, it is possible that God took them to an early death *for their sake* to prevent an escalation of sin in them and save them from eternal judgment (see 1 Cor 11:28–32). Seen in this way, God's judgment was merciful.

It is possible the judgment is severe precisely because of the times. The Jesus community is young and fragile. This is a time of extraordinary work by the Spirit of God. Luke depicts this "as a unique period,

---

3. Witherington, *Acts of the Apostles*, 218.
4. Witherington, *Acts of the Apostles*, 218.

the new people of God in Christ, filled with the Spirit, growing by leaps and bounds. There is no room for distrust, for duplicity, for any breach in fellowship."[5] We would call this time a spiritual awakening, a special pouring out of the Spirit leading to revival. Love and holiness permeate the fellowship. Deceit must be rooted out.

Even if we still may struggle with the fate of Ananias and Sapphira, it is important that we learn from it. God commands us to be honest and upright in all our interactions with one another. I have tried to take this passage seriously and sought always to be upright in my communication with others and to try not to do anything that threatens the unity of the Spirit among God's people. It's not always easy, but it is important, and our lives may depend on it.[6]

---

5. Polhill, *Acts of the Apostles*, 161, quoted in Peterson, *Acts of the Apostles*, 220.

6. Marshall, *Acts of the Apostles*, 114. The disciples for the first time are called "the church" in Acts 5:11. The word means an assembly and thus the people who make it up. While still Jews, the disciples have a new corporate identity as the church/assembly of God.

14

Extraordinary Signs
(Acts 5:12–16)

I HAD ALWAYS UNDERSTOOD miracles to be sudden, dramatic works of God, but later I learned that since the Jewish people believed God was always active in their lives, they looked for signs of his care every day in less dramatic ways. I want to share a sign, a direct intervention of God that I experienced on a previous trip to Israel.

I was completing a weeklong hike on the Jesus Trail in Galilee with a friend, David, when we finally reached the northern shore of the Sea of Galilee at Capernaum. It was mid-May; the afternoon sun was cruel. Hikers had been warned to get off the trail and seek shelter. We tried to, but the café where we had planned to cool down and grab lunch had been closed. We had no choice but to carry on.

Hungry and hot, we hiked with our heavy backpacks up an asphalt road from the northern shore of the Sea of Galilee, where Jesus had once healed the multitudes. The mid-afternoon sun beat mercilessly on our backs. Heat radiated from the asphalt. The air-conditioned room of our hostel waited for us a mile straight up the mountain.

Walking up the steep asphalt road, my feet slipped back and forth in my boots, tearing into the blisters from a week of hiking. To spare my feet, we decided to walk in the four-foot drainage ditch by the road so that my feet could grip the stones. I stopped every few minutes to catch an outline of shade under a bush and sip on water.

We had only covered a quarter of a mile. We tried without success to wave down passing cars for help. I knew I was not doing well, and I was concerned I might have a heat stroke, concerned enough to pray!

Our guidebook suggested that we repeat a short prayer as we hiked the Jesus Trail. I had forgotten that. Now in my desperation I prayed repeatedly the cry the blind beggar made to Jesus when he passed by him near Jericho. "Jesus, Son of David, have mercy on me; Jesus, Son of David have mercy on me; Jesus, Son of David have mercy on me."

I prayed this with faith ten to twelve times and then heard a machine coming up the road behind us. I turned and with relief and gratitude saw a John Deere tractor pulling a wagon. We waved down the driver from Indonesia, who was kind enough to stop and give us a lift. In my excitement, when I tried to climb out of the ditch, my backpack swung and threw me off balance. I stumbled and fell on the rocks.

My travel companion, David, extended his hand to help me up, threw my backpack on the wagon, helped me climb up, and off we went up the mountain to our hostel arriving in only five minutes. My blisters were still painful, but with water and rest in an air-conditioned room, I soon felt better.

As I recovered, I thought about the multitudes who in desperation had cried out to Jesus in this very place and had been helped. Now, in the same place, I had cried out in desperation to him, and he heard my cry. For me, this was a *sign* of his care.

I'm sure each of you have had interventions like this—some dramatic, some less dramatic. But each was a cry to God that came with an answer, or as the Jewish people would have said, *a sign*. I think it is good that we share such signs with one another to remind each other that God is good and active in our lives. What sign have you last experienced?

LUKE'S THIRD SUMMARY—SIGNS AND WONDERS

Luke writes another summary shortly after the second one (Acts 4:32–36). Why another one so soon? Recall that the major function of a summary is to show how the risen Lord Jesus meets opposition both from within and without the community of disciples so that the kingdom of God would continue to expand. Looking back, the deception of Ananias and Sapphira was detected and dealt with so that we now read of great numbers added to their community (Acts 5:14–15).

This summary emphasizes the many signs and wonders taking place through the apostles. Looking ahead, the acceleration of more signs and wonders through the apostles and more people joining their community leads to jealousy and increased hostility from the leaders of Israel (Acts 5:17–42). From this we learn that we must fight for unity in the church and expect opposition as we live out the gospel.

Strangely, while the people continue to highly respect the disciples, many seem fearful of joining them. Perhaps they sense that the increased hostility of their leaders against the Jesus people could lead to violent measures against them too, if they were to become disciples (Acts 5:13). Yet even the fear and reticence of the majority does not prevent great numbers of both men and women being added to the Lord (Acts 5:14).

MIRACLES PERFORMED THROUGH THE APOSTLES

The miracles taking place through the apostles occurred both in the temple courts and on the streets of Jerusalem so that crowds from the towns around Jerusalem are healed (Acts 5:15–16). The work of the Spirit is now so strong that even as Peter walked the streets of Jerusalem, people were healed as they were placed on the street for his shadow to fall on them. Strange. How are we to understand that?![1]

First, the passage suggests that this was a brief period of an unusual work of the Spirit, leading to many from the countryside of Jerusalem becoming disciples, thus fulfilling another phase of the mission's expansion (Acts 1:8). So, people weren't healed by encountering Peter's shadow throughout his life.

Second, something similar occurred when a woman touched the fringe of Jesus' garment to be healed (Luke 8:44) and later, when the Spirit worked so powerfully through Paul that even handkerchiefs and aprons that had touched him were taken to the sick for them to be healed (Acts 19:11–12). Again, this was an unusual time of the Spirit's work. But how do we understand these unusual works of the Spirit?

The text says that the crowds believed they would be healed by encountering Peter's shadow. There was a common ancient Greek belief that there was a kind of zone around people that was an extension of their soul, and that by encountering that "zone" or shadow, one was influenced

---

1. Schnabel, "Topography of Jerusalem," 30. The streets were likely the larger ones in Jerusalem. One was likely the 41-foot (12.5 m) wide street along the western wall that Peter used as he went back and forth from his residence to the Temple Mount.

for better or worse. But there is no evidence that first-century Jews, especially in Israel, believed this.[2] As we read on in Acts, we will see how Luke contrasts the work of the Spirit with pagan magic.

The crowds who sought Peter's shadow believed that God's Spirit worked so powerfully in him at this time that *as they came near him in faith, God would heal them*. This is not magic, and the healings were not automatic.

By way of application, Luke's readers would have associated Peter's shadow with the power and glory of God overshadowing Mary (Luke 1:35) and later Jesus at the transfiguration (Luke 9:34–35). "The shadow may thus recall what some sources call the Shekinah [glory of God]."[3] Paul writes, "And all of us, with unveiled faces, seeing the glory of the Lord as though reflected in a mirror, are being transformed into the same image from one degree of glory to another; for this comes from the Lord, the Spirit" (2 Cor 3:18). Paul also writes that believers are the aroma of Christ to those around them (2 Cor 1:15–16).

This means that to the degree that we live close to the Lord and are transformed into his image, his glory is present in us for all to see. And God will speak to those who take the time to reflect on what they see. A friend once encouraged my wife and me, with our ministry, to welcome international students to live with us with these words: "As soon as they enter your house, they sense something different. They sense the love and goodness."

The summary ends with the good news now spreading to the towns in Judea around Jerusalem. Jesus had promised that his disciples would be his witnesses in Jerusalem, Judea, and Samaria and to the very ends of the earth (Acts 1:8). The promise is being fulfilled. The mustard seed Jesus planted is growing into a great tree.

A FOCUS ON SIGNS AND WONDERS

Proclaiming the good news of Jesus by the power of God's Spirit is central to Acts. At the same time there are two main ways people are attracted to the message of Jesus. First, the disciples modeled what it means to be a truly restored community to those around them. We read several times that the disciples "had favor with all the people."

---

2. Peterson, *Acts of the Apostles*, 215.
3. Keener, *Acts, Vol. 2*, 1202.

The second major way of drawing attention to the gospel message is by the "signs and wonders" done through the apostles and other leaders as they proclaim salvation through Jesus. This is often stated in summary statements with individual stories and the many miracles done by Jesus helping to spark our imagination.

The Significance of Signs in Acts

Signs signify or point to something. In Acts, the apostles are careful to point out that they do not point to their innate power or godliness (Acts 3:12) but to the risen Lord Jesus Christ, who continues his compassionate acts of healing (Acts 3:15–16). It should not surprise us that God sends numerous signs and wonders to draw attention to his fulfilling his promise to bring salvation to the world.[4]

Signs of God's work in bringing salvation through Jesus match the significance of signs in the Old Testament. The purpose of signs for the people of Israel was not to prove the existence of God, for that was assumed. Rather they were given to point out that he is faithful and active on their behalf. God always shows himself through his created works and daily dealings in human affairs to care for his people. The "miraculous signs" are only more attention-grabbing.

The phrase "signs and wonders" is used at the exodus to describe the power and mercy of God when he delivers his people from bondage. Luke often uses this phrase. The phrase would have resonated, especially with the people of Israel, as it is used in Acts.

Because many people associate signs mainly with power, *it is important to emphasize that they also signify the compassion of God.* The Lord Jesus did not seek to dazzle people with the power at work in him but to heal and restore them. If God only wanted to draw attention to the gospel message, "explosions in the sky would have served just as well to draw attention (Luke 21:11; cf. Acts 2:19), *but the most common signs in Luke-Acts involve healing the sick or delivering those oppressed by demonic forces.*"[5]

In the Gospel of Luke, Jesus' ministry of healing is primarily "to the poor, the socially marginalized, and those without power," in

---

4. Witherington, *Acts of the Apostles*, 220.
5. Keener, *Acts, Vol. 1*, 545. Italics in original.

contrast to the elite who frequently opposed him.[6] Likewise, in Acts, Jesus continues to reach out in compassion to the poor through his disciples. Could this have implications for where signs and wonders occur today?

Signs as a Model for Ongoing Missions

Luke intends for both his Gospel and Acts to be examples of how God works to extend his kingdom to the ends of the earth. This is seen with the repeated emphasis on prayer, unity, generosity, Spirit-filled wisdom, boldness, and more. And the overwhelming abundance of "signs and wonders" also constitutes a pattern for how Luke expects God to continue to work in reaching the lost.[7]

In Acts, the Spirit is poured out for the "last days" (Acts 2:17), the time of salvation that stretches until Jesus returns. There is not the slightest hint in Acts that signs will not continue to accompany the proclamation of the gospel to the nations until Jesus returns.

I believe miracles continue today, but I confess I struggle with that belief. I have been close to charismatic and Pentecostal friends during what they call an outpouring of the Spirit, but I did not witness what I read in Acts.

To be honest, I have put off writing about "signs and wonders" because of my uncertainty of what to say, so I conclude with a few thoughts that I hope may be of help.

In Acts, signs and wonders are done through leaders who take the gospel to the nations—the twelve apostles, Paul, Stephen, Philip, and others. Perhaps this is why we read of more miracles taking place by evangelists in developing countries where the gospel is little known and where, I may add, they have inadequate medical care. Personally, I do not believe that it is because you or I have little faith.

Some would say that the apostles had a unique anointing of God's Spirit limited to them. I do believe the Spirit worked in a special way through them to plant the seeds of the gospel in the first century. Perhaps if we were to have another awakening in our country, we would see more of the miraculous. I believe so.

---

6. Keener, *Acts, Vol. 1*, 545.
7. Keener, *Acts, Vol. 1*, 539.

15

The Apostles Are Persecuted
(Acts 5:17–42)

IF YOU HAVE BEEN following my and Esuga's walk around the Temple Mount, you will be able to visualize the movement in this story.

Crowds flock from the countryside to Jerusalem to be healed by the twelve apostles on the great main street where the Sanhedrin meets. When the high priest and his colleagues see this public display of God's power attracting more and more people, they arrest the Twelve and put them in what was likely a large public prison "in the upper city where other official buildings were located."[1]

When the apostles are rescued by an angel at night, they return for several hours' prayer and sleep to the house where they stayed a few minutes away. They likely pray for boldness and some rest before returning to the Temple Mount early in the morning to continue teaching the people about Jesus.

When the Sanhedrin discovers the apostles are not in their prison cells but at the Temple Mount teaching about Jesus, they must again send the temple police to arrest them. Now the temple police must lead not only Peter and John (Acts 4:1–3) but all twelve apostles across the crowded courts of the Temple Mount down to the street to stand before the Sanhedrin. The apostles will soon be flogged in secret inside the chambers of the Sanhedrin, but for now they are led without violence across the temple courts because the Sanhedrin feared the reaction of the people!

1. Schnabel, "Topography of Jerusalem," 33.

THE SANHEDRIN TRIES TO SILENCE THE APOSTLES (ACTS 5:17-29)

As the Jesus movement continues to grow, so does opposition to it. The leaders of Israel fear they can't control it. With more and more signs and wonders done through the apostles and people streaming into Jerusalem from the surrounding towns, the rulers are now not only annoyed (Acts 4:2) but are filled with jealousy (Acts 5:17) and soon will become so crazy with rage that they want to kill the apostles (Acts 5:33). But their growing opposition will only make the disciples bolder and keep the good news spreading!

In a renewed attempt to intimidate and so silence the apostles, the rulers had put them in a public prison with plans to interrogate them in the morning. But the apostles are not long in prison. God demonstrates who is really in charge and sends an angel to release the apostles, the true leaders of the true Israel. The angel tells them, "Go, stand in the temple and tell the people the whole message about this life" (Acts 5:20). Emboldened now even more by their dramatic rescue and the angel of the Lord's command, the apostles rise before dawn and make their way to the temple to continue teaching about Jesus.

Notice the humor. While the apostles stand in the temple courts (which the Sanhedrin governs) proclaiming Jesus, the high priest and his closest advisors call together the entire Council of Israel to again warn them to stop teaching the people about Jesus! The Council gathers, waiting and waiting for the prisoners to be brought to them. As readers we are amused, for we know they aren't coming.

When the Sanhedrin discovers the apostles have somehow gotten out of jail, they have the temple police once again break their way through the crowds listening to their teaching to arrest them. But they cannot use violence since the Jesus movement has become so popular among the people that the temple police might be stoned, causing a major riot and leading Roman soldiers to pour out on the temple courts to bring order.

The Council, now even more annoyed, angry, and jealous, has the twelve troublemakers placed before them. Humiliated by the prison escape, angry their warnings have again been ignored, and jealous that the crowds continue to flock to the apostles and not them, they are eager to stamp out this growing Jewish sect.

The high priest leads the interrogation making two charges. First, they have deliberately disobeyed their orders to no longer speak of Jesus

(Acts 4:17, 18) but have instead filled Jerusalem with their teaching about him. Second, they proclaim God has raised Jesus from the dead and now reigns in God's Presence as Israel's Messiah and Lord. This makes them, the leaders of Israel, guilty of the most unimaginable crime of crucifying Israel's promised Messiah!

Rather than responding as a man on trial, Peter speaks as if putting the high priest and the Council on trial before the courts of heaven.[2] As we have come to expect, speaking for all the apostles, Peter responds to the first charge by saying, "We must obey God rather than any human authority." How will he respond to the accusation that the leaders are guilty of the Messiah's death? He teaches them about Jesus!

TEACHING THE COUNCIL (ACTS 5:30–32)

Peter teaches the Council the same message he has spoken to the people. He teaches about Jesus' death, resurrection, and exaltation as Lord and his giving of the Spirit. It is difficult to know if he expected any of them to repent and confess Jesus as their Lord, but, as previously (Acts 3:17–21), Peter says that God has exalted Jesus to "his right hand as Leader and Savior" so that even they would repent and be forgiven! Such is the grace of God that he would freely forgive the very men who led to the Messiah's cruel death by crucifixion.

At Pentecost, Peter had concluded his message by saying "that God has made him (Jesus) both Lord and Messiah" (Acts 2:36). Now he speaks of Jesus "as Leader and Savior." Since the term translated "Leader" was used for kings to denote rank and authority and thus can be translated "Prince," it is another way of speaking of Jesus as Lord.[3] Because Jesus was the Messiah sent to bring salvation, he was also called Savior.

The apostles back up their claim that God has raised Jesus from the dead and made him Leader and Savior by saying, "We are witnesses to these things and so is the Holy Spirit whom God has given to those who obey him" (Acts 5:32). The many signs and wonders done through the apostles *by the Spirit* can't be explained away (Acts 5:12), and they testify that their message is true.

The Spirit's Presence in the believer's heart confirms to them the reality of Jesus as Lord, while the outward signs of the Spirit witness to

2. Witherington, *Acts of the Apostles*, 232.
3. Keener, *Acts, Vol. 2*, 1219.

the reality of Jesus to others. God will give the Spirit to anyone who turns to him in obedience through Jesus.

Thus, the apostles teach Israel's high priest and Council that if they embrace their teaching about Jesus and turn in obedience to God, they too will receive the Holy Spirit! Do you see what is happening? The apostles have again been dragged in before the leaders of Israel and commanded to obey them, but the apostles, who, as we know, are the true leaders of believing Israel, boldly insist that the leaders of Israel obey their message about Jesus.

GAMALIEL INTERVENES (ACTS 5:33-42)

Hearing this fills the Council with such rage that they want to kill all the apostles, but God has placed a man among them, a Pharisee by the name of Gamaliel, to prevent it. A man of great learning and spiritual authority, he commands the respect of the Council. He stands and orders the apostles to be removed from the Council chamber to de-escalate the rage in the room and to grab the attention of the other leaders.

It is difficult to know with certainty how Gamaliel felt about the Jesus movement. Because he was a Pharisee, not a Sadducee, he shared the apostles' belief in a resurrection from the dead. But this does not mean he believed Jesus might be the Messiah, raised by God from the dead. He may speak more as a cunning politician, weighing popular opinion among the people to further promote himself as a leader in Jerusalem.[4] And again, since the Jesus movement was popular among the people, he may fear rioting in the streets.

Soon, one of Gamaliel's disciples, a young man named Saul, would not follow his teacher's wait-and-see approach. As a young, much more zealous Pharisee, Saul would try to stamp out this growing heretical movement with murderous violence.

But for a short time, Gamaliel's reasoning wins the day, and no one is killed. He reminds the Council that other men have appeared in Israel claiming to be the messiah and gained large followings. But when their leaders were killed (as Jesus was), their followers scattered and disappeared, which Jesus' disciples haven't! Instead, they keep growing! So, Gamliel tells the Council to wait and see what will happen to this new

---

4. Peterson, *Acts of the Apostles*, 227.

sect in Israel. If it is not of God, it, too, will fail. If it is of God, they "may even be found fighting against God!" (Acts 5:39).

While Gamaliel convinces the Council not to kill the apostles, many are still furious and have the apostles flogged. That meant thirty-nine whips on the back with "a strap of calf leather with interwoven thongs" to tear the flesh.[5] It seems the intent of the flogging is to finally silence the apostles, who are now for the third time ordered "not to speak in the name of Jesus" (Acts 5:40).

The young band of brothers leave the Council with deep lashes cut into their backs and blood everywhere. Not thinking for one second to reject Jesus, instead "they rejoice that they were considered worthy to suffer dishonor for the sake of his name" (Acts 5:41). Jesus had also been severely flogged before his execution. So, the apostles rejoice that in some small way they have shared in his sufferings.

---

5. Keener, *Acts, Vol. 2*, 1242.

16

Stephen and His Companions
(Acts 6:1–7)

THIS SHORT PASSAGE IS packed with challenges and insights for our life together as Jesus followers.

We read of:

- Disagreements due to different cultures and breakdowns in communication.
- The needy and the lonely feeling forgotten.
- Church leaders spread so thin that their most important tasks are neglected.
- The importance of finding new leaders with good character.
- How decisions are made for those most affected by them.

Because of Luke's purposes and lack of space on his scroll, he doesn't often take up problems in the early church, which his readers were aware of anyway, but this account illustrates problems that could arise with lessons on how to meet them.

The apostles are determined to not "neglect the word of God," to have ample time to "serve the word" (Acts 6:2, 4). This is often cited to support the need for pastors to have extensive time to prepare for "preaching the Word," that is, teaching from the Bible on Sundays and other occasions.

While time to study the Bible to build believers up in their faith is crucial, this was not the concern of the apostles here. The references to "speaking or serving the word," both here and in all of Acts, refer primarily to communicating the gospel to those who have not yet received it.[1] This is confirmed at the conclusion of the passage, when the problem raised was solved and allowed the apostles ample time to continue their witness all over Jerusalem. We read, "The word of God continued to spread; the number of the disciples increased greatly in Jerusalem, and a great many of the priests became obedient to the faith" (Acts 6:7).

Most seminaries today train pastors to preach, administer a church, and perhaps counsel Christians. What is missed in most seminary training is training for mission, *planting the seeds of the gospel* in our neighborhoods among those who do not yet know Christ. This is especially important for those who plant churches. They must resist the temptation to gather believers from other churches to start a church rather than laboring at the long, patient work of planting the seeds of the gospel in their neighborhoods. Alan Hirsch, a leader in the church as a missional movement, often says, "If we don't begin with mission, we never get around to it."

Recall that one of Luke's objectives is to show how the message about Jesus continues to spread despite forces opposing it. Those opposing forces are both *external* and *internal*. With threats and beatings, the leaders of Israel have tried without success to silence the apostles from speaking about Jesus. Now the enemy of all things good seeks to cause disunity to diminish the credibility of the community.

TENSION BETWEEN HEBREW AND HELLENIST BELIEVERS (ACTS 6:1–4)

The present passage begins by saying that "during those days" of continued witness, "the disciples were increasing in number" (Acts 6:1). With these words Luke points back to Gamaliel's claim that if the apostles' teaching springs from their wishful imagination that Jesus is alive and reigns as God's Messiah, their movement will die out like all others. More seriously, the leaders of Israel would be fighting against God (Acts 5:38–39)! As readers we know the movement will not die out and that Israel's leaders are in fact fighting against God.

So, failing to silence the disciples from speaking about Jesus, the enemy of God works *again within the Jesus community* (recall his attempt

---

1. Keener, *Acts, Vol. 2*, 1270.

with Ananias and Sapphira) to cause disunity and weaken its reputation for justice and compassion among the poor.

For the first time in Acts, we read of Greek-speaking disciples called Hellenists, who were a minority among the mostly Hebrew disciples, who spoke Aramaic. The Hellenist disciples were Jews from across the Roman Empire who had retired and moved to Jerusalem or had come to Jerusalem for a Jewish festival and stayed after becoming disciples of Jesus.

While both the Hebrews and the Hellenists are Jewish believers, united in their allegiance to Jesus, and while they both meet at the temple to worship, significant language and cultural differences naturally led the Greek-speaking disciples to gather in their own house churches with their own leaders, such as the seven we read of in this account.

The cultural and linguistic differences between the two groups, along with the continued rapid increase of disciples, caused the apostles, who oversaw the distribution of monies to the poor, to overlook the needs of the Greek-speaking widows. As immigrants these widows were even more socially disadvantaged among the poor.

There is no hint that overlooking the widow's needs was due to cultural prejudice. For when the legitimate complaint is raised by the Greek-speaking believers, the apostles act at once to right the wrong and suggest a solution that pleases the Greek-speaking believers.

As their Lord, the apostles show compassion for the poor. At the same time, now stretched to their limits, they realize that if they spend even more hours each day distributing food to them, their unique charge from Jesus to be his witnesses will be neglected.

So, with Spirit-given wisdom, the apostles ask the Greek-speaking disciples themselves to appoint persons of good standing for the task. The persons selected are to be "full of the Spirit and wisdom." The Spirit-led wisdom will give them the ability to discern the right thing to do to resolve the cultural and economic tensions that had developed between the two groups. To say that they were "full of the Spirit and wisdom" implies more than a special filling for one occasion. Those chosen walked so consistently with God that the Spirit's life in them characterized their lives.

The apostles' proposal both pleased the Greek-speaking community and freed the apostles to continue devoting themselves to prolonged times in prayer, empowered witness.

Since the passage ends saying many embraced the gospel (Acts 6:7), Luke implies that the internal conflict that threatened to both diminish the good reputation of the community and derail the apostles from their unique tasks has been met with Spirit-given wisdom among the leaders. So, the Jesus movement continued to grow in Jerusalem, extending even to a great many priests, who were likely not part of the official leadership of Israel.

While the purpose of this passage is to show us how a new threat to weaken the witness of the disciples is successfully met, it also provides the names of the seven young Greek-speaking leaders, who were appointed to distribute food to their widows. As with the apostles, their calling and abilities went beyond caring for the poor. Stephen and Phillip, especially, are soon singled out for their bold proclamation of the gospel, accompanied with signs and wonders.

SUMMARY OF STEPHEN'S SHORT MINISTRY (ACTS 6:5–7)

While all seven men are characterized by the Spirit's life and wisdom, Stephen is singled out as "a man full of faith and the Holy Spirit." Again, the expression suggests a person who walked so close and so consistently with God that the Spirit's power and faith characterized his life. Stephen would soon be charged with blasphemy. Luke wants us to see that such a person could not have blasphemed God or violated his law.[2] Stephen would need to be strong in faith and full of the Spirit when he is put on trial for blaspheming God and is stoned to death.[3]

Stephen's strong faith and awareness of the Spirit's power enabled him to do "great signs and wonders among the people" (Acts 6:8). As he proclaimed the word about Jesus (Acts 6:10), God confirmed the truth of his words with signs and wonders. As the risen Lord confirmed the witness of the apostles with signs and wonders to the Aramaic-speaking Jews of Jerusalem, so now he raises up young men like Stephen and Philip and confirms their witness with signs and wonders among Greek-speaking Jews.

Does this suggest that when the gospel goes out to new frontiers, God will grant signs and wonders to accompany the witness of godly leaders he raises up?

With the introduction of the Greek-speaking leaders in Acts 6:1–7, the Jesus movement develops in significant ways. First, as stated, Stephen proclaims Christ accompanied with signs and wonders just as the twelve

---

2. Peterson, *Acts of the Apostles*, 244.
3. Keener, *Acts, Vol. 2*, 1282.

apostles. That he did not belong to the select group of twelve apostles, who had known Jesus from the beginning and witnessed his resurrection, signals that the risen Lord Jesus is selecting additional leaders to extend the kingdom of God beyond Jerusalem. Barriers are about to be broken.

Second, opposition toward the Jesus movement escalates further. The apostles had first been warned not to speak about Jesus and then severely beaten (flogged) when they ignored the warning. But now Stephen will be stoned to death.

Third, Stephen's teaching becomes the final straw for the leaders of Israel. The Jesus movement is now beyond their control. So, with the people finally on their side in stoning Stephen to death, a popular uprising against the disciples drove them out of Jerusalem to the countryside of Judea and Samaria (Acts 8:1). But again, the leaders underestimate the power and love at work in the disciples. As they are scattered, they remain bold and speak about Jesus wherever they go (Acts 8:4). In all this we are to see the hand of God at work. Just as he used the sufferings and death of Jesus to accomplish his purposes, so now he uses the suffering of his people to extend his love and light to the nations.

Stephen's short ministry functioned as a crucial geographic and theological transition in the Jesus movement's witness to the nations. As mentioned, *geographically* God uses the death of Stephen and the persecution of the disciples to scatter them beyond the borders of Jerusalem to proclaim the word in all of Judea and Samaria. Much later we read that some of these very people who "were scattered because of the persecution that took place over Stephen, traveled as far as Phoenicia, Cyprus, and Antioch" to proclaim Jesus (Acts 11:19). Stephen's suffering became a geographic catalyst for the expansion of the Jesus movement.

As we will see in Stephen's teaching in Acts 7, it was primarily *his new theological insights* into the meaning of Jesus' death and the giving of the Spirit at Pentecost that leads to a new freedom and boldness in proclaiming Jesus among non-Jewish people. *It was friends of Stephen, driven from Jerusalem with his new theological insights, who first took the gospel to the gentiles, not Paul as we often assume (Acts 11:20–21), and curiously not the twelve apostles.*

I like to say that Stephen was a man ahead of his times, a man who taught some of what Paul would later teach. As he reflected on the meaning of Jesus' death and the giving of the Spirit, the Spirit showed him implications of these events that the twelve apostles had not yet seen. While Stephen and the apostles agreed on the core of the gospel, Stephen began to draw out implications from the gospel for the place of the Law of Moses and especially the temple in the life and mission of the Jesus movement.

I have always been fascinated and inspired by Stephen. We will now look in more detail for how his life and teaching become such a lightning rod for violent opposition.

17

Stephen Is Arrested
(Acts 6:8–15)

EARLY ONE MORNING, ESUGA and I went to the Western Wall to pray. You may have seen pictures of Jewish people placing their hands on the wall as they pray there. The Western Wall is only a small section of the entire 1590-foot (488 m) western retaining wall built by Herod. Because of its proximity to what was the holy of holies in the temple proper, it has become the holiest site in Judaism, so much so that when you pass through security to approach the wall, you will see a sign which says God's Presence resides there.

On a previous day, when we had walked up the ramp to the Temple Mount occupied by Muslims, we observed a sign from the Chief Rabbinate of Israel which said, "according to Torah Law, entering the Temple Mount area is strictly forbidden due to the holiness of the site." I wasn't sure how to understand this, so I did some research. Apparently, this prohibition has been made by all the great Torah scholars for a long time and applies to everyone, even the most conservative Torah-practicing Jews. The reason for the prohibition is that the ritual bath required to enter the Temple Mount cannot be performed today. However we understand these signs, it became clear to Esuga and me that place (or location) is important to the Jewish people. We would be careful to show respect.

Passing through security we entered the spacious plaza in front of the Western Wall and stopped to take in the hundreds of men with outstretched hands on the wall in fervent prayer. Then Esuga walked up, placed his hands on the wall, and began to pray with them as I watched from far behind. I did not join him to pray at the wall, because I wanted to take it all in and felt a bit intimidated from the signs.

My caution was confirmed when I observed a Jewish man tap Esuga on the shoulder and whisper in his ear. Esuga walked sheepishly back past me to grab a skullcap provided for tourists to pray at the wall. We were told this was near the place of God's Presence. In fact, for Orthodox Jews, by walking through a tunnel which runs along the Western Wall, they would come closer to God's Presence. This is because they believe one comes even closer to the Divine Presence once revealed in the holy of holies in the temple proper. According to the eighteenth-century Jewish scholar Jonathan Eybeschutz, "After the destruction of the Temple, God removed his Presence from his sanctuary and placed it upon the Western Wall where it remains in its holiness and honor."[1]

It was time for lunch, and we had many impressions to process. I appreciated traveling with Esuga for many reasons. He was generous, always helpful and patient, and had a good eye for maneuvering through the crowded, narrow streets of Old Jerusalem. But he also had a good eye for where to eat. Today it would be crepes in the Jewish Quarter of Old Jerusalem instead of our standard staple of chicken shawarma in the Muslim Quarter.

As I tore into my crepes and sipped on coffee, Esuga expressed his frustration and even criticism about how the Jewish people make the Western Wall, made of stones, the place of God's Presence. But he noted how Muslims and Christians can also make physical places sacred. Muslims do not allow non-Muslims to enter the Dome of the Rock or the El Aqsa Mosque built on the Temple Mount. Then there were the Christians—Esuga saw kissing stones inside the Church of the Holy Sepulcher, built on the site where Jesus was crucified and buried.

I asked Esuga to lower his voice for it was this kind of comment about the place of God's Presence that got Stephen stoned to death (Acts 6:14). We sat and talked for another hour about how religions make physical places sacred sites for God's Presence. I will share our thoughts in the next chapter. For now, read on in Acts to learn what Stephen taught about the place of God's Presence and why that got him stoned to death.

---

1. Eybeschutz, *Ya'arot Devash*, chapter 4.

SIGNS AND WONDERS BY STEPHEN

We have read that Stephen was not only full of the Spirit and wisdom but also full of the Spirit and faith (Acts 6:3, 5). His Spirit-produced faith prepares us to now read that "full of grace and power, he did great wonders and signs among the people" (Acts 6:8). The meaning of grace in this context refers to God's favor empowering him for ministry.[2] That God enabled Stephen to do great signs and wonders portrays him as a great prophet like Moses, who predicted the coming of the Messiah and was rejected.

Great signs and wonders by the apostles attested to their witness of the risen Lord Jesus, resulting in many becoming disciples (Acts 5:12–14). This had provoked jealousy among the leaders of Israel, leading to the persecution of the apostles. Also, Stephen became a target of persecution as he powerfully proclaimed Jesus with great signs and wonders.

His ministry causes a reaction from members of one of the Greek-speaking synagogues, called the Synagogue of the Freedman. The name suggests many were former slaves who had moved to Jerusalem from Africa (Cyrene and Alexandria) and Asia Minor (Cilicia and Asia). We will soon be introduced to Saul from Tarsus in Cilicia and will see that he was likely the main leader in opposing Stephen.

At first, they debated with Stephen, but when they realized they were not able to withstand the wisdom the Spirit gave him to speak, they secretly instigated some men to say that he blasphemed God and Moses.

Angry and humiliated from their defeat in debate, they seized Stephen to bring him before the Sanhedrin after first stirring up the people, the elders, and the scribes with false accusations against him. The false witnesses claimed that Stephen "never stops saying things against this holy place and the law; for we have heard him say that this Jesus of Nazareth will destroy this place and will change the customs that Moses handed down to us" (Acts 7:13–14). What lies behind their false claim?

Apparently, Stephen frequently taught things that threatened their core identity as Jews. N. T. Wright explains that "any first-century Jew could have told you there were certain key things, certain symbols, of what it meant to be God's people in the midst of a wicked pagan world, and it was absolutely vital that all Jews stuck by them" to maintain their fragile identity in a hostile world.[3]

---

2. Peterson, *Acts of the Apostles*, 238.
3. Wright, *Acts for Everyone, Pt. 1*, 103.

Wright goes on to specify *four key symbols* for Jewish identity at this period: *the temple, the law of Moses, the holy land with Jerusalem at the center,* and *circumcision,* the major sign of ethnic identity for the Jewish people. Most important of all, God was assumed to be tied to these symbols, so that to question them was to question God himself![4] This is why they can charge Stephen with blaspheming God. (To try to understand their mentality in the American context, consider the public reaction to someone who questions the American constitution or refuses to pledge allegiance to the American flag, or sing "The Star-Spangled Banner.")

But what was Stephen exactly teaching? Because the charges against him were false, it is difficult to discern the truth from how his opponents have distorted it. In his speech that follows (Acts 7:1–53), Stephen speaks positively of the roles of the Law of Moses and the temple in Israel's history. Yet, the fact that the charges against him centered on the Law of Moses and the temple suggests he was saying something about them that caused such a violent reaction. While the false witnesses deliberately distorted much of what Stephen said, there was an element of truth in the charges against him.[5] What was it?

Stephen was likely teaching that *God has now fulfilled the purposes for giving the Law and the temple.* They had their function for a time, but God has moved beyond them, fulfilling what they symbolized by sending Jesus. But to his opponents, "Stephen appeared to have violated the majesty of God by casting doubt on the sacredness and eternal significance of the law and the Temple for his people."[6]

With keen prophetic insight, Stephen sees that God is working out his grand story for all humanity, a story not bound by Jewish symbols. His opponents believe God will end history with Israel exalted among the gentiles, with the nations obedient to *their* Law of Moses, renewed worship at *their* temple, and with the Messiah reigning as *their* King in *their* land of Israel. In contrast, Stephen was likely teaching the implications of God's Spirit first coming to dwell in Christ and then in those who are joined to him by faith. God's Spirit dwelling in the disciples makes them the new Temple of God, making the Jerusalem Temple obsolete. We can see how this would lead to the charge of Stephen blaspheming God and "this holy place," the temple.

---

4. Wright, *Acts for Everyone, Pt. 1*, 103.
5. Peterson, *Acts of the Apostles*, 241.
6. Peterson, *Acts of the Apostles*, 241.

Stephen was also likely saying things about the Law that would later be emphasized by Paul. Somehow the death of the Messiah called for "a total reassessment of the role of the law in the life of God's people."[7] Later we will read Paul's explanation for a reassessment of the Law due to the death of Christ.

In short, Stephen was a pioneer thinker led by God's Spirit to lead the people of God out of the confines of Judaism, thus making the gospel available for non-Jews without converting to Judaism. While Stephen teaches that the Jewish national symbols have lost their significance and that one's identity should now be found in Jesus and the Spirit, they continue to find it in the symbols.[8] This was the great divide between Stephen and his opponents and will be the great divide between Paul and his opponents.

How did the twelve apostles view Stephen and his teaching? Why weren't they also put on trial for teaching against the Law and the temple? While there is no direct answer to this question in Acts, several factors indicate that they kept some distance from this young, Greek-speaking radical and his teaching.

THE APOSTLES AND STEPHEN RESPOND

We will soon read that due to the teaching of Stephen, all the disciples except the apostles were driven from Jerusalem (Acts 8:1). How were they able to stay in Jerusalem when others couldn't? And we have seen that due to language and cultural differences, the apostles, who led the Hebrew-speaking disciples in Jerusalem, did not have the closest contact with Stephen and the Greek-speaking disciples (Acts 6:1–6). In addition, the apostles have been teaching their fellow Jews that if they embrace Jesus as their promised Messiah, "times of refreshing may come from the presence of the Lord . . . and he may send the Messiah appointed" *for their restoration* (Acts 3:20).

Since the apostles were leaders of God's new Israel, and since there are frequent mentions of their teaching at the temple, and since they somehow are able to stay in Jerusalem when the other disciples are scattered, it seems *at this time* the apostles believed God would fulfill his literal promises to Israel, with Jesus returning to reign over believing Jews

---

7. Peterson, *Acts of the Apostles*, 243.
8. Wright, *Acts for Everyone, Pt. 1*, 104.

in Jerusalem with renewed worship at the temple and still following the Law of Moses.

In short, while they were persecuted for teaching Jesus was the Messiah, at that time the apostles lived more within the confines of Judaism and were not the lightning rod for hostility that Stephen was. Again, I ask you to consider how God has progressively revealed his truth even in the New Testament.

While the apostles and Stephen agreed on the core gospel message, the apostles did not yet see all the implications of the gospel Stephen had seen. Peter will later see them and address believers as living stones making up God's temple (1 Peter 2:4–5).

This does not mean, as some scholars have suggested, that Stephen and the Greek-speaking believers had a completely different theology than the apostles and the Hebrew-speaking disciples. They shared the same core beliefs of the gospel message, and Stephen possibly became a disciple when hearing the apostles teach the gospel at the temple.

Stephen was simply a man ahead of his time, seeing implications of the gospel that others hadn't. These implications would be especially relevant to the millions of non-Jews scattered throughout the Roman Empire and to taking the good news to the ends of the earth. Non-Jews can have Jesus as their Messiah, with the Spirit living in them, without becoming Jewish.

It is inevitable that our faith expresses itself within the confines of our culture with our unique forms and traditions, but from Stephen we learn that we must be careful not to absolutize our particular political beliefs and cultural preferences as part of what it means to be a Christian.

The last verse sets the scene for Stephen's speech in Acts 7. As Stephen stands alone before the Council of Israel and the false witnesses, they look intently at him, waiting for a response. They do not see fear but a face resembling that of an angel (Acts 6:15)! Apparently, there were enough traditions of angelic appearances to lead to the view of an angel's face illuminating a countenance of light, serenity, and goodness.[9] This is what the Council sees in Stephen.

Stephen's angelic countenance both confirms his innocence (Acts 7:55–56) and the reliability of his witness in contrast to that of his false

---

9. Wright, *Acts for Everyone, Pt. 1*, 106.

accusers. For generations to come he will stand as a model witness for disciples facing persecution and martyrdom.[10]

Viewing Stephen's countenance seems to calm his accusers for the moment, making them willing to listen to him.

---

10. Peterson, *Acts of the Apostles*, 244.

18

Stephen's Speech
(Acts 7:1–53)

I LEFT YOU IN the last chapter with Esuga and me eating crepes as we discussed how religions often put an unusual emphasis on holy places as a mark of their identity. This is a summary of what Esuga said, and I think it's quite profound.

> Human beings like to create places they believe are sacred and worthy of veneration. Then they construct regulations to honor and preserve the sanctity of their sacred places. "Don't enter if you're not one of us, don't touch, take off your shoes, face this way when you pray." But we simultaneously lack a profound sense of the immense worth of our fellow human beings. The radical nature of the gospel is to tear down any sense of identity tied to *our story and our sacred places* which erect barriers between us and together find our common place in God alone.[1]

Then Esuga looked across the table at me and began moving his hands back and forth toward my heart and back to his and said, "God is present in us and that is our place of identity. God dwells in us, not in walls of stone or sacred buildings. God is present in us as his portable sanctuary wherever we go."

To grasp this, sit back and imagine God's glory filling the holy of holies in the temple. Then watch yourself pull back the curtain before the holy of holies and walk in. You see God's glory; you breathe in his

---

1. Remarks from Esuga.

Presence to the very depths of your being. Then you hear God say, "My Presence is leaving this place to dwell within my people."

This is what Stephen knew happened on the day of Pentecost. This is what makes claims of holy places irrelevant. And this is what gets Stephen in trouble.

I have mentioned how I previously skimmed the sermons in Acts, and Stephen's speech, the longest in Acts, was no exception, but of course, in writing this book I knew I must study it carefully and try to understand it. Since Stephen is a first-century Jew speaking to other first-century Jews, his long speech rehearsing Israel's history may not at first seem relevant to us but it is. It has important implications for how many Christians tie their identity to a nation and its symbols.

STRUCTURE OF STEPHEN'S SPEECH

I found the speech a fun interpretive puzzle asking for answers to important questions. First, why does Luke devote so much space in Acts to this lengthy review of Israel's history? Second, how does the speech answer the charges made against Stephen? Finally, where is Stephen headed in the speech? What is his intent? I hope the following suggested answers to these questions will make your reading easier and more enjoyable in case you, too, have only previously skimmed it.

One reason Luke devotes so much space to Stephen's speech is to prepare us for the extensive conflicts Paul will have with Jewish disciples who want to force gentile believers to live by the Law of Moses and revere Jerusalem with its sacred temple. Another reason is to help later non-Jewish disciples, who knew little about the Old Testament, to be able to see how Jesus fulfilled promises to Moses, David, and other prophets. They would then be better prepared to answer Jewish challenges to their faith.[2]

Secondly, how does Stephen's speech answer the charges made against him? We will see that Stephen only indirectly defends himself. Instead, he puts his accusers on the defense. His main intent is to "develop a scriptural argument which charges Israel with consistently rejecting God and those sent to fulfill his purpose for his people (Acts 7:9–10, 23–29, 33–43). A terrible pattern of resisting God's prophets and disobeying

---

2. Gaventa, *Acts of the Apostles*, 120–21, quoted in Peterson, *Acts of the Apostles*, 245.

his law (Acts 7:44–50) had culminated in the betrayal and murder of the Righteous One (Acts 7:51–53)."[3] In short, Stephen, the Spirit-filled prophet raised up by God, exposes Israel's sin and challenges them to repent and receive their Messiah.

Despite all the miracles by the apostles, all the changed lives, all the prophecies of Israel's Messiah, the leaders of Israel persist in their unbelief. This explains why Stephen's indictment against them is so harsh. Their rejection of God's gracious offer of salvation brings to a climax the conflict that has been growing since Peter healed the lame beggar at the temple gate (Acts 3:1–10).

The structure of speech shows Stephen's skill in Greek rhetoric.[4] He begins by establishing common ground with his hearers (Acts 7:2–34), gradually moving toward his main points (Acts 7:35–50) before he concludes with an emotional appeal to his listeners to respond (Acts 7:51–53).

Stephen emphasizes the three great pillars that held Jewish society together: the land (Acts 7:2–36), the Law (Acts 7:37–43), and the temple (Acts 7:44–50), showing their fulfillment in Jesus and the giving of the Spirit.

It is helpful to read the speech and note the repetition of key words and phrases such as *rescue, ruler, reject, jealousy, and the places* where God appears. Noting these helps us see how Stephen builds his argument of God's sending Jesus to rescue his people and rule over his kingdom only to be rejected by Israel, like previous prophets.

Stephen moves from Abraham (Acts 7:2–8) to Joseph (Acts 7:9–16) and devotes most space on Moses (Acts 7:17–43) before he addresses the question of the temple (Acts 7:44–50) and ends denouncing Israel for her continuous rejection of the prophets, culminating with the rejection and murder of Jesus, the Righteous One (Acts 7:51–53). Note how Stephen uses Abraham, Joseph, and Moses to address Jewish identity on the Law of Moses, the land, and the temple. In the following comments, I focus on these themes as they relate to the accusations made against Stephen.

---

3. Peterson, *Acts of the Apostles*, 244.
4. Witherington, *Acts of the Apostles*, 261.

Abraham (Acts 7:2–8)

Without any hint of controversy, Stephen seeks to build common ground with God's call to Abraham and the promise that his descendants would worship him "in this place," that is, the land of Israel (Acts 7:7). He also says that God gave Abraham and his descendants the sign of circumcision as a mark of identity for the Jewish people. This is important to note since Stephen will turn the rite of circumcision against his accusers at the end of his speech, saying they have uncircumcised hearts (Acts 7:51).

Joseph (Acts 7:9–16)

Stephen then moves quickly to the patriarchs and Joseph. The patriarchs, that is the forefathers of Israel, were *jealous* of Joseph, "but God was with him and *rescued* him from his afflictions" (Acts 7:9–10). Further, God granted Joseph wisdom to become *ruler* over Egypt.

Stephen shows parallels between Joseph and Jesus. God chose Joseph and granted him favor and wisdom to rescue his people, but jealous of him, they rejected him. In the same way, the leaders of Israel were jealous of Jesus, rejected him, and orchestrated his death. As God rescued Joseph and made him ruler both over his people and all of Egypt, so, too, he rescued Jesus from death and made him Lord over all. Stephen does not yet draw this conclusion, but gradually, as his opponents listen, they begin to see it with growing anger.

While Stephen's emphasis is on Jesus, he also draws parallels between Joseph and himself, as a leader filled with the Spirit of Jesus, also full of grace and wisdom (Acts 6:3, 8) but now rejected by those to whom he has spoken the word of God. Yet he is confident that God will rescue him from death just as he did with Joseph and Jesus (Acts 7:55–56). By faithfully following the example of Jesus, Stephen becomes an example to others who will suffer for their loyalty to Jesus.

With Joseph, Stephen has prepared his listeners for what he now states more emphatically with Moses, who is given the most space in the speech. As you read about Moses, note the repetition of key words already used for Joseph.

Moses (Acts 7:17–43)

As we read about Moses, note how Stephen uses his story to now more directly address why he has been accused of blasphemy. First, he will show the Presence of God has never been tied to the temple. Then, he shows how Jesus was a prophet, like Moses, raised up by God but rejected by the people he was sent to rescue. And finally, he says that though God gave the law through Moses, Israel was unwilling to obey it.

First, just as with Abraham and Joseph, Stephen points out that God made his Presence known to Moses outside of the land of Israel, making wherever he chose to be present to be holy ground (Acts 7:30–33). While Stephen will soon acknowledge the role of the temple in Israel's history, he is building his case that *God's Presence has never been exclusively tied to the temple in Jerusalem.*

And just as with Joseph, he emphasizes that Moses was a type for Jesus (Acts 7:35–37). Moses said to the Israelites, "God will raise up a prophet for you from your own people as he raised me up" (Acts 7:37). If we recall what happened to Jesus, we see how he was a prophet like Moses. As Moses led Israel out of bondage from Egypt with signs and wonders, so Jesus performed wonders and signs, showing God was with him to liberate humankind from bondage to the deeper slavery of evil. And of course, as Moses was rejected by Israel as God's chosen ruler and judge, Jesus has been rejected by the very men Stephen addresses. Finally, from the very beginning, the people of Israel not only rejected Moses as their leader but also the law he received from God (Acts 7:38–43). They pushed Moses aside and said to Aaron, "Make gods for us who will lead the way for us" (Acts 7:40). This pattern of rejecting the word of God through the prophets he sent, and instead worshiping idols, continued throughout their history.

They said that Stephen was blaspheming God and the law of Moses! Stephen turns the tables on them. It is "the Jewish rulers, following their idolatrous ancestors" who were doing so.[5] Any defense Stephen has implied now turns into a direct denunciation.

---

5. Wright, *Acts for Everyone, Pt. 1*, 118.

THE QUESTION OF THE TEMPLE (ACTS 7:44-50)

Stephen now turns from key persons in Israel's history to specifically address the issue of the temple he has been accused of blaspheming. We have seen how he has already pointed out that God manifested his Presence in places outside of the land of Israel and the temple. Now he builds on these previous allusions.

In short, Stephen teaches *God's Presence has never been tied exclusively to the temple, and it is now found in members of the Jesus community in whom he dwells by his Spirit.* Stephen sees the implications of God's first coming to dwell in Jesus and now through the Spirit in his disciples. The functions the temple had in the story of Israel have been fulfilled in Jesus and his giving of the Spirit. Because his accusers reject Jesus and the work of the Spirit in his disciples, they do not see the Presence of God in them, even though they saw Stephen's face was like that of an angel!

Since God's home dwells within his people by the Spirit, "Wherever they are, there he is also."[6] This relativizes the temple in Jerusalem and any claim for a manmade structure to be "the house of God." This teaching was the basis for the charges made against him.

The question of the temple regarding Stephen's teaching contains "true and false thinking about God's presence."[7] Stephen is positive about the role the temple had in Israel's history. He agrees that God directed Moses to construct the tent of testimony and, later, Solomon to build the temple in Jerusalem, where God would choose to reveal his Presence to Israel. The temple had an important function in Israel's history. Yet Stephen quickly adds, "The Most High does not dwell in houses made with human hands" and quotes Isaiah where God says, "Heaven is my throne and what kind of house will you build for me" (Acts 7:48-49).

By this he attacks "an attitude that assigned permanence and finality to the Temple."[8] That God chose to manifest his Presence in the temple does not necessitate permanence to it. He attacks any thinking that ties God down to Jerusalem and the temple and so "expresses some claim upon God," limiting his freedom to act.[9] It was Jesus' claim to forgive sins up in Galilee apart from the temple in Jerusalem that began opposition to him (Luke 5:20-21).

---

6. Stott, *Message of Acts*, cited in Witherington, *Acts of the Apostles*, 139.
7. Witherington, *Acts of the Apostles*, 263.
8. Peterson, *Acts of the Apostles*, 263fn68.
9. Franklin, *Christ the Lord*, 105, quoted in Witherington, *Acts of the Apostles*, 274.

Stephen's teaching was especially relevant to the Greek-speaking disciples who will soon be driven out of Jerusalem to be scattered throughout the Roman Empire. For "this declaration of God's independence of the Jerusalem Temple is also a declaration of God's availability to all with or without the Temple."[10] Stephen's teaching thus paves the way for taking the gospel to the gentiles.[11]

Many Greek-speaking Jews had moved to Jerusalem to be near the temple, but now as Jesus' disciples they will leave, carrying the Presence of God with them. Taking Stephen's insights with them, they will pave the way for gentiles to become disciples apart from the law of Moses and worship at the temple in Jerusalem (Acts 11:19–21).

Saul, who stands among Stephen's accusers, will build on what he first heard from him. Stephen influenced many in his short life!

CONCLUSION (ACTS 7:51–53)

It only now becomes clear that Stephen has been building a case to put on trial before God those who try him in an earthly court. His denunciation may seem sudden and severe, but if we recall God's repeated witness to his accusers attested with signs and wonders by the apostles in Jerusalem, it is not at all surprising. Stephen knows the hard hearts of those he addresses and seeks to shake them as a last warning.

Having spoken about the temple, he now brings together other key points in his speech: circumcision (Acts 7:51), the rejection of God's prophets by Israel (Acts 7:52), and the law of Moses they had failed to obey (Acts 7:53). His accusers claim to be faithful Jews, the circumcised who revere the prophets and obey the law of Moses, but they are no more responsive to God than the uncircumcised pagans they so despise.[12] They stand like their ancestors, who both killed the prophets and never kept the law of Moses.

Stephen delivers a stinging indictment. They are stiff-necked, that is, "stubborn, unwilling to bend or rethink things."[13] Their hearts are uncircumcised, and their ears are blocked up so that they cannot hear and will not respond to God's message to them. They claim circumcision as

---

10. Tannehill, *Narrative Unity*, 93, quoted in Peterson, *Acts of the Apostles*, 263.
11. Peterson, *Acts of the Apostles*, 263.
12. Peterson, *Acts of the Apostles*, 264.
13. Witherington, *Acts of the Apostles*, 274.

their chief identity marker, setting them apart from gentiles, but they are no different from the pagan gentiles they deride as "the uncircumcised." They have been deaf to the word of God spoken to them first by Jesus, then by the apostles, and now by Stephen!

Most serious of all, showing solidarity with their ancestors who rejected and killed the prophets God sent them, they have rejected and killed Jesus, the Righteous One, sent to rescue them. Their rejection of Jesus (and now his apostles and Stephen) is part of a continuing pattern of disobedience to God. They are simply acting out "the pattern of rebellious behavior set by their ancestors."[14]

They are one with Joseph's brothers, who rejected his leadership and cast him in a well to die, and one with the Israelites, who rejected Moses as their leader and helped Aaron build an idol to worship. Finally, they have not kept the law of Moses they zealously boast of and condemn Stephen for not honoring.

---

14. Wright, *Acts for Everyone, Pt. 1*, 119.

19

The Stoning of Stephen
(Acts 7:54—8:1)

AFTER READING STEPHEN'S LONG speech, we may forget that he stands on trial before the Sanhedrin in their great chamber on the busiest street of Jerusalem running along the Temple Mount (Acts 6:12). After likely being beaten, he is dragged out on the street and then uphill "through the upper city past Herod's palace (praetorium) through a gate in the western wall to the site where executions took place, perhaps to Golgotha, a former quarry."[1]

Jesus had been sentenced to death by Pilate at Herod's palace and forced to carry his cross through the same gate to be crucified that Stephen is forced through by an angry mob of very religious leaders and those who join them. If Stephen was stoned to death at Golgotha outside the same gate where Jesus was crucified, he completes the picture of a disciple consumed with Christ and following in his footsteps.

My admiration for Stephen continues to grow since I first wrote a paper on him in my youth. A person saturated with God's Spirit, faith, and wisdom, yet a person who humbly administered care to needy widows. As a lifelong student of the Scriptures, Stephen has been my mentor in his readiness to question cultural, nationalistic interpretations added to the Scriptures. With fearless prophetic insight he maintains that our cultural expressions of faith must never be added to what it means to be a

---

1. Schnabel, "Topography of Jerusalem."

Christian. While the gospel is lived out in thousands of different cultures around the world, it must never be bound by any one culture.

Because of our calling and gifting, most of us will not be another Stephen. But we can all be so filled with the Spirit of Christ that others see Christ in us. With humility, by a careful reading of the Scriptures, we can evaluate our interpretation so that the living, loving Jesus is not hidden in our denominational boxes or wrapped in our nation's flag with his hand on our constitution.

STEPHEN SEES JESUS AT GOD'S RIGHT HAND

When the Council and Stephen's accusers hear "these things," i.e., that they are stiff-necked, uncircumcised law-breakers who have never lived by the law of Moses, they become insane with rage. Stephen, by contrast, is serene as he looks to heaven and sees the glory of God.

The account of Stephen's death completes the portrait of him as a prophet in line with the prophets of Israel, the twelve apostles, and especially Jesus, all rejected by Israel for speaking the words of God. But the parallels between Stephen and Jesus are especially prominent. Some four years earlier, Jesus stood on trial where Stephen now stands and was unjustly accused by the leaders of Israel.

Stephen doesn't look at the rage in the faces of his accusers but up to heaven, where he is granted a vision of the glory of God. Unlike some previous prophets who had been granted a vision of the glory of God, Stephen also sees someone else. He sees Jesus, the Son of Man, standing at God's right hand, sharing his glory, and reigning over his kingdom!

That Jesus *stands* suggests he is ready to receive Stephen to be with him in heaven, just as he had received the thief crucified beside him. But Jesus standing also suggests he is an advocate for Stephen in the heavenly courtroom, ready to vindicate him and judge his accusers who hold a trial on earth.[2]

Now when his accusers hear Stephen say that he sees Jesus, the Son of Man, at the right hand of God, they cover their ears (which Stephen has said are blocked up anyway!) and shout out loud curses to drown out any more words of blasphemy. The scene now becomes frightful.

If the entire Sanhedrin of seventy-one has joined the false accusers, some one hundred enraged men, now an uncontrollable mob, rush

---

2. Keener, *Acts, Vol. 2*, 1441.

toward this solitary prophet to stone him to death without giving him a formal verdict or sentence.

The main reason for their rage is that Stephen has identified Jesus as the Son of Man, reminding them of what Jesus said when he stood before them on trial. Jesus had said, "But from now on, the Son of Man will be seated at the right hand of the mighty God" (Luke 22:69). Thus, Stephen affirms the fulfillment of Jesus' words. Jesus is alive and reigns as Lord over God's kingdom, as Daniel and other prophets had predicted of the Messiah. This defied the leaders of Israel politically, claiming an alternate kingdom and authority to theirs.[3]

It is one more word of blasphemy. For "the idea that a human being could be at the right hand of God in heaven, especially a crucified manual worker from Galilee, was unthinkable."[4] In addition, this young Greek-speaking Jew claims that they, the leaders of the nation and interpreters of Israel's religion, are enemies of God, working against his purposes, and continuing to persecute the people of the Messiah they have crucified.

The false witnesses now take the lead in stoning Stephen. He is stripped of his clothing and pushed off a cliff roughly twice his height. Then one of them would have aimed for his heart with a large stone, followed with more stones, to finish him off and release the rage of the false witnesses.[5]

As the rocks crush and slash his body, Stephen continues his gaze to heaven and entrusts himself to the care of the Lord Jesus. Jesus had entrusted his spirit to the Father (Luke 23:46). Now Stephen prays, "Lord Jesus, receive my spirit" (Acts 7:59). In a matter of minutes Jesus would receive Stephen into his presence.

Stephen continues to show that the Spirit of Jesus permeates his being. As Jesus had prayed that God would forgive those who crucified him (Luke 23:34), so now Stephen cries out in a loud voice, "Lord, do not hold this sin against them" (Acts 7:60).

There had been countless Jewish martyrs in the centuries before Stephen, killed mainly at the hands of the gentiles. When they met their deaths, they normally shouted out curses to their torturers. "Keep on and see how (God's) mighty power will torture you and your descendants,"

---

3. Keener, *Acts, Vol. 2*, 1440.
4. Witherington, *Acts of the Apostles*, 276.
5. Keener, *Acts, Vol. 2*, 1454.

one was recorded as saying. Curses like this were "typical of many Jewish stories of people being tortured and killed for their belief and way of life."[6]

The love and forgiveness ruling in Stephen's heart are expressed in words as he asks the Lord to not hold this sin against them. When the love and forgiveness that ruled in Stephen's heart rules in the hearts of Jesus' followers, they have changed the course of history. Jesus teaches his disciples, "Love your enemies, do good to those who hate you, bless those who curse you, pray for those who mistreat you" (Luke 6:27 NIV). Where Jesus' disciples have lived by this central command to love even their enemies, they have changed neighborhoods, cities, and even countries. When they haven't, they have caused God to be blasphemed (Rom 2:24), ruined the reputation of his true people, and ignored their witness.

SAUL ENTERS THE STORY

Luke has briefly introduced Barnabas into the narrative (Acts 4:36–37). Now he introduces Saul (Acts 8:1), who will be his companion in extending the Jesus movement to the gentiles. Saul is now a young man, most likely in his late twenties.[7] Saul had moved from Greek-speaking Tarsus to Jerusalem to study under the famous Jewish scholar Gamaliel (Acts 5:34–39) and had likely recently completed his studies under him. As an eager graduate, he is ready to apply his learning with strict Pharisaic zeal.

The false witnesses who stoned Stephen had laid their outer garments at the feet of Saul. This was a cultural expression showing Saul's prominence among the more zealous Greek-speaking Jews in Jerusalem[8] and suggests that he oversaw the stoning of Stephen.[9]

Saul was also likely among those who had debated with Stephen (Acts 6:10) and was present at Stephen's trial when he gave his speech to the Council.[10] Putting these details together shows the remarkable influence Stephen's short ministry had on Saul. There is no doubt that Saul first heard some of his "more liberal ideas" about the temple and the law from Stephen. While he now violently rejects Stephen's teaching, later,

---

6. Wright, *Acts for Everyone, Pt. 1*, 123.

7. Keener *Acts, Vol. 2*, 1447. Contrary to popular assumptions, most of the apostles had begun to follow Jesus in their teens and are now in their early twenties.

8. Keener *Acts, Vol. 2*, 1445.

9. Keener *Acts, Vol. 2*, 1452.

10. Witherington, *Acts of the Apostles*, 265.

after Jesus appears to him (Acts 9:1–6), he will remember, embrace, and build on it.

But Stephen's way of being also influenced Saul. He had been among those who had looked intently at the face of Stephen and saw a radiance like that of an angel (Acts 6:15), and now he sees how Stephen dies, praying for his murderers, not cursing them. Thus, Stephen's example influenced Saul's conversion.[11] But for now, Saul fights for his God, becoming the leading persecutor of the Jesus movement. Leading the stoning of Stephen is only the start of his efforts to eliminate the Jesus movement from Jerusalem and Judea before it spreads any farther.

A FOCUS ON SAUL'S HOME IN TARSUS

Saul was born and raised in Tarsus before moving to Jerusalem after turning thirteen. Then three years after his conversion, now in his early twenties, he is sent back to Tarsus, located in the regions of Cilicia and Syria, where he spends some ten years (the so-called silent years). After this, Barnabas travels to Tarsus to bring him back to Antioch as a coworker in the ministry (Acts 11:25–26). With all those years Saul spent in Tarsus, it is helpful for us to know more about the city and how it influenced Saul's life.

Tarsus is 590 miles (950 k) north of Jerusalem at the northeast corner of the Mediterranean Sea, around the corner from Antioch. It was the capital of Cilicia and a wealthy city due in part to its location on a main trade route and its location in the middle of a fertile plain that stretched from the mountains in the north down to the Mediterranean Sea.

Tarsus was a "city of culture and politics, of philosophy and industry," rivaling Athens as a center of philosophy, in part because "half of the philosophers of Athens had gone there a hundred years earlier."[12] At this time many Stoics, some of whom Saul may have debated during his "silent years" in Tarsus, have returned to Athens, where he will again debate the Stoics.[13]

As Paul later traveled the Roman Empire, the reputation of Tarsus as a city of learning would have affected how people viewed

---

11. Keener *Acts, Vol. 2*, 1444.
12. Wright, *Paul*, 11.
13. Keener, *Acts, Vol. 2*, 1650.

him, just as it does us when we learn that a person has attended a prominent university in a famous city.[14]

The Jewish people in Tarsus were a minority of several thousand in a city of one hundred thousand.[15] We can assume, just as in other cities in the empire, that the Jewish people in Tarsus lived close to each other both for their safety and for the convenience of buying kosher food.[16] Their strict requirements for kosher food, circumcision, and not working on the Sabbath as all others did made them seem aloof "and prevented them from fully socializing into the larger society."[17]

Growing up in a strict Pharisaic home in the Jewish quarter of Tarsus, young Saul was keenly aware that the Jews around him took note of how well he obeyed the Jewish law. Later he could say that regarding the law he followed it like a Pharisee, faultless regarding legalistic righteousness (Phil 3:5–6). Many wealthy Jews gave into the pressures of gentile culture (it was good for business) but not Saul and his family. They stood out in their determination to live faithfully to the Jewish laws.[18]

Growing up as a strict Pharisee, young Saul would not have freely mingled with gentiles. Yet his work with the family business as a leatherworker/tentmaker required polite conversation with their gentile customers. Unlike Jerusalem, which had mostly all Jews, young Saul felt the cultural pressures of refusing invitations from gentiles for a meal and perhaps even offers of marriage to a daughter.

In the family workshop young Saul heard the politics and philosophies abreast in the Roman Empire. He would have especially been provoked to learn that the gentiles prayed to Caesar as a god, even claiming that he was the savior and source of universal peace for the empire. Young Saul passed pagan temples and shrines on every corner of Tarsus knowing well of the immorality and worship of idols that took place in them,[19] but he kept himself separate, pure. Thus, living outside the land of Israel, young Saul with his keen mind became familiar with other ethnicities and cultures. As he observed

---

14. Keener, *Acts, Vol. 2*, 1651.
15. Wright, *Paul*, 14.
16. Wright, *Paul*, 14.
17. Jeffers, *Greco-Roman World* 215.
18. Barnett, *Jesus and the Rise*, 260.
19. Wright, *Paul*, 23.

them, he evaluated their ideas and practices based on his deep understanding of the Jewish Scriptures. His innate ability for careful reasoning developed into what we later read in the carefully structured arguments of his letters.

"Saul's background in Tarsus uniquely equipped him for the work to which God had called him. Few others in the world at that time could have been what this man was."[20] He was fluent in biblical Hebrew and the Aramaic of the Middle East "in addition to the ubiquitous Greek, which he spoke and wrote at great speed."[21]

Saul grew up in a wealthy family, and just as wealthy, prominent families send their children to the best universities today, he was sent to Jerusalem to receive the highest possible training in the Torah. He left for Jerusalem with yet another asset for his future work. He was a Roman citizen. In provincial cities like Tarsus, Roman citizenship "was limited to the wealthiest and most distinguished local citizens," and Saul was one of them.[22] Saul carried the passport he would need at times to save his life as he traveled the empire.

---

20. Barnett, *Jesus and the Rise*, 262.
21. Wright, *Paul*, 15.
22. Barnett *Jesus and the Rise*, 261.

20

Driven from Jerusalem
(Acts 8:1–4)

I REMEMBER THE UNEASE I felt when I first realized that the apostles believed they must remain in Jerusalem to proclaim Jesus to the people of Israel, with the hope that they would believe and Jesus would return to reign in Jerusalem over a renewed Israel. It is a mystery to me that Jesus did not teach them this would not happen from the beginning (see Acts 1:6–7), but this and other truths would later be revealed.

Then there was the unease I felt in seeing how very slow the apostles were to leave Jerusalem (because of their belief that Jesus would return to reign from there) and go to the nations with the good news of Jesus.

Finally, there was my unease in seeing how the apostles seemed to distance themselves from Stephen and his teaching *at this time* about the law and the temple, important identity markers for the Jewish people.

This unease was wrongly based (in my view) on the belief that the apostles knew from day one everything we read in Paul and Peter's letters.

Then I had to decide if I should write this? Would it create doubts for some readers? Would it show disrespect for the apostles? So, when I met with four colleagues who have PhDs in biblical studies for advice on this book, I raised these questions to them. One of them, who has spent his life researching and teaching the New Testament at a local seminary, responded at once to say that I should include these insights in the book, for it is part of our history recorded in Acts—it is what happened. And as he often points out in his teaching, God has not given us "a flat Bible" with the same theological truths in each book from beginning to end. Rather, *God has chosen to progressively reveal* his plan of salvation in the Scriptures. This means even the apostles did not see everything from the beginning that was later revealed. All this will be most vividly seen in the debate in Acts 15 about the role of the law.

Of course, not all matters were debated. The reason I stressed the core content of the gospel in Acts 2 is because all the believers agreed on it (which sadly they don't today). The six facets of the gospel in the Acts sermons contained "an outline of the faith that was commonly held, especially as applied to missionary situations."[1]

I confess my frustration with Christians who read the Bible through the lens of their theological grid with no openness to question any part of it.

PERSECUTION IN JERUSALEM

On that day, the day Stephen was stoned to death, a severe persecution spread beyond the apostles to all the disciples in Jerusalem. Opposition to the Jesus movement from the leaders of Israel had been mounting since Peter first healed a lame beggar at the temple gates (Acts 3:1–10). Now the people, who once favored the disciples, have joined their leaders in persecuting them (Acts 6:12). A storm of persecution swept through the streets and alleyways of Jerusalem, seeking any who belonged to the Jesus community.

Luke writes that "all except the apostles were scattered" from Jerusalem. This caught my attention and raised questions. Did every single disciple except the Twelve leave Jerusalem? *How* were the apostles able to stay? *Why* did they stay? And, as mentioned earlier, what was their relationship with Stephen? Jesus had instructed the apostles to be his witnesses in Jerusalem, Judea, Samaria, *and to all nations* (Acts 1:8), but some four years later, they seemed determined to remain in Jerusalem.

How are we to understand all this?

First, Luke often uses "all" as hyperbole. For example, we may say, "All of Europe watched the World Cup finals yesterday." (See Luke 1:6; 2:1; 5:17; 7:17; and Acts 1:1 for some of Luke's hyperboles.) I follow those scholars who believe he uses hyperbole here and that because Stephen was an outspoken leader among the Greek-speaking disciples, they were

---

1. Leith, *Creeds*, 13.

the main target for persecution and forced to flee Jerusalem. No doubt many of the more temple-focused, Torah-adherent, Hebrew-speaking disciples were also scattered but not permanently as we later read of them back in Jerusalem.[2]

How and why were the twelve apostles able to stay? Since the risen Jesus appeared to them and poured out the Spirit on them, they had been fearlessly bold, defying orders to keep silent about Jesus. This led to increased persecution. Yet due to the violent death of Stephen, they may have gone "underground" a brief time to regroup while the streets of Jerusalem returned to normal. Yet remaining in Jerusalem to also face possible death was an act of courage because normally "ancients more often persecuted ringleaders first."[3]

While the apostles and Stephen held to the same core truths of the gospel, at this time the Twelve likely distanced themselves from what they perceived as his more radical teaching about the temple and the law. This made it easier for them to stay in Jerusalem, and it may explain why they were not mentioned as present at Stephen's burial. "It was probably more dangerous for the apostles to emerge from hiding than for others."[4]

I have already addressed *why* they were so determined to stay in Jerusalem. *They believed they must stay* as the chosen leaders of the renewed people of Israel. They still believed Jesus would soon return and reign from Jerusalem over the nations with a renewed temple. "They did not leave their posts; they were still contending for the soul of Jerusalem from which they would presumably rule" (Luke 22:30).[5] So they thought at this time.

In addition, Luke may want to point out that the gospel was taken to the gentiles by the more culturally open members of the Jesus movement, not the Jerusalem church which would become increasingly nationalistic (see Acts 21:20–24).[6] The gospel is most often spread by those who break out of their culture-bound mindsets.

---

2. Peterson, *Acts of the Apostles*, 276.
3. Keener, *Acts, Vol. 2*, 1469.
4. Keener, *Acts, Vol. 2*, 1471.
5. Keener, *Acts, Vol. 2*, 1469.
6. Keener, *Acts, Vol. 2*, 1468.

THE DISCIPLES ARE SCATTERED

Like a flood of displaced refugees, thousands of disciples fill the roads leading out of Jerusalem to the countryside of Judea, Samaria, and beyond. As they leave, they take the message about Jesus with them. They become Jesus' witnesses in Samaria and beyond, not the apostles. Luke writes, "Now those who were scattered went from place to place, proclaiming the word" (Acts 8:4).

We recall that Joel's prophesy said that when God poured out his Spirit on all his people, *all would prophesy, speaking of God's mighty work through Jesus* (Acts 2:11, 17–18). With the apostles still in Jerusalem, those scattered are even more emboldened to proclaim the message of Jesus. Displaced, they suffer hardship, but they see their refugee status as an open door to take the good news to regions where Jesus is not yet known. It seems God has waited until now for them to be dispersed.

For several years they have devoted themselves to apostolic teaching, filling their hearts and minds to obey all Jesus said and did. They have lived in generous, caring community with one another. They have gathered daily in house churches, praying in unity, and sharing the life of the Spirit, and they have experienced the power of God working through signs and wonders by Stephen and the apostles (Acts 2:42–47).

While Luke will now highlight the role of Philip, an outstanding leader among those dispersed, he wants us to see that *all* the disciples were active in spreading the gospel and establishing small Jesus communities.

"The community life, which found its strength in house meetings and spread its influence from that joyful and caring context (Acts 2:46–47), was now systematically dismantled."[7] The only "church" the disciples knew was small, simple, Spirit-filled gatherings in houses with believers connected to one another throughout the week. It was not complicated; it did not require "paid professionals" trained at a seminary. Through ordinary believers, the life and message of Jesus flows in streams to the countryside of Samaria and beyond.

SAUL "FIGHTS FOR GOD"

But Saul is blind to the work of God. The leader who oversaw the stoning of Stephen now turns his rage against all the disciples (Acts 7:58, 8:1, 3).

---

7. Peterson, *Acts of the Apostles*, 277.

He does not agree with his teacher, Gamaliel, who had urged the Jewish leaders to let the Jesus people alone, warning that they might be fighting against God (Acts 5:38, 39). Saul believes that because of this tolerant approach, the movement has continued to grow, allowing radicals like Stephen and his friends to influence even more people with an even more dangerous teaching undermining the nation of Israel.

Enough. The entire Jesus movement must be rooted out with force. Even though they have been flogged, they have ignored orders to not speak about this man Jesus, so they must be killed or put in prison to be silenced. And Saul will do it. Saul will fight for God.

He silenced Stephen. Now he will silence all the disciples. With the support of the Council (Acts 9:1), he hunts them down, entering house after house in Jerusalem to drag both men and women off to prison, not caring that he separated children from their parents (Acts 8:3). "Just as the disciples had been meeting from house to house (Acts 2:46; 5:42), now Saul persecuted them from house to house."[8] He likely broke into their houses when they met in the evenings for worship and prayer to maximize his capture. Because homes were viewed as private and mainly the sphere of women, Saul's savage hostility against the disciples is even more deplorable. At the same time, his targeting of women shows their courage and important role among the disciples.[9]

Stephen had been dragged outside the city walls and crushed to death under a hail of rocks. Saul approved. He believed this "was the kind of action the Torah required. This was what 'zeal' was supposed to look like."[10] From that moment, the young Saul knew what had to be done.

Jesus' followers had fled Jerusalem after Stephen's death, continuing to spread their poisonous message. Wherever they went, they established new groups, "little revolutionary cells, propagating this new teaching, putting Jesus in the center of the picture, and displacing the ancient Israelite symbols, up to and including the temple itself. From Saul's point of view, if the compromisers in the old biblical stories had been bad, this was worse. This could set back the coming kingdom. This could call down further divine wrath upon Israel."[11]

Saul will fight for God, and with God on his side he is confident he will win the battle for the right religion. As readers, we know he will lose,

---

8. Keener, *Acts, Vol. 2*, 1482.
9. Keener, *Acts, Vol. 2*, 1483.
10. Wright, *Paul*, 38.
11. Wright, *Paul*, 38.

for already the persecution he launches leads to the kingdom of God, spreading to Samaria! Soon Saul will see he is fighting against God, just as Gamaliel had warned.

21

Philip in Samaria
(Acts 8:5–25)

WITH THE JESUS MOVEMENT now moving out of Jerusalem, travel becomes more prominent in Acts. Philip travels to "a city in Samaria" (Acts 8:5, 8). Luke does not specify which city in Samaria, but it was the main city where most Samaritans lived. That would make it Shechem (modern-day Nablus), with the smaller village of Sychar (modern-day Askar) just to the east. Sychar is where Jesus met the woman at the well (John 4:1–42).

To trace Philip's travels, Esuga and I rented a car in East Jerusalem from a Palestinian company and headed up to Samaria. Our destination, Nablus, was only thirty miles north. Philip traveled by foot, making his trek a few days. Ours took us only an hour and a half once we found the right road! We spent half an hour driving around Jerusalem looking for Route 60, which runs straight north to Nablus. Google Maps had us driving four hours all the way around the West Bank to get to Nablus. Frustrated from driving in circles, Esuga finally downloaded Waze, which directed us to Route 60, straight north to Nablus.

Built over Israel's ancient roads, Route 60 ran up the spine of the mountain ridge, running north to south through Israel. I looked at my map of Ancient Israel on my lap. Jericho was only twelve miles east, deep down in the Jordan Valley. Joppa, where Peter would soon visit, was by the Mediterranean Sea, thirty miles to the west. Israel is a small country.

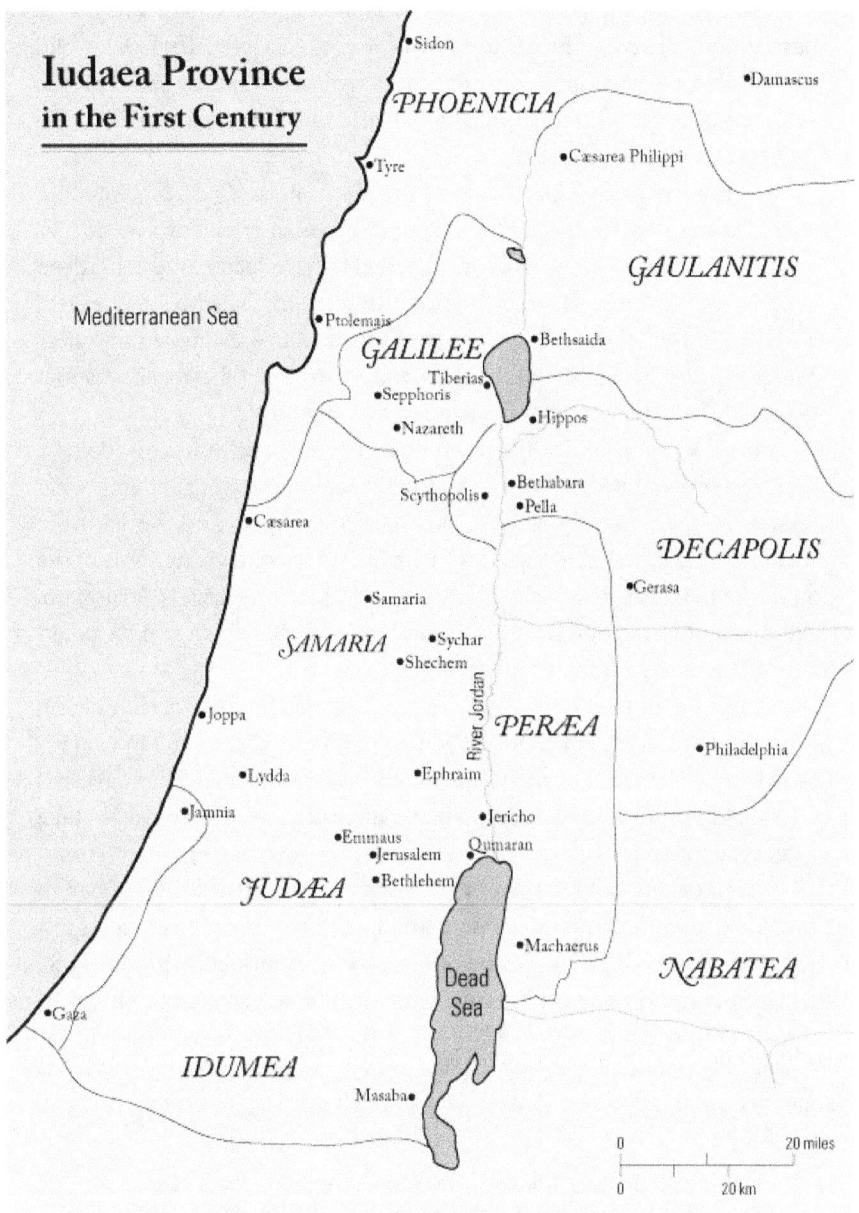

Figure 4: Map of First-Century Israel.
This photo by unknown author is licensed under CC BY-SA.

More a student of the New Testament, I was only vaguely aware of all the prophets and kings and armies from surrounding nations that had traveled this highway. I peered east and west at the small villages we passed and turned to Esuga to say that I wished Cyndi Parker, an Old Testament scholar from our church, was with us to tell us about all the prophets of Israel who traveled this ancient road. Later, back in Philadelphia, I met with her to ask about it.

Cyndi shared that 60 percent of the events in the Old Testament occurred along this road! Both Samuel and Jeremiah were born in villages along it. Abraham stayed near it in Bethel, where Jacob later fell asleep and dreamed of angels ascending and descending a ladder to heaven, and here in Bethel the great prophet of social justice, Amos, prophesied. We drove past Shilo, unaware that it was where the tabernacle was first placed and where Samuel was raised as a young boy.[1]

I still struggled with the nasty virus I brought with me on the trip. A persistent cough dampened my spirit, keeping me from reliving what I knew of the ancient road we traveled. Esuga liked to drive with the windows down, so I held tightly to my map as I tried to locate some of the Samaritan villages Peter and John visited on their way back to Jerusalem. I had run out of cough drops in Jerusalem, so I asked Esuga if we could stop at a Jewish settlement to buy some.

In few minutes, we spotted one, pulled off the highway, and soon found a pharmacy. But when I asked for cough drops, the woman who assisted me explained they did not use cough drops in Israel. She suggested a strong liquid form of cough medicine instead. I bought a bottle to take a generous swig.

Back on the road, a map in my right hand and the bottle of cough medicine in my left, my spirits were lifted, but I continued to cough. I unscrewed the cap of the medicine bottle and took another generous gulp. Esuga shared how the rolling hills with their small, scattered villages in the distance reminded him of Nigeria. I glanced out the window, but his words didn't register. I started coughing again and took another generous drink of the medicine. Then I leaned my seat all the way back to listen to the wind.

Half an hour later the car jolted to a stop. Startled awake, I saw we had stopped at the Palestinian checkpoint for entering Nablus. There was a sign warning Jews from entering Nablus, but we passed through without questions since our rental car had Palestinian plates.

---

1. Personal conversation with Cyndi Parker, Sept. 21, 2021.

Nablus, or ancient Shechem, where Philip proclaimed Jesus, was high in the hills of Samaria, nestled between two mountains. As the first capital city of the Northern Kingdom, it too featured prominently in Israel's history. We drove the winding streets up and down the hills until we reached our hotel in the Old City.

The following day we drove up a long winding road to Mount Gerasene, where the Samaritans once had their own temple. There were several hundred Samaritans still living in the village on Mount Gerasene, and today they would celebrate Passover, as they did every year. We found our place in the crowd to watch sheep led in to be sacrificed and older Samaritan men in their long ornate robes chanting prayers in unison. We witnessed a hint of Passover in Jerusalem at the time of Jesus and the apostles.

Before leaving, we trekked to the very top of the mountain to see where the Samaritan temple once stood. Ruins are still there but the gates were locked because of the Passover celebration. So, we sat on large boulders outside the walls high up on the mountain and scanned the hills and valleys below. This was Samaria. This is where the Samaritans flocked to hear Philip proclaim that God had sent the Messiah to die as our Passover lamb.

PHILIP BREAKS BARRIERS FOR THE GOSPEL

Jesus has said the apostles would witness of him first in Jerusalem, then Judea and Samaria, and finally to the ends of the world (Acts 1:8). They have been bold, fearless, and effective in their witness in Jerusalem, but they remain stationed there because of their beliefs. So, it is Philip, a companion of Stephen, that God leads to take the good news to the Samaritans. While the apostles follow up and confirm Philip's work in Samaria, there is no hint in the text that they send him.[2]

Philip, like Stephen, was a Greek-speaking Jew, filled with the Spirit, wisdom, and faith (Acts 6:3, 5; 8:5–6). We are to assume he shared Stephen's more open teaching concerning the temple and the Law, which contributed to his ability to go beyond the more closed culture of Judaism and take the gospel to Samaria. In addition, since Greek was his mother tongue and the main language of Samaria, he was better able to

---

2. See Acts 8:4–5, 39–40.

communicate with the Samaritans than the apostles.[3] These factors make Philip better qualified to cross cultures with the gospel.

Like Stephen, Philip is a boundary-breaker. Stephen broke the gospel out of the theological confines of Judaism, and Philip acts on the implications of Stephen's teaching to take the gospel across the religious and cultural boundaries between the Jews and the Samaritans.

Jesus' encounter with the Samaritan woman (John 4:1–42) prepared the way for Philip's ministry in Samaria. Jesus had told the Samaritan woman he was the Messiah and that a time was soon coming when God would be worshiped neither at the temple in Jerusalem nor in Samaria but rather in Spirit and in truth (John 4:21–24). Her witness became instrumental for many from her town believing; thus, she becomes Philip's processor in Samaria.[4]

Besides the challenge of a different language and different culture, there were other challenges for the gospel to take root in Samaria. The Samaritans had their own temple for worship on Mt. Gerizim. Would they now be required to travel to the temple in Jerusalem where the Jewish disciples worshiped?

Since Philip likely agreed with Stephen that God's Presence was not tied to the temple but resided in anyone anywhere who turned to Jesus, he was the right person to assure them they need not make pilgrimages to the temple in Jerusalem. The Spirit had come to dwell in them, just as Jesus predicted, making them God's living temple.

Yet another challenge—of all the Jewish Scriptures, the Samaritans only believed in the five books of Moses. This means they lacked the rich teaching of the prophets, who predicted the coming of the Messiah to reign over God's eternal kingdom. With only part of the Jewish Scriptures to build on, it would be easy for them to deviate from apostolic teaching, causing a major split in the movement as soon as it moved outside of Jerusalem. But the greatest challenge to Samaritan belief was the threat of syncretism, the assimilation of new beliefs and practices into their previous pagan beliefs.

While officially the Samaritans believed in the same God as the Jews, in practice, Greek religions, which included magic done by dark forces, had influenced their popular culture for more than a century.[5] Thus, there was the threat of the Samaritans joining their belief in Jesus

---

3. Keener, *Acts, Vol. 2*, 1494.
4. Wall, "Acts of the Apostles," 137.
5. Keener, *Acts, Vol. 2*, 1513.

to their Hellenistic, pagan beliefs in magic, rampant in Samaria as illustrated through the "divine man" called Simon.[6]

Note how the account shows the risen Lord Jesus acting through his Spirit to overcome these challenges through Philip, Peter, and John so that all Samaria accepts the word of God (Acts 8:14).

A FOCUS ON PHRASES FOR THE GOSPEL

You may have already noticed this, but in case you haven't, I want to make an important point. For variety and to economize space, Luke uses many different phrases to summarize the one gospel message in Acts. It is important to note this so that we avoid reducing the gospel to our favorite phrase or read different meanings into the variety of phrases used by Luke to communicate the one and same gospel.

Philip's proclamation in Samaria provides a good illustration of the variety of phrases used for the one, and the same, gospel message. For example, Philip proclaims "the word" (Acts 8:4), "the Messiah" (Acts 8:5), and "the good news about the kingdom of God and the name of Jesus Christ" (Acts 8:12). Then we read that the apostles learn that Samaria had accepted "the word of the Lord" (Acts 8:14) and that they proclaimed, "the good news" (Acts 8:25). Each phrase is an abbreviation of Peter's detailed gospel message on Pentecost and elsewhere.

Luke can also summarize the gospel message with the phrase "the word of God," meaning all that God had accomplished through Jesus (see for example, Acts 4:31; 6:7; 11:1; 13:5, 7, 42). The gospel is also summarized as "the word of this salvation" (Acts 13:26), "the good news about the Lord Jesus" (Acts 11:20), "the good news of the kingdom of God and the name of Jesus Christ" (Acts 8:12), "proclaiming the kingdom" (Acts 20:25), and "preaching the kingdom of God and teaching about the Lord Jesus Christ" (Acts 28:31).

The variety of phrases used for the one gospel message reminds us that when we come across them, we should not look for differences in meaning but rather different expressions of the six-faceted gospel we explained in Acts 2 (see chapter five in this book).[7]

---

6. Peterson, *Acts of the Apostles*, 283.
7. See Thompson, *Acts of the Risen Lord*, 100–101.

PHILIP AND SIMON (ACTS 8:5-13)

The story falls into two parts. The first part focuses on Philip's ministry in Samaria and introduces the false prophet, Simon, as an antithesis and threat to Philip's witness (Acts 8:4-13). The second part focuses on Peter, who both confirms and supplements Philip's work as he prays for the Samaritans to receive the Spirit and confronts Simon, who seeks to purchase the greater power of the Spirit (Acts 8:14-25).[8]

First Philip, filled with the Spirit and emboldened with Stephen's example, doesn't flee to the mountains to hide when driven from Jerusalem but treks straight north to the chief city of Samaria (Acts 8:5-8). There he proclaims the word about Jesus, accompanied by signs just as the apostles and Stephen.

This is not yet the witness to gentiles at the ends of the earth (Acts 1:8), for despite their many deviations from Judaism, the Samaritans were regarded as Jews on the fringe of Judaism. It was true they were Jews who had intermarried with gentiles, making them ethnically strange and religiously deviant, with their own temple and rejection of all the Jewish Scriptures except the books of Moses.[9] But they were, nonetheless, Jews.

Like the apostles, Philip proclaimed Jesus as the Messiah through whom the kingdom of God had come to earth. We read he "was proclaiming the good news about the kingdom of God and the name of Jesus Christ" (Acts 8:12).[10] The crowds listened eagerly to the good news of the kingdom of God coming with Christ, as they saw the signs done through Stephen.

First Stephen, and now Philip, showed that God calls people besides the apostles to proclaim the gospel accompanied with signs and wonders. *What distinguishes the twelve apostles* is not their witness accompanied by signs and wonders but that they were with Jesus from the very beginning of his ministry to the end and can verify that God raised him from the dead (Acts 1:21-22). In addition, because they were with Jesus throughout his ministry, their teaching was reliable. But Stephen, Philip, and other apostolic-like evangelists in Acts show us that God continues to raise up leaders to take the gospel to unreached peoples.

---

8. Witherington, *Acts of the Apostles*, 281.

9. Witherington, *Acts of the Apostles*, 280.

10. I mentioned earlier that by writing of the kingdom of God both at the beginning and at the end of Acts, Luke intends his readers to see that everything in between refers to the kingdom of God. This is a literary device called an inclusio.

As he proclaims the same message as the apostles, Philip demonstrates his continuity with the believers in Jerusalem. Faithful to apostolic teaching, he is not a maverick starting his own movement as soon as he leaves Jerusalem. His message is the same as the apostles, and so is the power by which God authenticated it. When the crowds listened eagerly to Philip's message about Jesus, *they saw and heard the power of the Spirit* at work through him. They saw many who were lame or paralyzed healed. And they heard "unclean spirits, crying with loud shrieks" when they came out of the many who were possessed by them (Acts 8:7). Then they heard joyful shouts of praise to God filling the city as multitudes were delivered from darkness. The darkness that had long covered Samaria was now driven out and replaced with holy light.

The mention of the many who were possessed by unclean spirits prepares us to read of Simon, who had kept Samaria in darkness. In contrast to Stephen, he is portrayed "as a satanic figure, whose power is manifest in magic and idolatry."[11]

The contrasts between Philip and Simon are clear. First, Philip puts Jesus in the center of his message, while Simon proclaims himself as "the power of god that is called great" (Acts 8:10). Many scholars believe Simon was making a claim of deity, since "The Great Power" was how the Samaritans designated the supreme deity.[12] Thus, Simon may have claimed to be the manifestation or incarnation of the one true God.[13] Since Jesus was sent to show us what God is like, Simon is portrayed as an antichrist figure, competing with allegiance to Jesus.

Second, while God authenticated Philip's witness with signs by the power of the Spirit, Simon actualizes the power of Satan with magic, forbidden among the Jews because of its association with demons and idol worship. In fact, the unclean spirits Philip delivered the Samaritans from likely had their source in Simon, who used the power of Satan.[14] This is the first of many power encounters in Acts between the kingdom of light and the powers of darkness using magic.[15]

One last contrast between Philip and Simon—amazed by his magic, the crowds had previously eagerly listened to Simon; now amazed at the signs of the Spirit, they eagerly listen to Philip's teaching about Jesus.

11. Peterson, *Acts of Apostle*, 278.
12. Keener, *Acts, Vol, 2*, 1512.
13. Wright, *Acts for Everyone, Pt. 1*, 129.
14. Garrett, *Demise of the Devil*, 60, quoted in Peterson, *Acts of the Apostles*, 283.
15. Peterson, *Acts of the Apostles*, 278.

Though steeped in darkness, Simon surprisingly believes the message about Jesus and is baptized. Amazed by the great miracles taking place through Philip, Simon follows him everywhere. We will see, however, that a true change of heart did not accompany Simon's claim to faith. He seemed more motivated to possess the power at work through Philip for personal gain and glory. It is so sad how people use faith for profit.

PETER AND JOHN COME TO SAMARIA (ACTS 8:14-17)

Philip temporarily fades into the background when the apostles Peter and John arrive from Jerusalem to complete his work. Luke describes their role as first praying for the Samaritans to receive the Spirit (Acts 8:14-17) and then exposing the darkness of Simon's heart (Acts 8:18-24).

When the apostles in Jerusalem learn that all Samaria has accepted the word about Jesus, they sent Peter and John there. It doesn't seem they are sent to inspect Philip's ministry. Rather, they had learned that even though the Samaritans had embraced Jesus as Lord and Messiah and had been baptized, the Spirit of God had not come to dwell within them when they believed.

This was unusual. For the Spirit had always come to dwell in a person when they believed. Strangely, this had not happened with the Samaritans. So, when Peter and John came to Samaria, they met with the believers to pray for the Spirit to come and dwell within them.

The text indicates that the experience of the Samaritans in not receiving the Spirit when they believed was *an exception*. That is the very reason the apostles sent Peter and John to Samaria. Something was not normal. So, when Peter and John prayed for them with the laying on of hands (expressing identity and concern for them), the Spirit came to dwell in them just as he had with the first disciples on the day of Pentecost.[16]

If this was an exception of receiving the Spirit at the time a person (or, here, an entire region!) confesses Jesus as Lord, we must ask why.

---

16. Some have built a teaching on the Samaritan experience, making it the norm. In short, they teach two stages in the work of the Spirit. First, the Spirit works to bring about repentance and the new birth in a believer, but only later, as "a second blessing," the Spirit fills them with spiritual gifts for power and ministry. I believe this teaching errs in making the norm out of what is an exception and can cause spiritual confusion with its two-tiered, "haves and have nots" spirituality. Yet I have met those who have become spiritually alive through their "second blessing" experience. I believe this was due to their full surrender to God. God will fill their fully surrendered hearts, despite their theology.

Why did God deliberately withhold giving the Spirit to the Samaritans until days later, when the leading apostles came from Jerusalem to pray for them to receive the Spirit?

I agree with those who believe God did this because of the centuries-long deep division and animosity between the Jews and the Samaritans. Left alone, the Samaritans could be tempted to build their own brand of messianic belief from their limited Scriptures and the influence of magic in the region, but by only receiving the Spirit when the lead apostles from Jerusalem came to pray for them, they acknowledged their identity with the church in Jerusalem and their submission to the authority and teaching of the apostles.

At the same time, the Jerusalem disciples could be tempted to look down on the Samaritans as culturally and spiritually inferior to them. So, to ensure unity and respect for one another, God sent Peter and John *to see the Samaritan believers receive and experience the very same Spirit they had on the day of Pentecost.* As leading apostles, they could correct any pride or suspicion from any disciples in Jerusalem. In short, God broke the norm of giving the Spirit when one believed to help the Jewish and Samaritan disciples see that they were one body of believers united in their Messiah.

A PRETENDER IS EXPOSED (ACTS 8:18-24)

Simon reenters the story. He has witnessed a greater power than his magic and joined the Jesus movement. But his motives seem marred as he follows Philip everywhere, not listening to him teach but dazzled by the great miracles taking place through him (Acts 8:13). His hidden, unresolved desire for power, money, and fame now comes to light when he sees the Spirit of God come upon the Samaritans as Peter and John lay their hands on them and pray. We can assume Simon sees the outward manifestation of the Spirit's falling on the Samaritans as they possibly prophesy, speak in tongues, and praise God with joyful hearts, as on the day of Pentecost.

Simon sees and so wants this power. To him it appears to be a new and more powerful kind of magic which one can purchase with money and control with prayer and the laying on of hands. Simon still wants to be someone great in Samaria, greater than before, with this superior power he now witnesses. Because he was able to conjure up manifestations of dark spiritual powers through his magic, he may believe Peter, too, is a magician with control over the power he sees at work through him.[17]

So, Simon extends his hands filled with silver coins to Peter. This was dangerous and deceitful. Money easily threatens to erode genuine faith among the people of God. Simon's manipulative ways that made him popular among the Samaritans has the potential to lead the Samaritans back into false religion, *now with the veneer of true faith*.[18]

With prophetic insight Peter sees that Simon is a pretender who has expressed belief but without true repentance and a change of heart. His need for forgiveness goes deeper than a specific sin. A deep-seated obsession for control, prominence, and prosperity must be rooted out with genuine repentance.[19] So Peter rejects Simon's offer of silver to tell him he will perish with his money unless he roots out the bitter poison ("gall of bitterness") and the captivity to sin that fills his heart. With a true repentance, he can be forgiven. But Simon does not really want to change; he only wants to escape God's judgment. He asks Peter, "Pray for me to the Lord, nothing of what you have said may happen to me." He is like "a cornered criminal, frightened at the prospect of punishment although not obviously remorseful over his crimes."[20] No longer the Great Power of Samaria, he is reduced to a small, frightened man, pleading in the presence of the power at work in Peter and John.

The Samaritan mission concludes with Peter and John staying in Samaria for a time, teaching about the Lord, and proclaiming him in the villages of Samaria on their way back to Jerusalem. Due to Simon's long influence in the region and the danger of syncretism, Philip would have been happy for the apostles to build on his evangelistic ministry with teaching about Jesus. And since Philip is an itinerant evangelist soon led by the Spirit to other places, the apostles' time in Samaria will enable them to continue to support the work there.

With this account, Luke wants us to understand Samaria has been reached with the gospel so that we can now anticipate how God will continue to break barriers to extend his kingdom to the ends of the earth (Acts 1:8), perhaps by using those we may not expect.

---

17. Peterson, *Acts of the Apostles*, 288.
18. Peterson, *Acts of the Apostles*, 278.
19. Peterson, *Acts of the Apostles*, 289.
20. Peterson, *Acts of the Apostles*, 290.

22

Philip and the Eunuch
(Acts 8:26–40)

OF ALL THE STORIES in Acts, this one about a black official from faraway Ethiopia fascinates me most. Suddenly we leave the world of Judaism and meet one "fascinating, multifaceted character who defies easy classification."[1] As an Ethiopian he was idealized in ancient writing as a man of great piety and beauty.[2] Studying his journey caused me to better recognize the handsomeness, beauty, and piety of the many African Americans in my neighborhood in Philadelphia.

But then I realized the story emphasizes more often that he was a eunuch (mentioned five times) than that he was from Ethiopia. Castrated and likely dismembered, he may have had, as other eunuchs, a shrill voice and other effeminate characteristics.[3] The ridicule he received for being considered neither a man nor a woman[4] caused me to feel compassion for the man.

THE EUNUCH'S TRIP

I write more about this fascinating man in the following comments, but first let's look at his journey. I know you will understand why Esuga and

1. Spencer, *Journeying Through Acts*, 101.
2. Spencer, *Journeying Through Acts*, 102.
3. Keener, *Acts, Vol. 2*, 1570.
4. Keener, *Acts, Vol. 2*, 1570.

I did not try to retrace the travels of the Ethiopian eunuch. The journey from his home alone in what is now central Sudan up the Nile River to Alexandria, Egypt, covered 1,250 miles.[5] Then he had to travel from Alexandria to Jerusalem by wagon, through deserted wastelands filled with wild animals and robbers.

Travel itself from his home to Jerusalem would have taken him three to four months.[6] If we include possible business ventures in Alexandria and elsewhere for Queen Candace and a prolonged stay in Jerusalem, his destination, he could have been away from home for half a year. Not many would have made such a long journey, but as we will see, he hungered for God, and he hungered to belong.

We think of Ethiopia as a nation in the horn of Africa, but at that time it applied to all of Africa south of Egypt, especially to ancient Nubia.[7] Nearly all scholars are convinced he was from the Nubian kingdom of Meroe, several hundred miles south of modern Egypt in Sudan.[8] "Nubian civilization stretches back to perhaps before 3000 BCE, and Nubian kings sometimes ruled Egypt (and vice-versa)."[9] The eunuch lived in a strategic location for trade, where the wealth of Africa's interior was transported up the Nile to Egypt and then over the whole of the Mediterranean.

The wealth the eunuch oversaw was so extensive that an ancient "novelist could claim that Ethiopians cared little for gold or jewels, heaps of which the royal palace had in storage."[10] Supervising this vast wealth for Queen Candace gave the eunuch a high socioeconomic status in his society,[11] and because of his extensive travels for trade, he likely knew at least some Greek and was able to converse with Philip. He must have been highly trusted and respected by the queen for her to allow him to travel so far for such a long time.[12] Then again, he likely engaged in business for her as he traveled up the Nile to Egypt.

Given his status and wealth, the Ethiopian eunuch likely traveled in a four-wheeled covered wagon pulled by oxen or horses, rather than the two-wheeled chariot we may be familiar with from the movie *Ben*

---

5. Keener, *Acts, Vol. 2*, 1551.
6. Keener, *Acts, Vol. 2*, 1552.
7. Keener, *Acts, Vol. 2*, 1535.
8. Keener, *Acts, Vol. 2*, 1551.
9. Keener, *Acts, Vol. 2*, 1572.
10. Keener, *Acts, Vol. 2*, 1573.
11. Keener, *Acts, Vol. 2*, 1573.
12. Keener, *Acts, Vol. 2*, 1572.

Hur. The covered wagon allowed him to take ample supplies, making the trip more comfortable.[13] "Further, a royal treasurer with means to travel such a long distance in comfort might also have companions, or servants, traveling with him for safety on the road."[14]

The driver of the wagon sat in the front with the Ethiopian eunuch sitting in the back reading, as was common when traveling. Scripture scrolls (measuring up to 145 feet) could be cumbersome to unroll and hold with one hand while unrolling more pages.[15] When Philip runs up to the wagon to sit beside the eunuch, he may have helped hold the scroll as they read Isaiah.

Now to the story. It begins with young Philip walking alone on a desert road toward Gaza.

The Spirit now leads not one of the apostles but Philip, a desert traveler in exile from Jerusalem, to break yet another boundary for the good news of Jesus.[16] The story's "theological importance is that the Spirit acts ahead of the apostles (as in Samaria, Acts 8:12, 14; and Antioch, Acts 11:19–24)."[17]

The Spirit has led Philip *north* to reach *the entire region of Samaria*. Now an angel of the Lord directs him *south* on a desert road to *one man from the edge of the known world*. We sense the good news will go everywhere, even beyond the Roman Empire. When Paul begins his missionary travels, Luke's controlling geography in Acts becomes clearer, from Jerusalem to Rome. But this story hints at the future expansion of the gospel beyond the empire's borders and will inspire later evangelists.[18]

The Spirit led Philip from a successful ministry to all of Samaria to one man on an isolated road in the desert. What made this man so special that God leads Philip to him? Understanding who the man was will help us to understand God's heart for all peoples. Notice how much the direction and initiative of God permeates the story (Acts 8:26, 29, 32, 36, 39–40). God wants this man and his people to know him!

---

13. Keener, *Acts, Vol. 2*, 1579.
14. Keener, *Acts, Vol. 2*, 1580.
15. Keener, *Acts, Vol. 2*, 1583.
16. Spencer, *Journeying Through Acts*, 101.
17. Keener, *Acts, Vol. 2*, 1541.
18. Keener, *Acts, Vol. 2*, 1541.

WHO IS THE EUNUCH?

We read the unnamed man was from Ethiopia and a eunuch in charge of the entire treasury of the queen of Ethiopia. This alone reveals much about him and how Luke's readers viewed him. Suddenly we meet in the narrative someone who is not Jewish nor a Roman gentile yet a gentile nonetheless. Again, he is "a fascinating, multifaceted character who defies easy classification."[19] Yet we know enough about him to understand why God leads Philip to him.

First, he is *an Ethiopian*. As an Ethiopian he was tall, black, and handsome. Ethiopians "were idealized in ancient classical writings as people of great piety and beauty."[20] Regarding this beauty, "Herodotus extolled the 'burnt-skinned' Ethiopians as the tallest and most handsome of all humankind."[21]

While class and ethnic prejudice existed in antiquity, "skin color, and in particular black and very dark brown skin color, was not to any significant degree the case or basis of such prejudice so far as we can tell."[22] Humanity was not divided between "blacks" and "whites," "a legacy primarily of the Western slave trade and ideologies generated to justify it."[23]

Since Ethiopia was "renowned in Greco-Roman lore as the farthest outpost of the known inhabitable world,"[24] the story suggests that since Jesus has been proclaimed in Jerusalem, Judea, and Samaria, he will now be proclaimed to the ends of the earth (Acts 1:8), and God chooses this black eunuch to be the first to hear. (In that he was only one man from a faraway land, the apostles in Jerusalem likely made little of his conversion, even if they had learned of it from Philip.)

Second, even though he is drawn to the God of the Jews, the Ethiopian eunuch was most likely not Jewish but *a gentile*. Somehow, likely on a previous journey, he had encountered the Jewish faith and purchased a copy of their Scriptures. But since he was a gentile, he was treated as an outsider in Jerusalem (the color of his skin was not an issue). As a gentile he was denied entrance to the temple and full access to the God of Israel.

---

19. Spencer, *Journeying Through Acts*, 101.
20. Spencer, *Journeying Through Acts*, 102.
21. Spencer, *Journeying Through Acts*, 102.
22. Witherington, *Acts of the Apostles*, 295.
23. Keener, *Acts, Vol. 2*, 1563.
24. Spencer, *Journeying Through Acts*, 101.

The Ethiopian eunuch was not only a handsome, dark-skinned gentile from a country at the edge of the known world; he was also *a high-ranking official* in charge of the queen's treasury. This meant he was a man of personal wealth and prestige in his society. His wealth is revealed by the fact that instead of walking, he traveled in a covered wagon with the aid of servants and that he possessed a scroll of the Jewish Scriptures.

In addition to his wealth, we can add that since he reads the Scriptures, he was an educated man. With low literacy rates at this time, he must have "come from an elite class in Nubia, which afforded him education."[25]

Finally, and most important to the story, he is *a eunuch*. After first being identified as an Ethiopian eunuch, he is then only referred to as eunuch (four times). While as a castrated *official* he had a more honorable status than others, castration was not normally an honorable state. Those castrated were regarded as effeminate and were despised by most. When seeing a eunuch, a superstitious person (as most were) would retrace their steps and start their day over to evade bad luck.[26]

"Calling a man a 'eunuch' was an insult to his manhood. Castration was thought to remove a man's status as a male, and eunuchs were considered neither men nor boys (nor for that matter, women); one lacking some male traits might be subject to ridicule as a eunuch. Eunuchs (at least those made so before puberty) tended to have shriller voices and other effeminate characteristics."[27]

By emphasizing that the Ethiopian is a eunuch, Luke highlights his marginal status in Judaism and hence the crossing of an additional barrier in Acts beyond the main Jew/gentile barrier.[28]

Given the bias against eunuchs "in a world that worried very much about preserving the male from any hint of effeminacy,"[29] how would Luke's readers respond to God's choosing him as the first non-Jew to receive the good news? How do we?

Imagine how the conservative religious establishment in Jerusalem had looked upon him. As a castrated male they would have "placed him in a position of extreme, irrevocable dishonor and impurity."[30] "Unable to

25. Keener, *Acts, Vol.* 2, 1580.
26. Keener, *Acts, Vol.* 2, 1569.
27. Keener, *Acts, Vol.* 2, 1570.
28. Keener, *Acts, Vol.* 2, 1571.
29. Keener, *Acts, Vol.* 2, 1570,
30. Spencer, *Journeying Through Acts*, 103.

procreate or be circumcised (assuming he was dismembered), he had no hope for acceptance and a place in the Jewish community."[31]

His hopes *for belonging* by his long pilgrimage to Jerusalem have been dashed, for he had learned that he was "socially and religiously 'worthless' in leading segments of Israelite society."[32] He is still a man on the margins of Judaism, with his hopes for belonging unfulfilled. But there is yet another reason I admire the man. Despite being despised and ostracized by religious people, the eunuch does not give up his search for God because of bad religion. He can separate the living God from the lives of those who claim to worship him. He remains focused, humble, and hungry for God. He is a man on a spiritual quest and will not quit. Disappointed with the Judaism he experienced in Jerusalem, he still searches their Scriptures. (It doesn't seem that he encountered any of the disciples.)

He still seeks God and remains hopeful as he ponders the identity of a man that he identifies with in the prophet Isaiah, *a man also humiliated, despised, and deprived of justice* (Isa 53:3, 7–8), yet a man who, after his suffering, is exalted by God (Isa 52:13). The eunuch is drawn to this man and ponders "the relevance of the mutilated, humiliated, ostracized servant of God to his own deviant social position."[33]

Now that we know more about the Ethiopian eunuch, his longings, and disappointments, let's pick up in the story as he travels back to Ethiopia from Jerusalem. Leaning over the scroll in his chariot, his lips move slowly as he reads from the Jewish Scriptures sitting on his lap. He reads in Isaiah of an unidentified servant.

Now the passage of Scripture that he was reading was this:

> Like a sheep he was led to the slaughter,
> and like a lamb silent before its shearer,
> so, he does not open his mouth.
> In his humiliation justice was denied him.
> Who can describe his generation?
> For his life is taken away from the earth. (Acts 8:32–33)

---

31. Spencer, *Journeying Through Acts*, 103.
32. Spencer, *Journeying Through Acts*, 103.
33. Spencer, *Journeying Through Acts*, 104.

PHILIP MEETS THE EUNUCH

Philip has obeyed the Lord and walks on a desert road toward Gaza. As he walks, wondering why God has sent him there, a chariot passes by. The Spirit directs him to approach it. Running up to the chariot, he hears a man reading from Isa 53! More divine direction.

When Philip asks if he understands the prophecy of Isaiah, the man replies that he needs someone to help explain the meaning to him. An educated man of high standing speaks to a young stranger walking alone on a desert road and asks him for help! How humble he is, how hungry to know God.

The eunuch then invites Philip to climb up and join him in the chariot to explain the identity of the servant who is despised, humiliated, and deprived of justice. Starting with Isa 53 and from there to nearby prophecies, Philip explains how Jesus is the servant of God written of by Isaiah.

He, too, like the eunuch, was despised, rejected, and deprived of justice. He, too, was humiliated, with no physical descendants when his life was taken from him. Philip showed how Jesus "sympathizes with the plight of social and religious outcasts and opens a way for them into the household of God."[34]

See how the message of Jesus is good news to the Ethiopian eunuch.

Philip likely moved back in the scroll to where Isaiah also says that God's servant would be a light to the nations, reaching to the ends of the earth (Isa 49:6). The servant brings light to the eunuch and his people from far-away Ethiopia. He has poured out his life in death to bear their sins so they could be forgiven, cleansed, and come close to God (Isa 53:12).

We can assume Philip showed the eunuch where Isaiah speaks of the time when *God will bring the eunuchs near him in his temple and give them an everlasting name, a name better than the sons and daughters of Israel (Isa 56: 4–5)!* The time Isaiah spoke of has come.

As both a gentile and a eunuch, the Ethiopian had been deprived of entrance to the temple in Jerusalem, where he had been told God revealed his Presence. But he learns from Philip that God now dwells in anyone, anywhere who turns to him through Jesus. God's Spirit comes to dwell in the eunuch, making him (and likely the servants with him and those in Ethiopia with whom he will share the good news) his temple. He has found his place with God and his people. His longings are fulfilled.[35]

---

34. Spencer, *Journeying Through Acts*, 104.
35. Wall, "Acts of the Apostles," 137. Just as the Spirit came to dwell in the Samaritan

This is how the message about Jesus was good news to the eunuch. The Spirit of God awakens the eunuch's heart to believe the good news of the servant of God, Jesus. For as they travel along the desert road, they come to water. The eunuch commands his servant to stop the chariot and asks Philip to baptize him. When they come up out of the water, the Spirit suddenly takes Philip to another place, and the eunuch will never see him again, but with the Spirit dwelling in him, his heart swells with joy as he continues his journey home.

The Spirit leads Philip to proclaim the gospel in coastal towns all the way up to Caesarea, where he eventually settles and starts a family (Acts 21:8–9). Because Lydda and Joppa were two of the towns he would have visited on the way up to Caesarea, the Spirit again leads Philip ahead of Peter, just as in Samaria.[36]

GOD'S PURPOSE FOR INCLUDING THIS STORY

The account of the Ethiopian eunuch illustrates the relentless pursuit of God, driven by his boundless love for all peoples, to include all ethnicities in his family. Soon God will instruct Peter to speak the gospel to the gentile Cornelius and his household (Acts 10–11).

As the first gentile to believe, the Ethiopian's conversion anticipates their more formally recognized inclusion in the church. In that sense he is a prototype and an inspiration for future evangelists like Philip to take the gospel to peoples beyond the known world of the Roman Empire to all of Africa and east to Asia.[37]

We will now read of how God calls Saul, who will be an apostle to the gentiles (Acts 9). We will then read how God leads Peter to speak the gospel to the gentile Cornelius and his family (Acts 10).

---

believers, marginalizing the need to worship at the Jerusalem Temple, so, too, the eunuch, prevented from entering the temple, has become a living temple, taking God's Presence with him to Ethiopia.

36. Keener, *Acts, Vol. 2*, 1596.
37. Keener, *Acts, Vol. 2*, 1534.

A FOCUS ON THE MIND AND MOTIVES OF SAUL: WHY WAS HE SO VIOLENT?

I have written about Saul's upbringing in Tarsus and will later write more about this remarkable man. But at this point in the story, it would be helpful to understand why Saul was so full of rage against the disciples of Jesus. Why was he so zealous to rid the world of the Jesus movement? I am indebted to the New Testament scholar and historian N. T. Wright, who points out we can learn something of Saul's mind and motives to destroy the Jesus movement if we understand his strict Pharisaic upbringing.

Saul was born and raised in a strict Jewish home in Tarsus before he moved to Jerusalem in his late teens "with his head full of Torah and his heart full of zeal."[38] As a devout Jew, he had come to study in Jerusalem as a teen under Gamaliel, one of the greatest rabbis of that time.[39] Jerusalem was the center of the world for the Jewish people. Here God would fulfill his eternal promises to them, and Saul moves there to help him.

Saul was not only Jewish; he was a Pharisaic Jew. This not only meant praying to the one true God of Israel; it also meant acting on your prayers by fighting against anyone who, like Stephen, minimized Israel's law and their sacred temple. Saul rejected the wait-and-see, non-violent approach to the Jesus movement of his teacher, Gamaliel.[40] For Saul this was a sign of weakness based on fear and preserving the status quo.

While they had waited, Stephen's friends—Philip and others—had continued to spread their blasphemous message to town and villages in Judea and even up to the much-hated Samaritans. What is this sect that includes Samaritans? Who else will join them? They must be stopped, and Saul will do it.

Saul will fight under *the banner of zeal, violent zeal*. Since it was God's will to establish his kingdom on earth for Israel in the land of Israel, Israel must be faithful to him and ready to fight for him. Those who are truly zealous for God, the Torah, and the temple would not just say their prayers; they would sharpen their swords to fight—fight

---

38. Wright, *Paul*, 34.
39. Wright, *Paul*, 35.
40. Wright, *Paul*, 35.

against any Jew who compromises obedience to the Law and the sacredness of their temple.[41]

Many in the Jesus sect did just that. "Wherever they went, they established groups, little revolutionary cells, and propagated this new teaching, putting Jesus in the center of the picture and displacing the ancient Israelite symbols, up to and including the Temple itself."[42]

Saul believed this could set back the coming of God's kingdom for Israel. It must be stopped—and now. Saul believed he had been chosen by God to eliminate the Jesus sect so that God's kingdom would come to Israel. When he looked down at Stephen being crushed to death under a hail of rocks, Saul was satisfied. *This is what zeal for God looks like.*

So, Saul set off for Damascus with his Bible in his head, zeal in his heart, and documents from the chief priest in his bag. Believing he was a modern-day righteous warrior in Israel's history, he would rid Damascus of the disciples.[43] Such was the mind and such were the motives of Saul. His cataclysmic turn around on the road to Damascus will not be a Sunday school conversion.

---

41. Wright, *Paul*, 36.
42. Wright, *Paul*, 38.
43. Wright, *Paul*, 39.

23

Saul's Change of Direction
(Acts 9:1–31)

SAUL TRAVELED ABOUT 135 miles from Jerusalem to Damascus, likely by foot, based on inferences in the story. Walking roughly twenty miles a day makes for roughly a six-day travel. Saul and the men with him headed east down to Jericho, where they crossed the Jordan River to pick up the Great North Road, the trade route from Egypt. To avoid traveling through the largely gentile towns along this road, they likely crossed back into Israel, south of the Sea of Galilee, and continued up through Capernaum and other cities where Jesus ministered.[1]

This caught my attention. So, I pulled out my maps to trace their travels. This is speculation, but if they did travel about twenty miles a day, Saul would have spent at least one night where Jesus ministered for three years. Did he learn more about the teaching of "this Jesus of Nazareth," adding to his zeal to stamp out the movement he started?

We read that Jesus appears to Saul at the end of his week's journey shortly before he comes to Damascus (Acts 9:3). This is the first geographical reference in the story and prompted me to think why Jesus chose to appear to Saul so close to Damascus and not right outside of Jerusalem, or in Galilee?

A clue came in learning what Damascus symbolized for the Jewish people. It was the gateway through which Israel's long list of enemies had swooped down on their land to destroy them, and now Roman troops were

---

1. Wright, "Road from Jerusalem," 226.

stationed there, ready to again invade Israel when necessary. Damascus represented a threat to Israel's very existence, with Rome itself hovering over them.[2] Yet here in Damascus, Jesus calls Saul to become a witness to the enemies of Israel, gentiles across the Roman Empire. Through the gospel Saul will see enemies of Israel united in Christ as one family.

The other reference to location in the story is when Saul, blinded by the light of Jesus, is led by hand to a house on "the street called Straight" (Acts 9:11). The street, 50 feet (15m) wide with colonnades on each side and visible still today, was the main street in Damascus in Roman times.[3] This is the only street Luke mentions in Acts. Why does Luke include its name?

A clue is in the abundance of literary allusions for it in Luke's writings. John the Baptist had said the crooked roads shall become *straight* for the coming of salvation through the Messiah (Luke 3:4–5). And later, the false prophet, Bar-Jesus, will go blind *for making crooked the right ways* of the Lord (Acts 13:9–11).

Saul will speak to Bar-Jesus from experience, for he too had twisted God's straight road and was blinded for it. But the risen Lord will remove his blindness and put him on the right path to belong to the people of the Way, the Straight Street to God's Way (Acts 9:2).

SETTING THE SCENE

When we last read of Saul, he was seeking to destroy the Jesus movement by breaking into their houses (house churches) in Jerusalem, dragging both men and women off to prison (Acts 8:3). We are meant to see the irony of it all. While Saul seeks to eliminate the Lord's disciples, the Lord has led Philip to take the good news to the Samaritans and then to a leading official from Africa!

Saul now realizes the persecution he led in the stoning of Stephen has not stopped the disciples from spreading their message, so he redoubles his efforts. He doesn't stop to think that the words of his teacher, Gamaliel, might be right. He might be fighting against God. Impossible. Inconceivable for Saul. All faithful Jews knew that their Messiah could not be crucified and certainly would not reign for God in his Presence,

---

2. Wright, "The Road to Damascus." In Beitzel, *Lexham*.
3. Keener, *Acts, Vol. 2*, 1652.

sharing his glory, and no true Jew would ever minimize their law and sacred temple, as Stephen had.

Still this traitorous sect continues to spread and must be stopped. Saul believes he is called by God to do just that. Believing he has contained the Jesus movement in Jerusalem (Acts 8:1–3), he now heads north to Damascus. His mission is clear and simple. He will hunt down every man and woman who belongs to this sect and bring them, bound in chains, back to Jerusalem and throw them in prison with the other disciples. As he secures his tent and provisions on his donkey to begin the weeks-long journey to Damascus, little does he know how his life will be completely turned around.

JESUS APPEARS TO SAUL (ACTS 9:1–19)

After Stephen's death, Saul still breathes "threats and murder against the disciples of the Lord" in Jerusalem (Acts 9:1). He had led the charge in murdering other disciples besides Stephen. Now learning that the Jesus movement has spread to Damascus, he asks the high priest for papers granting him permission to seek out any who belong to the Way there.

Full of resolve, Saul plans to break into their houses and synagogues, bind the disciples, and bring them back to Jerusalem to be placed in prison. As in Jerusalem, both men and women will be seized, leaving their children behind.

After some six days of travel, as he nears Damascus, Saul's life is suddenly turned around. Was he praying? Was he planning how he would execute his plans? We don't know. But suddenly a light from heaven overpowers the blazing Middle Eastern sun and surrounds him. Overwhelmed, Saul falls to the ground and hears a voice from the light speak to him, "Saul, Saul, why do you persecute me?"

When Saul asks who addresses him, the answer must have shocked him to the core of his being. The voice says, "I am Jesus, whom you are persecuting." Saul's heart races, his mind thrown into confusion. How could Jesus be alive and speak from heaven? Was he reigning as Lord in God's Presence, as Stephen had claimed? And what does he mean by saying I am persecuting *him*? What kind of relationship does he have with his followers?

It will take time for Saul to process all the implications of his encounter with Jesus, but he knows at once that Jesus is alive and reigns with God as Lord. In fact, the entire episode emphasizes Jesus is Lord. He is not only referred to as Lord six times, but throughout the account he demonstrates his lordship. He tells Saul to get up, enter the city, and wait to be told what to do.

He directs Ananias to get up and go to the house of Judas to find Saul. The risen Lord Jesus sends, chooses, and gives visions to the man who will be his primary witness to the gentiles.

Blinded by the light, Saul, the once-mighty warrior against the Jesus movement, is now led into Damascus by the hand like a helpless child. He has traveled to Damascus to lead Jesus' disciples, bound in chains, back to Jerusalem, but instead he is led into Damascus to become one of them.

Still blind, he stays for three days in the house of a man called Judas, who lives on the main street in Damascus called Straight. He neither eats nor drinks and barely sleeps as he prays and reflects on his encounter with Jesus. He now believes Jesus is God's Messiah, but his brilliant mind races with questions as he thinks through the Jewish Scriptures, looking for answers for why the Messiah must be crucified.

During the three days, the Lord gives Saul a vision. A man named Ananias will come to pray for him and restore his sight. Saul doesn't object. The Lord then gives Ananias a vision. He is to get up and go to the house of Judas and pray for Saul to regain his sight. Ananias objects. Help murderous Saul regain his sight so that he can do in Damascus what he has done in Jerusalem? But Ananias, too, must bow to the Lord's direction.

Ananias will later tell Saul what the Lord had revealed to him. "He is an instrument whom I have chosen to bring my name before gentiles and kings and before the people of Israel; I myself will show him how much he must suffer for the sake of my name" (Acts 9:15–16). The Lord chose Philip to share the good news with the first gentile, an Ethiopian, and soon he will lead Peter to share it with a household of gentiles in Caesarea, but Saul will be sent as the apostle to gentiles throughout the Roman Empire.

Growing up among gentiles in Tarsus as a Roman citizen and fluent in Greek, Saul is uniquely prepared by God to be his witness to the gentiles. No one could ever claim that the apostle to the gentiles was a liberal Jew, uninterested in Israel's law and traditions, for God chose "a hardline, fanatical, ultra-nationalist, super-orthodox Pharisaic Jew" to reach them.[4]

---

4. Wright, *Acts for Everyone, Pt. 1*, 145.

Ananias obeys the Lord. He enters the house of Judas, perhaps with a degree of fear and hesitation, remembering Saul's intentions to do in Damascus, but the Lord has spoken to him, so with faith he affirms to Saul that the Lord has sent him to pray for Saul's sight to be restored and for Saul to be filled with the Holy Spirit.

Saul is baptized in the name of Jesus and, after eating, he regains his strength. Saul, the persecutor of the Lord's disciples, becomes Saul, the Lord's disciple. Saul the persecutor will become Saul the persecuted.

We speak of Saul's conversion on the road to Damascus, "but it was more like a volcanic eruption, thunderstorm and tidal wave all coming together."[5] He will still be a man of zeal but zeal to proclaim the love of God in Jesus.

SAUL PREACHES IN DAMASCUS (ACTS 9:19–25)

The disciples Saul had come to persecute have become his family. He now knows they belong to Jesus and since he, too, now belongs to Jesus: he is their brother. For several days he stays in their homes, worships with them, and learns more about the life and teachings of Jesus.

Saul had heard the gospel in his debates with Stephen. So, when Jesus revealed himself to Saul on the way to Damascus and gave him three days to process that he was alive, he knew immediately what Stephen said was true and began to proclaim the good news of Jesus in the synagogues of Damascus, saying Jesus is "the Son of God."

This is the one time the title "Son of God" is used for Jesus in Acts. As in the Gospels, the title Son of God is another way of claiming Jesus was the Messiah. Even here, proclaiming Jesus was the Son of God is paralleled with "proving that Jesus was the Messiah" (Acts 9:22). So, it seems to have the same messianic sense here as in Luke's Gospel.

While the title Son of God is interchangeable with the title "Messiah," it adds the important nuances of Jesus' obedience and submission to God as his Father, the Father's delegated authority to Jesus, Jesus' intimacy with God, and God's fatherly love and protection.[6]

Those who heard Saul proclaim Jesus as Lord were amazed, the word often used in both the Gospels and Acts as a response to miracles. Saul's sudden turnaround was just that, a miracle of the risen Lord.

5. Wright, *Acts for Everyone, Pt. 1*, 142.
6. Keener, *Acts, Vol. 2*, 1671.

Because Luke writes a compact, flowing history of the gospel's movement from Jerusalem to Rome, he does not include an interesting detail Paul later mentions in Galatians (a detail with important implications for us). There, he writes that shortly after his conversion, he "went immediately into Arabia and later returned to Damascus" (Gal 1:17).[7]

Because Saul (Paul) will later write that he spent three years in Damascus (Gal 1:18), it appears he left Damascus relatively soon after his conversion to then return and stay for three years.

Why would Saul leave Damascus so soon after his conversion? And what did he do in Arabia?

I agree with most scholars that Saul's mission to the gentiles has not yet begun (this becomes clearer later in Acts); thus, he did not travel to Arabia to proclaim Jesus to gentiles. Keener sums up the three main reasons for Saul's soon departure from Damascus to Arabia. He "could have preached to Jews among the Nabateans, could have gone as a recluse for a time, or could have been discipled by Jewish believers in the Hellenistic cities there."[8]

Most of us know Saul as Paul, a mature, godly man, through his writings and can forget that he, too, was once a new believer who needed to learn about Jesus and mature in his faith. While we should not discount that Saul proclaimed Jesus to Jews in Arabia at this time, I suggest Saul soon realized in Damascus that he needed to seek solitude in Arabia to further digest his conversion and understand how the Jewish Scriptures were fulfilled in Jesus. In addition, he could have been discipled by Greek-speaking disciples, forced out of Jerusalem and now settled in Hellenistic cities in Arabia.

His time away in solitude to grow in understanding the Scriptures increased his confidence and power in witness when he returned to Damascus for three years. We read that he grew "more powerful and confounded the Jews who lived in Damascus by proving that Jesus was the Messiah" (Acts 9:22). Eager young evangelists can learn from Saul's example.

His ministry during these three years is now so effective that some unbelieving Jews in Damascus plotted to kill him. Only after a miraculous escape with the aid of his followers, Saul travels back to Jerusalem three years after he had left.

Remember who he was when he left Jerusalem and why he left.

---

7. At this time Arabia referred to the Nabatean kingdom which stretched from Damascus southwest to the Suez.

8. Keener, *Acts, Vol. 2*, 1682.

SAUL IN JERUSALEM (ACTS 9:26-31)

Most of the disciples in Damascus were Greek-speaking Jews who had fled Jerusalem due to the persecution of Stephen. They were still a targeted community and had little contact with Jerusalem. Thus, when Saul returns to Jerusalem three years later, the Hebrew-speaking disciples may have only heard rumors, if anything, about him, so when Saul seeks to join the Jesus movement in Jerusalem, they were suspicious and afraid. They only know violent Saul, the persecutor of the church. Does he want to infiltrate their community to continue to purge them from the earth? Deep fears do not die quickly.

Somehow Barnabas, introduced earlier in the story as a man who encourages (Acts 4:36-37), has learned the truth about Saul's radical change and came alongside him to help welcome him into the fellowship of believers. He first brought Saul to the apostles and described how the Lord appeared to Saul on his way to Damascus and how Saul had spoken boldly in the name of Jesus to the Jews in Damascus. From the apostles the word spread quickly to the rest of the disciples.

Likely with tears flowing and pleas for forgiveness, Saul joins the community he once persecuted and boldly proclaims the Jesus he once blasphemed. Soon he returned to the Greek-speaking synagogues where he had debated with Stephen and now debates the very men who had once joined him in having Stephen stoned to death. Despite the dramatic change in Saul and his skill in showing how Jesus fulfilled their Scriptures, they remain unbending. One of their own, their former leader, has left them to join this dangerous sect of Jews. He is more dangerous than Stephen had been, and he, too, must be stopped.

When some disciples learned of a plot to kill Saul, they got him out of town at once. They joined him up the coast to Caesarea, where they sent him off on a ship to Tarsus, where he grew up and still had family. We will not read of Saul again until some ten years later when Barnabas travels to Tarsus to bring him to Antioch to assist in the work there (Acts 11:25).

Luke ends the story of Saul's transformation with a short summary (Acts 9:31). Throughout Judea, Galilee, and Samaria, the believers lived in peace and grew strong in their faith. They lived in great awe of the Lord's work among them, and, in the comfort of the Holy Spirit, they were increasing in numbers. Does Luke imply this was in part due to Saul? I believe so.

Like Stephen, he had stirred up a hornet's nest among the Greek-speaking Jews that could lead to another major persecution. It would be better if Saul returned home to minister in Tarsus, for his own safety and for the peace of the movement in Jerusalem. Saul agreed.

Perhaps Luke wants us to see how Saul's ministry in Jerusalem led to increased faith among the disciples. Once an enemy of Jesus, Saul has been transformed and now channels his zeal with love and his great intellect and knowledge of the Scriptures to boldly make Jesus known. If the Lord's love and power is so vast that it could change Saul, the disciples found courage in knowing he could change anyone. Saul's boldness was infectious.

Luke has further introduced Saul, who becomes the lead apostle to the gentiles. Before Luke continues with Saul's travels, he returns to the ministry of Peter, who leaves Jerusalem for a town near the coast.

A FOCUS ON SAUL'S SILENT YEARS

While Luke doesn't write about Saul's life and ministry during the next ten years, we learn partly of it based on brief comments in Galatians and what we know elsewhere of his life.

While sailing from Caesarea back to Tarsus, Saul may have dreamed of his family also embracing Jesus as Israel's risen Messiah. He would support himself with the family leather trade, and the family would support him in proclaiming Jesus as Israel's Messiah. It is likely, however, that Saul's family soon disowned and disinherited him, a cause of pain for his entire life.[9]

Jesus had taken hold of young Saul, who could not keep silent about him (Acts 9:20, 22, 28–29). In his letter to the Galatians, the more mature Paul says that during this time he not only proclaimed Jesus to the Jews in Tarsus but also in the synagogues in all the region of Cilicia and nearby Syria, where Antioch was the chief city (Gal 1:21–23).

Most scholars believe that during this time the Jews fiercely rejected Saul and his message of a crucified Messiah. Since we don't read elsewhere of the many floggings Saul received from the Jews, these likely occurred at this time (2 Cor 11:24–25), and since Paul in his letters and Luke in Acts are largely silent about this time of his

---

9. Barnett, *Jesus and the Rise*, 262.

life, his ministry likely bore little fruit. This may explain why he is ready to drop everything to join Barnabas in Antioch when he learns of the great number of Jews and gentiles who had embraced Jesus.

During these years Saul likely supported himself by setting up shop to work with leather in Tarsus or wherever he traveled. From his father he had learned the trade of using leather to make tents, awnings, and other leather products. "Tentmaking was a portable trade. As long as he had his working tools, he could set up shop in any town, buying his raw materials locally and offering his regular products for sale."[10]

When not proclaiming Christ in the synagogues of a city, he would "spend most of his waking hours with his sleeves rolled up, doing hard physical labor in a hot climate."[11] He would converse in his small, cramped shop with those who came to purchase his products.

It is easy to assume that since the Lord had called Saul at his conversion to be a witness to the gentiles (Acts 9:15–16; Gal 1:11–18), during this time he planted churches made up of Jews and gentiles, much like we later read in his missionary journeys. But if this had happened, the news would have surely spread quickly to Jerusalem, as it later does when friends of Stephen first teach gentiles about Christ, with great numbers believing (Acts 11:20–22). *It seems rather that Saul's witness to any gentiles at this time was limited and without success.*

We can easily forget how thoroughly Jewish young Saul was. He grew up in a very sheltered Jewish culture, and even though he had some contact with Greek culture, "his Jewishness probably created limitations in his perspective" of what gentiles in the church would look like.[12]

It's more plausible that Saul only progressively came to understand what it would look like to include gentiles with their cultural background in the church and that he only fully envisioned this when he later sees it in Antioch (Acts 11:23–25). It will only be after immersing himself in a successful work of seeing Jews and gentiles

10. Wright, *Paul*, 68.
11. Wright, *Paul*, 69.
12. Krayer, "Moving Beyond," 6.

in the same church in Antioch that he and Barnabas are ready to be sent out to plant churches which include gentiles.[13]

While Saul knew from his conversion that he was called to be a witness to the gentiles (Acts 9:15), he did not know *when* that mission would begin and *all that it would mean.* For he knew from the Scriptures that the call of a prophet could take years before it materialized.[14]

Saul's limited witness and success to gentiles during his silent years is more than a question of interest. We learn from it that we must learn the culture of those we seek to reach and be careful not to impose our culture (for Saul, his Jewish culture) on the church that is birthed.

Young, zealous Saul had been sent from Jerusalem to Tarsus for his own safety and for the safety of the disciples in Jerusalem (Acts 9:28–31). Rather than calling this time the "silent years" of his life, perhaps we should call them *the formative years,* for during this time Saul prayed and reflected on the Scriptures, matured from a young man in his early twenties to a more mature man in his early thirties, and grew in his understanding of what gentile mission would look like.

When Barnabas (who likely maintained some contact with Saul during these years) comes to Tarsus to look for Saul, he finds a mature young leader prepared by God to minister with him to the Jewish-gentile community of believers in Antioch.

---

13. Krayer, "Moving Beyond," 7.
14. Keener, *Acts, Vol. 2,* 1680.

24

Peter to Lydda and Joppa
(Acts 9:32–43)

As MUCH AS I enjoyed exploring Old Jerusalem to feed my imagination for the events of Acts, it was small, crowded, and often tense due to politics. I was ready to tie my hiking boots and head down the mountains to the Mediterranean where Peter went "here and there among all the believers" (Acts 9:32).

We had bought the "Israel Trail Map" for this hike, and I had pored over it again and again in my little box before going to sleep to find out how we could pick up Peter's trail fifteen miles outside Jerusalem. We only needed to take a bus to drop us off near the Israel National Trail and hike it to Lydda, where Peter first went.

I was in good spirits when we left our hostel and headed through the Damascus Gate to the bus station. I jammed my tent, maps, books, food, and all my clothes deep into my large backpack and my toiletries, water, health bars, and all else into the smaller one I carried on my chest. Acts doesn't say the places Peter visited before he came to Lydda, but a straight walk there from Jerusalem was twenty-five miles. The bus would take us halfway there. I was ready to leave Jerusalem and sleep on the ground in the open air.

As we climbed the steep steps out of the Old City up to the street, first doubts hit me. This would not be a day hike; I was now carrying everything I had taken with me. I could already feel the straps from my backpack cutting into my shoulders with the thirty-five pounds in it, with another ten on my chest pushing down through my legs to my feet.

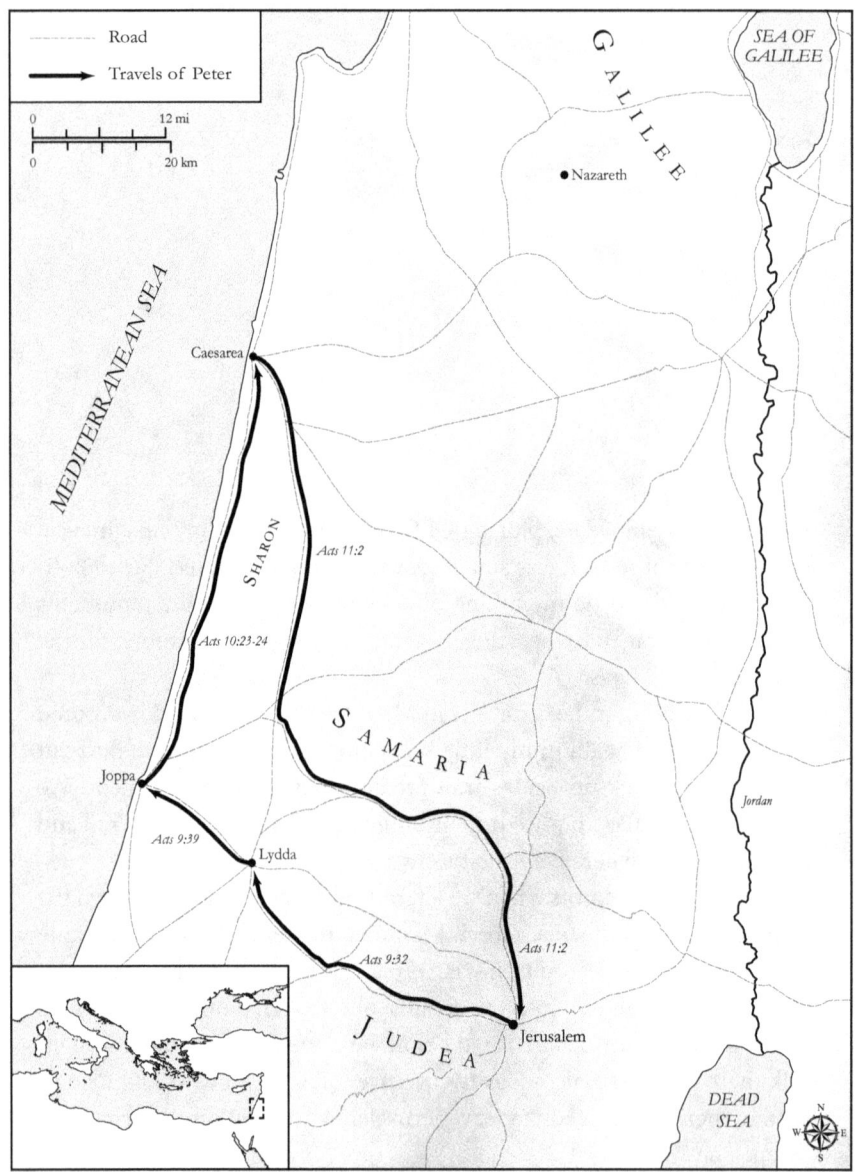

Figure 5: The Travels of Peter. Open Bible Maps.

What made me think this would be a fun adventure? The twenty miles a week I ran in a T-shirt and shorts had not prepared me for this. Peter hadn't carried this much weight, since he would lodge in the homes of disciples along the way.

Then as we crossed the street to find our bus, it began to rain. By the time we reached the bus station it was pouring down. My backpacks and everything in them would soon be soaked. We quickly found shelter at the station.

While I watched our gear, Esuga, good brother that he is, ran through the downpour to locate the bus that would take us near the trail. Ten minutes later he returned soaking wet to say we would have to take two buses to get near the trail. It would take hours before we even began our ten-mile hike to a campsite in woods near ancient Lydda.

First the weight on my back, then the rain, now the delay. I was ready to take a shuttle directly to Joppa, where Peter would end up. Wanting to encourage me with my research, and for the sheer adventure of it, Esuga was still ready to hike. I'm still glad we didn't. I had too much to carry, rain or shine.

When I later shared this story with Cyndi Parker, who has led dozens and dozens of tours in Israel, she pointed out that Peter was not able to jump on a shuttle when it rained. Part of experiencing the land as the disciples had meant hiking in the heat and rain. Next time, I promised I would—but without carrying a heavy backpack.

We soon boarded a shuttle to arrive forty-five minutes later in Tel Aviv. We caught a bus to settle into an Airbnb in northern Tel Aviv, two blocks from the Mediterranean Sea and three miles north of Joppa, where Peter would stay. I threw the weight of my backpacks on the floor and myself on the bed, only then realizing how tired I was from over a week of intense exploring.

The next day we would see Joppa, where Peter stayed and learned of God's plan to include gentiles in the family of believers.

The next morning after a late breakfast, I put on my running shoes and shorts for what would be my first and only run on the trip. I could never get Esuga to run with me in Philadelphia because of his bad memories of intense workouts when he trained for soccer. But now he was ready to run three miles in the sun by the sea, down the coast to Joppa.

A mile or so into the run I realized it would not be a good one. My cold lingered, and my stiff legs reminded me that I had not run in over a month. Then, too, Esuga, much younger than me, ran at a faster pace than I felt comfortable with. But what could I say? I was supposed to be the runner, not him.

Half an hour later we came to ancient Joppa (modern-day Joffa), where Peter had stayed in a house by the sea (Acts 10:6). While we do not know the specific location of the house he stayed in, old Joppa is very small and juts out into the sea, so we can easily imagine the general area.

After catching my breath, I found a café by the sea and, as usual, ordered coffee and a pastry. While I sipped my coffee and Esuga drank from his water bottle, we looked at Old Joppa on the cliffs above us. I reminded him of the significance of what happened in a house up there two thousand years ago.

Peter, along with all the Jewish disciples, would not even enter the homes of non-Jews (gentiles), whom they viewed as "unclean," but from a house up on that cliff, God shattered Peter's closed worldview and directed him up the coast to the gentile city of Caesarea, to enter a house filled with gentiles to share the gospel and welcome them into God's family.

This was the biggest event since Pentecost, for now non-Jews who turned to Jesus were included with the Jewish disciples as equal members in God's family.

We still had to run the three miles back to our Airbnb. The Mediterranean sun was even more fierce. I ran even slower.

PETER REENTERS THE STORY

When we last read about Peter, he was following up Philip's ministry in Samaria, and from there he returned to Jerusalem (Acts 8:25). Now, five years later, he traveled through the countryside west of Jerusalem to strengthen those who had become disciples. Even now he builds in part on the ministry of Philip who had preached the good news in all the towns along the coast on his way up to Caesarea (Acts 8:40).

Luke records two miracles through Peter resulting in many turning to the Lord. It seems Luke records the details of these two miracles because of their similarity to ones done by Jesus (e.g., Luke 5:17–26; 7:14–15; 8:54–55) and ones much earlier by the prophets Elijah and Elisha (1 Kgs 17:17–24; 2 Kgs 4:32–37). Luke may want to remind us of Peter's continued role as a leading apostle when he gradually fades from the account and Paul's ministry becomes the focus.

But Luke also uses the two miracle stories to bring Peter back into the account, to locate him near Caesarea. Here, for the first time, he will proclaim Jesus to gentiles and witness their receiving the gift of the Spirit, just as he and his fellow Jews had on the day of Pentecost.

THE HEALING OF AENEAS IN LYDDA (ACTS 9:32–35)

As Peter travels from Jerusalem down the central mountain range through towns in the countryside to strengthen the disciples, he finally arrives at Lydda, about 25 miles (40 km) down the road from Jerusalem. The brief healing story of a man named Aeneas recalls the power to heal that comes from the authority of the risen Lord Jesus. Peter says to the bedridden paralytic, "Aeneas, Jesus Christ heals you; get up and make your bed!" (Acts 9:34).

As we see throughout Acts, a significant miracle attracts the attention of the people and leads many to believe in Jesus. In fact, all those living in Lydda and the surrounding plain of Sharon now turn to the Lord.

PETER IN JOPPA (ACTS 9:36–43)

Peter remains in Lydda as the scene shifts to Joppa, twelve miles further west on the coast of the Mediterranean. There we are told that a woman by the name of Tabitha (which means "gazelle") lies dead in the upper room of a house. The character of Tabitha is recorded in detail, while that of Aeneas is not even mentioned. This, along with the length of the story, again illustrates Luke's emphasis on the important role of women in the Jesus movement.[1]

I have always pictured Tabitha as an elderly widow sewing clothes with other elderly widows, but the passage does not say she was a widow, and even if she was, widows at this time could be quite young. What we do know is that she imitated Jesus by devoting her life to helping the needy.

We read that she "was always doing good and helping the poor" (Acts 9:36). Her good works and acts of charity consisted in part in making clothes for poor widows and their children, and she likely invited the poor to her home for meals and fellowship.

She was likely wealthy and owned the house where her body now laid lifeless in the large upstairs room, where she is surrounded by

---

1. Witherington, *Acts of the Apostles*, 330.

widows who weep over her. The upper room where she lies reminds us of the upper room where the first disciples met and continued to gather for worship. This suggests the disciples may have met in her house for prayer and worship. Thus Tabitha, who had perhaps learned of Jesus through Philip's visit to Joppa, had been a central person among the community of believers, which still might be small in numbers (Acts 8:40).

Now when the disciples in Joppa learn that Peter is in nearby Lydda, they summon him to come down to Joppa to pray for Tabitha. We sense that Peter did not regard the raising of Tabitha from the dead lightly, for he asks the widows who weep for her to leave the room so that he can pray in quiet.

After a time of prayer, Peter turns to the dead body of Tabitha and says, "Tabitha, get up." This is what Jesus had said to the daughter of Jairus (Luke 8:54–55). The same kingdom powers that were at work to bring the daughter of Jairus back to life are now at work through Peter. We can assume there was great joy as she is presented alive to the widows and other disciples. This miracle, too, becomes known, resulting in many turning to the Lord.

Peter stays in Joppa for some time and lodges with a man named Simon, who Luke adds was a tanner. Jews avoided touching dead animals and tanners, "because their contact with the hides of dead animals which were considered unclean by more scrupulous Jews."[2] So why does Luke mention this?

He may want to show that Peter was liberally minded enough to live and eat with a Jew who more scrupulous Jews would consider unclean. Still, we will see that he was not liberally minded enough to even consider entering the house of the gentile, Cornelius. It will take patient convincing from God for that.

A FOCUS ON CAESAREA

While we don't read of Jesus visiting Caesarea, it is mentioned often in Acts. Philip ended up here after his witness to the Ethiopian eunuch (Acts 8:40). Then, later in Acts, Paul will stay there with Philip on his return to Jerusalem (Acts 21:8–9). We recently read that he was sent by ship from Caesarea to Tarsus (Acts 9:30), and we will soon read that Herod Agrippa I (a grandson of Herod the Great) will

---

2. Witherington, *Acts of the Apostles*, 333.

receive praise as a god at the great theater in Caesarea, which seated four thousand spectators (Acts 12:20–23). Finally, later in Acts, after Paul is arrested in Jerusalem, he is sent to Caesarea and spends two years in a cell there, at Herod's palace by the sea (Acts 23:33–35). Closer to our story in Acts, it is here that the Roman centurion Cornelius lives and embraces the faith when Peter is led to visit him.

But Caesarea was not an ancient Jewish city. Its history and the reasons for its creation hold important lessons for us, even today.

Herod the Great built Caesarea on barren land by the sea as Rome's capital and as his main residence as the Roman governor of Israel. Built thirty miles north of Joppa on the coast of the Mediterranean, Caesarea became a monumental showcase for Rome. It was built like most major Roman cities, complete with a "system of paved streets, sophisticated water and sewer systems, a theater, bathhouse, palaces, temples, and an impressive harbor."[3]

Since most of the shoreline along the coast of Israel is straight, the creation of the gigantic harbor at Caesarea was especially an impressive building achievement. The Romans had learned to create a dry cement mix that could be poured into wooden molds, set in the sea, and harden under water. The cement mix was poured into immense wooded frames that came from logs transported from forests in Europe.[4] And the cement mix itself, transported from Italy, required at least forty-four shiploads of four hundred tons each!

Herod spared no effort, no expense, to create a magnificent city by the sea.

But who paid for it, and why spend twelve years (22–10 BC) to basically build from scratch what would become the largest city in Israel? Because Herod was on friendly terms with Caesar Augustus, he was able to persuade him to finance the project (with taxes from around the empire). So, Herod named the city in honor of Caesar.

Caesar's reason for backing Herod's project was to build a strong military presence in Caesarea "to keep the Middle East as peaceful as possible, because Rome depended utterly on the grain that was shipped, throughout the sailing season, from Egypt."[5]

3. McRay, "Caesarea Maritima," 176.
4. Hale, *Classical Archeology*, 138.
5. Wright, *Acts for Everyone, Pt. 1*, 158.

Herod's reasons were more spiritual and cultural. He built Caesarea as an attempt to straddle "the Roman world and the Jewish world, to somehow pull these two forces together."[6] It combined Roman engineering, Greek civilized thought and art, and Jewish faith and tradition, for the purpose of bringing Jews and gentiles together. But Herod's vision was never fulfilled. Jews and gentiles living in Caesarea frequently quarreled over equal civil rights.

Even though twenty thousand Jews settled in Caesarea, gentiles dominated the city. It was basically a gentile city, created with Greco-Roman architecture and culture right in the land of Israel. "Although Jewish inhabitants controlled more of the city's wealth and claimed that Herod, its builder, was a Jew, the Syrian 'Greeks' who lived there argued that its statues and temples indicated that it was designed for Greeks."[7]

This makeup of the city made it politically volatile. While the Jews were allowed to build a synagogue, a monumental temple built to the worship of Caesar as a god dominated the harbor for all sailing in to see who was in control.

Thus, tensions often ran high between the Jews and the gentiles in Caesarea. They came to a head in AD 66, when a mob of young gentile men "performed a pagan sacrifice just outside the door of the synagogue on the Sabbath, touching off a riot that spread to Jerusalem."[8] This led to riots in Jerusalem, with the Jewish authorities banning sacrifices to pagan gods, including the emperors who insisted on being revered as gods.

When news of the riots in Jerusalem spread through Israel up to Caesarea, *gentiles in Caesarea massacred all twenty thousand Jews living there!* Herod's vision to unite Jews and gentiles in Caesarea had failed.

John Hale concludes a lecture on Caesarea with these sober words. "In Caesarea, two forces collided head-to-head, *and an explosion occurred that would not just color the rest of ancient history but have repercussions in the modern world, as well.*"[9] We still see these

---

6. Hale, *Classical Archeology*, 139.
7. Keener, *Acts, Vol. 2*, 1733.
8. Hale, *Classical Archeology*, 140.
9. Hale, *Classical Archeology*, 140. Italics mine.

two forces colliding head-to-head in Israel. They do not know what would bring them peace for it is hidden from them (Luke 19:42).

As I learned more about the racial tensions in Caesarea, I could better understand Peter's reluctance to travel there. More importantly, I came to see the wisdom of God in breaking the Jew/gentile barrier in Caesarea. What Herod failed to accomplish by building pagan temples for gentiles alongside a synagogue for Jews, God did by joining them together in Christ (Eph 2:14–17).

God chose Cornelius, a gentile Roman soldier in Caesarea, who would normally side with other gentiles against the Jews, to become the first example of how God intends to unite all humanity in Christ.

25

Peter and Cornelius
(Acts 10:1–33)

I<small>N THIS ACCOUNT</small> P<small>ETER</small> and six other Jewish disciples accompany three gentile men straight up the coast from Joppa to Caesarea. Since the road they traveled was flat and straight, the journey was easy, but they split it up into two days (Acts 10:23–24).

I will write now about my hike alone between Caesarea and Joppa, which I planned to divide up into three days. I should point out that there is little of historic interest between Joppa and Caesarea for our story in Acts. But if you want to read about my adventures and misadventures hiking and camping the sand dunes by the Mediterranean Sea, read on.

Esuga's wife, Lisa, had now flown over to join us. After we saw the ruins of Caesarea, they continued to Galilee after dropping me off south of Caesarea near the Israel Trail. It was late afternoon, with the sun descending to the sea, but I only had five miles to hike to the Israeli city of Hadera. There, according to my guidebook, I could put up my tent in woods across from the train station of Hadera. Strange. Camp out in woods across from the train station in a city? But trusting what I read, I headed out.

I enjoyed every minute of my travels with Esuga, but I also liked to head out on my own with vague plans to see what each day would bring my way. I had emptied my backpack of all but the essentials I needed for my three days on the trail and left the rest with Esuga and Lisa.

I hiked the opposite way of Peter in our story, but it was close to the way he walked. While I mostly hiked the sand dunes near the sea, Peter walked a well-worn ancient road a few miles inland for quicker and easier travel. The road Peter and company walked went straight up the coastline close to today's Highway 2. Though my trail was well-worn and not straight, it seemed hard to get lost if I hugged the shoreline with the sea.

It was already cooling off as I said goodbye to Esuga and Lisa, threw my pack on my back, and headed through the woods toward the sea. Alone on the trail. No more crowds. Happy as a lark, I began to sing. I felt a strong sense of the Lord's Presence. Nothing to do but put one foot in front of the other, enjoy the scenery, and look forward to exchanging stories with other hikers at the campsite in the evening.

But only thirty minutes later, I lost the trail near a park by the sea. I came to a bridge crossing into the park and asked three men there if they knew where the trail was. They were kind but could not help me. I missed Esuga, who had kept me on the right path.

On my own now and not particularly fond of reading detailed descriptions of trails in guidebooks, I came up with a plan. If I kept close to the sea on my right, I would eventually see Hadera, my destination. The happiness returned. For over an hour I enjoyed walking the dunes and watching the sun set over the sea.

But it was quickly getting dark, so I left the path on the dunes (which I later learned was the Israel Trail!) and walked over to a small asphalt road leading directly into the city. The darkness now enveloping me, I picked up my pace, the lights of Hadera in full view a few miles south.

Since I had lost the trail, I know I should have consulted my guidebook, but I reasoned the train station would most likely be near the center of the city with places to eat nearby. All I needed to do was walk straight into the city and ask for directions.

When I came into the city, I stopped to ask a woman walking her dog the location of the train station. It was a mile south of the city in the woods! She directed me to a bus I could take to the train station. I was tired now but hopeful of what was ahead.

I got off the bus and walked half a mile down the road to the remote station across from the woods. Seeing no tents, no hikers huddled around campfires sharing their stories, I approached a security guard at the entrance to the station to ask where I could camp. He grunted that I could camp in the woods directly across. I looked over and saw nothing but the dark woods and a few picnic tables but decided not to engage him in further conversation. I noted he wore a winter coat.

I carried my gear into the woods. No hikers. No tents. I was alone except for a few Israeli girls in their mid-teens, singing their hearts to the tune of their favorite Israeli artist, who they listened to on their phones. I enjoyed their singing as I put up my tent then boiled water for tea and sat at the picnic table to enjoy the cheese sandwich I had saved from the morning.

This was turning into a bit of an adventure, and I liked it. I had hiked off alone to see what the day would bring and found myself with a spot in the woods to sleep. In the morning I would get coffee and a sandwich at the train station.

Due to the lack of space in my backpack and the mild weather in Israel at the coast this time of year, I did not bring a sleeping bag or a pad to lay on. So, taking off my boots, I climbed into the tent and stretched out on the ground with my pants and three layers of shirts on to keep me warm. Happy and relieved, I soon fell asleep to the voices of the teenage girls, still singing as they drove off.

Suddenly I woke up in the middle of the night, chilled to the bone. I panicked, knowing I had no way to get warm. I quickly put on my boots and headed across the road to the train station to ask the security guard, now bundled up in his winter coat, if I could go inside to warm up and get some hot tea. "This is a cold station," he said, meaning it was not heated. He added it was closed now. There was no one inside selling food and drinks at this hour.

Panic. What will I do outside of town at 3:00 a.m. to get warm?

Then I spotted a single taxi approaching the station. As I ran over to the driver, the guard yelled to him, "Take him to Yellows." I didn't know what Yellows was, but I assumed it was a place I could get warm. Climbing into the warm cab, I greeted the driver, a man worn with years. When he learned I lived in Philadelphia, he went on and on and on about a girl from Philadelphia he almost married. Then he went on and on about all his favorite basketball players from the Philadelphia 76ers through the years. I was happy for the warm cab and the conversation.

A few minutes later he pulled up in front of Yellows, a gas station with a small store inside selling snacks, sandwiches, and hot drinks! After paying for the ride and wishing the driver well, I went inside to find only a young, college-aged student managing the station.

I told him I was hiking the Israel National Trail, camping across from the train station, and had woken up freezing. "Nobody hikes that trail except for foreigners" was his only reply. That explained why I saw only one other person on the trail and camped alone in the woods. (Later I learned that many Israelis do hike the trail but apparently not this guy's friends.)

Relieved to be warm, I bought hot coffee and a sandwich to enjoy. But my relief was short-lived. Halfway into my sandwich I realized that to stay warm I would need to sit on this plastic chair half asleep for four more hours until daylight.

So, I looked up at the few aisles in the store stocked with chips and cookies and candy and bottles of soda. Not much help. But always in search of a solution, I got up and walked up and down the aisles. You won't believe this. Finally, I found the solution to my troubles on the bottom shelf in the last aisle of the store. Three sleeping bags and a few sleeping pads for sale.

Of all the highs and lows of my travels, this was by far the highest high because I was so low. Without chiding the attendant for not telling me they were there, I bought a sleeping bag and pad and then walked the mile back to the train station in the middle of the night with not a soul in sight, and I began to sing again in anticipation of a warm sleep.

Climbing into the tent, I stretched the sleeping pad out over the cold ground and crawled into my new sleeping bag. Warm, grateful, and hopeful, I soon fell fast asleep. In the morning I would have breakfast at the station and then find the trail to continue south toward Joppa. (My hike to Joppa continues in chapter twenty-six.)

THE CONTEXT

Peter traveled the countryside west of Jerusalem but avoided the cities on the coast with larger gentile populations.[1] He is now in Joppa, unaware of the world-changing event he will soon witness, when God directs him to visit a house filled with gentiles in Caesarea.

We recently read how God led Philip to share the good news with an Ethiopian eunuch, who became the first gentile to believe. Yet he returns home, far from the land of Israel. If Philip informed the apostles of his conversion, it seems to have had little impact on them to take the gospel to the ends of the world (Acts 1:8).

---

1. Keener, *Acts, Vol. 2*, 1705.

Now God leads Peter to share the good news with not just one gentile from a distant land but with an entire household of Roman gentiles living in the land of Israel. But Cornelius and his household are not like the typical immoral, idol-worshiping gentiles Paul will reach; they were devout worshipers of Israel's God.

It will be a long step *geographically* to reach gentiles throughout the empire, those "from Britain and Spain in the west to Parthia, India and Egypt in the east," but once the disciples accept God's purpose to include gentiles into their family, it will be a short yet difficult step to accept them *culturally*.[2] The greatest barrier of all to taking the message of Jesus to the ends of the earth is about to be broken.

God has transformed Saul to take the gospel to the gentiles, but he is in Tarsus under training for the task. While God continues to prepare him for his mission, he leads Peter and the Jerusalem disciples to welcome gentiles as equal members in God's family. They, too, must be transformed because this new step in the mission, for breaking through deeply ingrained patterns of culture, prejudice, and beliefs developed through the centuries, takes time and considerable debate. It is always so with new movements of God's Spirit. The amount of space given to gentiles becoming officially recognized as equal participants of the promises of God shows its importance (Acts 10:1—11:18).

The message God now revealed to Peter is this: *By being joined to Jesus by the Spirit, gentiles share the exact same kingdom blessings (salvation) God had originally promised only to the people of Israel.*

Living two millennia later, when most who believe in Jesus are gentiles, this seems so obvious. We have read where Paul later writes that though gentiles were once "excluded from citizenship in Israel and foreigners to the covenants of promise" (Eph 2:12), now through Christ they are "heirs together with Israel, members together of one body, and sharers together in the promise of Christ Jesus" (Eph 3:6). What is obvious to us now was a seismic new revelation for first-century Jewish believers.

GOD PREPARES CORNELIUS WITH A VISION (ACTS 10:1–8)

This account is filled with movement: up and down stairs, in and out of houses, up and down the coast of the Mediterranean Sea, and most significantly, movement from heaven to earth: visions, visits from angels,

---

2. Wright, *Acts for Everyone, Pt. 2*, 167.

and the guidance of the Holy Spirit. It is always God initiating the movement; Peter and Cornelius only respond.

With Peter in Joppa, God begins the process to move him up the coast to Caesarea, a predominantly gentile city and the location of Roman government for all Judea. There lives a man named Cornelius, a Roman military officer in command of one hundred troops. He and his troops are stationed in the land of Israel to keep the Jewish population in check. As a Roman officer, he is feared by all, especially by Jews in the land of Israel.

Cornelius is not a typical Roman officer. He is described as a man who feared Israel's God, meaning he respected, honored, and worshiped him.[3] His love for God is demonstrated by his frequent prayers and his generous gifts to the poor. As a centurion he earned sixteen times that of regular soldiers, and he could have used his position and power to further build his wealth by exploiting the poor. Cornelius chose instead to help relieve them of their burdens.[4]

Following his example, his entire household—wife and children, other relatives, servants, and perhaps some soldiers under his command—are devoted to God. They are all depicted as practicing most of the typical duties of a Jew.[5] Still, Peter as a Jew would not enter Cornelius's house to pray and share a meal with him. Such was the Jewish mindset, even among the Jewish disciples.

Devout though they were, Cornelius and his household were still only God-fearing gentiles, forever separated from the nation of Israel—from socializing with them, from worshiping alongside them at the temple in Jerusalem, and most importantly, from participating in the promises God had exclusively given them.

But God sees Cornelius's heart. His devotion to God and generosity to the poor "ascended as a memorial before God" (Acts 10:4). He could not join the Jews in Caesarea to offer sacrifices at the temple in Jerusalem, but just as with the Samaritans and the Ethiopian eunuch, that no longer matters, for God accepts the sacrifices of his life. God is acting "to break down barriers between Jew and gentile *by treating the prayers and alms of a gentile as equivalent to the sacrifice of a Jew*."[6] As Stephen taught, the Spirit makes the heart his temple.

3. Peterson, *Acts of the Apostles*, 326.
4. Spencer, *Journeying Through Acts*, 119.
5. Witherington, *Acts of the Apostles*, 347.
6. Witherington, *Acts of the Apostles*, 348.

Looking into his heart, not his ethnicity, God grants Cornelius a vision. An angel tells him God has received his worship and acts of charity. He is told to send men to Joppa to find a man called Peter. Later we learn the angel had also told Cornelius that a man named Peter would come and share with him the message of salvation (Acts 11:14).

It is interesting to follow God's direction in the story and how people respond. Cornelius responds at once to God, knowing something of what will happen when Peter visits his house. Peter, as we now read, resists the command of God, and when he finally reluctantly agrees to enter Cornelius's house, he is still uncertain why he is there (Acts 10:29)!

GOD PREPARES PETER TO VISIT CORNELIUS (ACTS 10:9–23)

Cornelius obeys the Lord's command and sends three of his men to Joppa to locate Peter. While en route, the Lord directs Peter to receive them, which proves to be a more difficult challenge. About noon, shortly before the three men arrive at the house of Simon the tanner, Peter climbs the outside stairs of the house up to the roof to pray in quiet. While praying, the Lord gives him a vision of unclean animals and directs him to kill them and eat them. In contrast to Cornelius, who responded immediately to God, Peter resists. Peter refuses to obey the Lord. Peter!

Think about that. Think about how our culture keeps us from obeying the words of the Lord.

Peter refuses because God has given the Jewish people food laws separating them from their non-Jewish neighbors. This was the logic of the food laws: "the people you sit down and eat with are 'family,' and the Jewish 'family' has been called by God to be separate so as not to compromise with the idolatrous nations around them."[7]

Because of Peter's initial resistance, the Lord must again explain that he has now made clean what Peter considers unclean. Then a third time Peter receives the vision of unclean animals and is told to eat. Finally, he no longer resists the Lord and begins to reflect on the meaning of the vision.

While he ponders the meaning of the vision, the three "unclean" gentiles arrive. Hardly a coincidence, Peter now knows the meaning of the visions of unclean animals. He obeys the Spirit of God and is ready to go with the men to Cornelius's house. For the first time in his life, Peter

---

7. Wright, *Acts for Everyone*, Pt. 2, 160.

invites gentiles into a home to share a meal and provide lodging for the night. He must have felt uneasy, but now he obeys the Lord.[8]

The next morning Peter and six other Jewish disciples (Acts 11:12) begin the thirty-mile trek up to Caesarea with the three men. This must have been an awkward two-day trek for Peter and the six other Jewish men. Did they find lodging in a Jewish house? What kind of food did they eat? Perhaps, as they walked, the three men shared more of Cornelius's devotion to God.

I especially like to think about what went through Peter's mind as they walked. At this point he only knows he is to visit Cornelius but not why (Acts 10:29). God continues to patiently prepare him for the most significant ethnic breakthrough since he first called the people of Israel to be his special possession. Peter will soon learn God's plan to *enlarge (not replace)* his people to include anyone who fears him and lives in obedience to Jesus the Lord.

PETER ENTERS THE HOUSE OF CORNELIUS (ACTS 10:24–33)

Cornelius and Peter now meet. Cornelius greets Peter at the door. Knowing something of his prominence as an apostle and knowing he will share the good news of salvation with his household, Cornelius falls at Peter's feet as an act of respect. This is a highly unusual gesture for a Roman centurion to pay any Jew, especially one lacking political clout, wealth, and formal education. But this act, too, shows the humility and spiritual insight of Cornelius. Though Peter is a common Jew, Cornelius honors him as an apostle devoted to God. But Peter will not be bowed to even as an act of respect. He says to Cornelius, "Stand up; I am only a mortal" (Acts 10:26).

They enter the house. Peter is overwhelmed to see it filled with perhaps forty to fifty gentiles, all standing eager to hear from him. The six Jewish companions stand behind Peter, eyes wide open, their nostrils taking in the scents of a house packed with gentiles.

Peter speaks first. God has prepared him for this moment. He says they know that he and his Jewish companions would not previously enter

---

8. The multiple references to houses and hospitality in the account highlights that the people of God are a family and that the social separation between ethnicities has come to an end. God is creating a new community on earth centered on Jesus, a community unlike anything that has ever existed.

their house, but God has shown Peter that Jews are no longer to regard gentiles as unclean and separate themselves from them.

Then, turning to address Cornelius, he asks, "Now, may I ask why you sent for me?" (Acts 10:29). Peter still doesn't know what is about to happen!

Cornelius now speaks. He tells Peter that four days ago an angel from God appeared to him, commanding him to send for Peter who would tell them the message of salvation (Acts 11:14). Peter now knows he is to proclaim the good news of Jesus to non-Jews with the expectation that they would receive it.

A FOCUS ON THE MINDSET OF PETER AND THE JERUSALEM DISCIPLES

As I have worked through Acts and seen how the Jewish disciples at this time resist accepting gentiles as equal members in God's family, I have tended to judge them for what seems like an intolerant, ethnocentric mindset. But when I tried to put myself in their shoes and better understand the promises given to them in Scripture and their current history, I became much more sympathetic to why it was such a struggle.

It is good to recall that God had chosen Israel to be his own unique people out of all the nations of the world. He gave their father, Abraham, the rite of circumcision to distinguish them from other nations. Through Moses, God gave them the law so that they would worship him alone in righteousness, separate from the idolatrous nations around them. In this way they would be a light to the nations—if only they keep separate from the gentiles. Instead, they often worshiped the idols of the nations, forsook God's commandments, and were sent into exile because of it.

Now they were on high alert to keep separate and live by the law of Moses.

They knew the prophets did say the nations would come to Jerusalem in the last days to worship the true God, but they never said gentiles would join with them fully in the promises given to Israel. And Israel assumed that if non-Jews wanted to partly share in God's salvation in the last days, they would have "to take upon themselves Jewish identity, to renounce their own ethnic past and embrace

Judaism lock, stock, and barrel."[9] That meant being circumcised and living by the food laws and all the other laws of Moses. *For the Jew, circumcision and food laws were the politically charged, nationalistic equivalents of our national flags,* especially at this time *when Israel felt the threat of losing its national identity* under the repressive rule of the powerful Roman military.[10]

Here is the point. If we read through the Old Testament with attention to all the unique promises given to Israel, and if we realize the threat to Israel's national identity at this time, it is easier to understand why Peter and the Jewish disciples struggled to accept gentiles into the family without their first becoming Jewish—lock, stock, and barrel. But what they failed to understand was that they were chosen and given the law *"for a particular period and a particular purpose."*[11] Israel was chosen to prepare the way for a much greater purpose. Now, with the coming of the Messiah through whom all the promises of God are fulfilled, the period of preparation has achieved its purpose and is a thing of the past.

It helped me to recall that the fact that non-Jews sharing in the exact same promises given to Israel was not revealed in the Old Testament. That is why Paul calls this new work of God a mystery, meaning it had not been revealed to Israel in their Scriptures and has only now been revealed to the apostles (Eph 3:5–6). This made me more sympathetic with the resistance of the Jerusalem disciples to accept gentiles as full members in the family. They didn't expect this new work of God.

The Jewish mindset at this time explains why God must patiently give vision after vision to resistant Peter and seemingly drag him up the coast to the gentile city of Caesarea to enter a house packed with gentiles. In fact, the work of God to break Peter from his closed, nationalist mindset is emphasized in the story as much as the salvation of Cornelius and his household! *God must shake his people from their closed mindset so that others can enjoy the life of God.*

---

9. Wright, *Acts for Everyone, Pt. 2*, 163.
10. *Acts for Everyone, Pt. 2*, 175.
11. *Acts for Everyone, Pt. 2*, 163.

26

Gentiles Receive the Gospel
(Acts 10:34—11:18)

W㎞㎞㎞㎞ When I last wrote about my hike from Caesarea to Joppa, I was warm and sound asleep in my newly purchased sleeping bag from Yellows. At 7:00 a.m. I woke up suddenly from the sound of people parking their cars nearby to catch one of the commuter trains that speed up and down the coast. I turned over and slept for another hour then crawled out of the tent to assess my situation over a cup of hot tea and remnants of a stale sandwich from the night before.

I simply needed to take down my tent, pack up my belongings, and find the trail headed south. According to the trail guide (which I finally decided to read), I had a fifteen-mile hike to Netanya, where I would spend the night on the beach. But it would be another hot day in the high eighties.

I took another sip of tea and looked across the road at the commuters boarding the express train headed south. Once the idea hit me, I didn't think twice. Peter would understand. I had not slept well, and it would be a hard day hiking fifteen miles across sand dunes in the heat.

Half an hour later I sat comfortably in an air-conditioned coach headed south. The express train got me to Netanya in just ten minutes instead of the ten-hour hike I had anticipated. I caught a bus to the beach, where I would spend the night in my tent.

It turned out to be a long, lonely day. The beach was packed with families and friends enjoying the holiday together. I tried reading, but it was too hot to concentrate.

Finally, as the sun began to set over the Mediterranean Sea, I asked where hikers could camp. I was pointed to a desolate spot half a mile away at the far end of the beach, under cliffs hanging over the sea. I walked down to look. Dark and desolate. Again, I would be camping alone. Why was no one hiking the Israel Trail?!

I walked back to the center of the beach and stopped to ask for help from a parasailer packing up to leave. He said I could put up my tent anywhere on the beach. I thanked him, found a good spot by the shore, and put up my tent. It was another cold night, but I had my sleeping bag from Yellows. The beach café would open at 8:00 a.m. for breakfast. Thinking about my morning coffee and a fresh sandwich, I soon fell asleep to the roar of the waves.

I woke in good spirits and, after eating a hearty breakfast by the sea and packing up, I found the trailblazer at the end of the beach.

After hiking inland through two nature reserves, the trail again led up to sand dunes with great views of the sea. I walked the dunes, drinking in the morning—the roar of the waves, the cliffs, the spring wildflowers.

After four hours hiking the dunes in the midday heat, I grew weary. Increasingly I felt the thirty pounds on my pack pushing through my body down to my feet. Hiking in the deep, uneven sand made the going even more difficult. I realized why Peter walked the ancient road on firm ground a mile inland, but I had no choice but to press on.

In time the path led to a small beach, where I found families celebrating the Passover weekend. Desperate for shade, I asked a family if I could sit in the back corner under their large canopy. While they watched their children play in the sand, I relieved myself of my backpack and sat on a three-legged stool I carried with me. As I watched the waves and listened to the wind picking up out at sea, exhaustion overwhelmed me.

Seeing my weariness and feeling pity, the mother of the children offered me three large Joppa oranges. I thanked her and shared that I was headed for Joppa today. She replied, "You still have a long hike ahead of you. Think you can make it?" How should I take that? It was time again to assess my situation.

When dark clouds suddenly filled the sky and the wind picked up, people began to pack up and leave. I followed them up the narrow path to the top of the dunes. There, straight before me, I saw a sign pointing to the trail across the dunes by the sea. It was hot with no shade. Then, glancing to my left, I saw another sign across a field by the road. The yellow arch of McDonald's.

Ten minutes later I sat on a soft-cushioned booth in air conditioning to consume a quarter pounder with large fries and a Coke. I caught a bus across the street from McDonald's and was in Tel Aviv thirty minutes later. Again, Peter would understand. After all, I was in my early seventies and hiking across the dunes.

Peter and his companions had walked the thirty miles from Joppa to Caesarea in only two days (Acts 10:23–24). In three days, I had only hiked ten miles. But I had set out to see what the days would bring, and I was happy I did.

Down the road from McDonald's I boarded a bus to Tel Aviv and found a room at the hostel recommended by my trail guide. The next morning, I met up with Esuga and Lisa, who would fly back to Philadelphia while I continued my travels in Turkey with two of my daughters. My flight to Istanbul left at 4 a.m. I checked in around 11:00 p.m., found a dark corner in the waiting area, unrolled my sleeping pad, and used my sleeping bag for a pillow. Thank God for Yellows.

I slept well knowing I had completed the first major leg of the trip. Tomorrow—Turkey, to trace Paul's first missionary journey.

PETER PROCLAIMS THE GOOD NEWS TO GENTILES (ACTS 10:34–44)

This is the fourth of Peter's gospel messages in Acts (condensed, as in the others) and is a good one for us to know well since it is addressed to non-Jews and omits the many references to Jewish history, as in the previous ones. Still, it includes the important events of the gospel.

It can be helpful at this point to reiterate the sixfold facets of the one gospel from Peter's sermon at Pentecost and show where they appear in this sermon.

The gospel consists of:

1. The Spirit-empowered life of Jesus (Acts 2:22)
2. Jesus was crucified according to God's Plan (Acts 2:23)
3. God raised Jesus from the dead (Acts 2:24–25)
4. God made Jesus both Lord and Messiah (Acts 2:32–36)
5. The exalted Jesus pours out the Spirit (Acts 2:33)
6. Jesus will return to judge the nations (omitted in Acts 2)

With all eyes focused on Peter, he speaks at once—no meal, no time for rest. Celebration will come later. First, he must proclaim Jesus. He begins by saying that he now knows (or "has come to realize")[1] that God, who has never shown partiality to the rich and powerful, does not show partiality regarding nationality. For what God promised to the people of Israel is now available to all who fear him and "does what is right," that is, confess Jesus as Lord and seek to live in the world as he did (Acts 10:34–35).

Peter then makes his first point. "You know the message he sent to the people of Israel, preaching peace by Jesus Christ—he is Lord of all" (Acts 10:36). By living close to Galilee, where Jesus had ministered, Cornelius knew something of the life and message of Jesus, but he did not know that the Jewish Messiah was also sent for him as a gentile. Even though Peter will give a more complete understanding of the gospel, more importantly, for the first time ever, he shares it with gentiles, with the understanding that they, too, can receive it.

God's purpose is to bring peace in all its dimensions through Jesus, *who is now Lord of all.* In this context, we are reminded that Jesus is Lord over Cornelius the centurion and the feared military might of Rome. To confess Jesus as Lord of all is a declaration of our trust in him and allegiance to live for him above all else.

After beginning with God's intent to bring peace to the world through the Lord Jesus, Peter expands upon the good news. God came to dwell in Jesus by his Spirit when Jesus was baptized, to anoint him with power and authority. By the power of God's Spirit in him, Jesus "went about doing good and healing all who were oppressed by the devil" (Acts 10:38).

Sadly, our confessions of faith overlook that the Spirit-filled "life and character of Jesus were an important part of early evangelistic preaching."[2] The life and character of Jesus both reveal what God is like and what we are to become as his disciples. While no one can live without sin as Jesus did, confessing him as Lord means we saturate ourselves with his life in the four Gospels and seek to live as he did.

The compassionate healings of Jesus were *signs* of the great rescue and restoration accomplished by his death. Peter says, "They put him to death by hanging him on a tree" (Acts 10:39). By dying for us Jesus

---

1. Peterson, *Acts of the Apostles*, 335.
2. Peterson, *Acts of the Apostles*, 337.

delivered us not only from the fear of death but also from the power of sin in us and evil all around us.

Peter then states another familiar theme in Acts. He and all the apostles are witnesses that God raised Jesus from the dead (Acts 10:40, 41). The resurrection of Jesus proves that he is the Messiah; thus, all that he taught was true.

On one occasion after his resurrection, Jesus appeared to the apostles and commanded them to preach "that he is the one ordained by God as judge of the living and the dead" (Acts 10:42). Judgement is another aspect of the gospel often omitted today. Perhaps this is due to the hell, fire, and brimstone sermons in the past. But at the appropriate time and in the appropriate way, we should warn people that they will one day stand before Jesus to be held accountable for their lives. The just judgment of Jesus is good news, for one day evil and all its effects will be banished so that only love, light, goodness, and peace will fill God's universe and the world we will live in.

Peter has stated the main points of the Gospel story and apparently wanted to say much more (Acts 11:15), but as he continues to speak, the Holy Spirit falls on Cornelius and all those gathered (Acts 10:44)!

Apparently, as they listened to Peter, the Spirit moved their hearts to embrace the good news without any appeal or pressure. This, too, demonstrates God's will to include gentiles in his family. No one could ever say that Peter pressured the gentiles to believe the good news!

GENTILES RECEIVE THEIR OWN PENTECOST (ACTS 10:44-48)

When the gift of the Spirit promised to Israel fell on the Jewish disciples at Pentecost, they received the many blessings of salvation. This is the reason that the six Jewish believers with Peter are astounded when they see the Spirit also poured out on a house filled with gentiles.

They see gentiles experiencing what they did at Pentecost! They see them experiencing the same joy and intimacy with God. This was evident by their speaking in tongues, just as they had on the day of Pentecost (now not likely in known languages as then), and by praising God for the gift of salvation.

The witness of these six Jewish men will be crucial when Peter is soon summoned to Jerusalem and criticized for associating with gentiles and offering them the gift of salvation, for people will question how unclean gentiles could be fit vessels for God's Spirit.

Peter takes charge. Seeing that they have received the same Spirit and the same gift of salvation as the Jewish believers, Peter orders the entire household to be baptized. Their baptism was a public confirmation of their commitment to Jesus as Lord and a sign of becoming part of God's family.

Peter and his six fellow Jews baptize Cornelius and his family, extended family, servants, and some troops under his command. Imagine the joy, the celebration. This is a sign of God's new world. Boundaries are broken—cultural, ethnic, religious. A new society is born, a new kind of community for the world to see.

Peter and the other Jewish disciples were invited by Cornelius to stay with them for several days! Their fellowship as one people in one house completes the picture of their unity in Christ. What went through their minds as they shared meals and the Lord's Supper together? Surely, they realized they had witnessed the beginning of God's new work in the world.

PETER REPORTS TO JERUSALEM (ACTS 11:1–18)

Though Peter remained in Caesarea a short time, the startling news of gentiles turning to the Lord soon reached the other apostles and disciples in Jerusalem. We would expect celebration with Peter's news upon returning, but instead, we read, "The circumcised believers criticized him, saying, 'Why did you go to uncircumcised men and eat with them?'" (Acts 11:2–3).

Because all Jewish men were circumcised, some interpreters believe the entire church challenged Peter's actions. I agree, however, with those who identify "the circumcised believers" as an influential group of strict Pharisees who have become disciples (Acts 6:7). This same group will later insist that gentiles must be circumcised and live by the laws of Moses if they were to be saved (Acts 15:1–6). From this same group, some will travel to pester and persecute Paul as he welcomes gentiles into God's family solely by their allegiance to Christ apart from the law (Gal 2:12).

For now, Peter silences their criticism by recounting the unmistakable acts of God that demonstrate his plan to include gentiles into the family. First, there was the vision when God commanded Peter not to consider unclean what he had made clean (Acts 11:5–10). There was the Spirit commanding him not to make a distinction between Jews and gentiles (Acts 11:12). Then there was Cornelius's report of an angel's appearance, commanding him to ask Peter to come to his house to give the message of salvation (Acts 11:13–14). *Most importantly of all, Peter and his six companions saw the Spirit of God falling on the house of the gentiles just as he had on the Jewish disciples on Pentecost* (Acts 11:15).

Peter closes his argument with these words: "If then God gave them the same gift that he gave us when we believed in the Lord Jesus Christ, who was I that I could hinder God?" (Acts 11:17). This sounds much like Gamaliel's challenge to the Jewish Council, when he said if the Jesus movement is from God, you will not be able to stop it and "you will only find yourselves fighting against God" (Acts 5:39). Sadly, we will see *believers in Jesus* fighting against God! We will see many who profess Christ fighting against God, even today.

But for now, Peter succeeds and silences any more criticism from the circumcised party so that all praise God for pouring out his life to the gentiles. I suspect the circumcised party was not enthusiastic in their praise.

SUMMARY

Cornelius is a bridge figure to reach the nations in Acts. He is not the immoral, idol worshiper most gentiles were in the Roman Empire. It seems God uses the conversion of Cornelius and his household to prepare the Jerusalem disciples for Paul's more radical mission to gentiles scattered throughout the empire.

Now that the apostles know there are no longer any ethnic barriers to the good news of Jesus, we would think they would call a council and make plans to leave Jerusalem to be Jesus' witnesses to the ends of the earth (Acts 1:8). But they don't. Ten years after God sent Peter to the house of Cornelius, we will read that they are all still in Jerusalem (Acts 15:4)!

As we read Acts, we can reflect on the reasons for their reluctance and how they hinder the gospel even in our day.

A FOCUS ON ANTIOCH SYRIA

The City

If you look at a modern map of the Middle East, you will find tucked away in Turkey, at the northeast corner of the Mediterranean near the Syrian border, the modern day city of Antakya. This was ancient Antioch. The city was devastated by an earthquake in February 2023. It was built much like a typical Greco-Roman metropolis, with theaters, palaces, eight temples to worship the Greek and Roman gods and one, of course, to offer sacrifices to the emperor.[3]

Since this was the metropolis where many gentiles first turned to the Lord, it became Paul's home base for mission, and I was eager to learn more about it.

With a population estimated at five hundred thousand, Antioch was the third-largest city in the Roman Empire, following only Rome and Alexandria.[4] It was strategically located on the edge of a large, fertile plain near a busy commercial road, transporting goods from Asia throughout the Mediterranean.

Built on the banks of the Orontes River, goods from Antioch could also be transported fifteen miles west down the river to the harbor on the Mediterranean to be shipped throughout the empire. This important harbor functioned as the main gateway to and from the city and is from where Paul and Barnabas will sail and return after the journey recorded in Acts 13 and 14.

With at least eighteen ethnic sections in Antioch, deep divisions disrupted social integration and prospects for peace. This is the major reason Antioch was so prone to riots.[5] The gradual growth of small Jesus communities, built up of the diverse ethnicities and united in their love for Jesus and one another, was bound to stand out and create curiosity.

The Jewish population of Antioch in the first century is estimated at twenty thousand to thirty thousand. As was common for most ethnic groups, they would have lived near each other in their own part of the city, where they built synagogues to preserve their

---

3. Keener, *Acts, Vol. 2*, 1835.
4. Jeffers, *Greco-Roman World*, 287.
5. Jeffers, *Greco-Roman World*, 158.

faith and unique identity. Due to Antioch's proximity to Jerusalem, Jews there would have kept a stricter way of life than those farther away in the empire.

Archeologists have discovered the prestige and influence of the Jewish people in Antioch by excavations along its grand central street. Two miles long and paved with marble, "the street was one of Antioch's claims to fame."[6] Assuming some wealthy Jews became disciples, they would have generously contributed to the famine relief for the disciples in Judea that we read about at the end of Acts 11. In addition, larger numbers of disciples could gather in their more spacious homes for worship.

Living Conditions

Understanding the physical realities of everyday life in Antioch for most of its inhabitants helps us understand how the message about Jesus was received as good news, bringing peace and giving hope.

Rodney Stark has reconstructed the living conditions of Antioch, with its "extraordinary levels of urban disorder, social dislocation, filth, disease, misery, fear, and cultural chaos that existed."[7] Much of the filth, disease, and misery in a city the size of Antioch was due to the cramped quarters of the estimated five hundred thousand dwellers. Stark estimates that in Antioch 195 people were packed into only an acre and compares these crowded conditions with New York City, with only 37 people living within an acre.

Insulae, a type of ancient apartment building, housed most of the people. They were built close to each other and went up to five stories. The poor majority were packed as extended families into the smallest apartments of roughly one hundred square feet on the top floors.[8] With few windows, the room was dark and damp.

Water piped from the aqueducts outside the city ran mainly to public fountains, the homes of the very rich, and to public baths not accessible for all. Most people had to carry their water jugs down the steps of their apartment and walk the streets to a public fountain to fetch their water. Very little was available for scrubbing floors,

---

6. Jeffers, *Greco-Roman World*, 288.
7. Stark, *Rise of Christianity*, 149.
8. Beers, *Week in the Life*, 40.

washing clothes, or bathing.⁹ With poor ventilation, no running water, and open ditches on the streets used for pouring slops and chamber pots from several stories up, disease quickly spread.¹⁰ The pungent stench from sewage running down the streets rose through open windows everywhere.

Disease, the constant companion of cramped and filthy quarters, meant "illness and physical affliction were probably the dominant feature of daily life."¹¹ Signs of sickness were seen by all on the streets of Greco-Roman cities—swollen eyes, skin rashes, and lost limbs were common.

Since Greco-Roman tenements lacked both furnaces and fireplaces, cooking was done over small wood or charcoal braziers, also the only source of heat.¹² We watch the History Channel and marvel at the remains of Roman monuments and temples constructed with stone. But most structures in Greco-Roman cities were built close to each other and "consisted primarily of wood-framed buildings, plastered over," making them highly flammable.¹³ "The most dangerous apartments were those on the top floor, where the structural defects of thin walls and poor building materials placed occupants at the greatest risk from collapse or fire."¹⁴

In these tiny apartments built all over the city, many of the disciples lived and gathered as the church. The wealthy lived in the larger, more stable apartments on the bottom floors, with artisans residing in the middle floors. The wealthier who became disciples would receive the poorer members into their more spacious homes for meals and worship.

Luke writes twice that a great many people came to the Lord in Antioch (Acts 11:21, 24). I like to imagine Saul and Barnabas learning their way around Antioch, crisscrossing the city with its half a million inhabitants, up and down the stairs of the apartment buildings, trying to remember where the disciples lived and met.

---

9. Stark, *Rise of Christianity*, 152.
10. Beers, *Week in the Life*, 40.
11. Stark, *Rise of Christianity*, 154.
12. Stark, *Rise of Christianity*, 151.
13. Stark, *Rise of Christianity*, 159.
14. Beers, *Week in the Life*, 40.

In addition to cramped living conditions, natural and social disasters also contributed to the disease, death, and perpetual state of anxiety in Antioch. Antioch was extremely vulnerable "to attacks, fires, famines, epidemics, and devastating riots."[15]

During the six hundred years Antioch was under Roman rule, it was attacked eleven times, to be plundered and sacked on five of those occasions; it was burned entirely, or in large part four times—three times by accident and once by the Persians; there were six periods of major rioting by hostile factions that racked the city and led to major fires; it experienced hundreds of significant earthquakes during the six centuries, with eight so severe that they nearly destroyed everything and caused a large number of fatalities; at least three major epidemics plagued the city, causing probably 25 percent of the people to perish; and finally, there were at least five serious famines.[16]

Stark did the numbers with these disasters and found that *Antioch could expect a natural or social catastrophe on the average of every fifteen years*! Think of how the COVID-19 epidemic affected our lives for a few years. Then consider our outlook on life if a major epidemic, wide-scale rioting, fires, and a breakdown in food and water supplies struck our cities every fifteen years. Where would we put our hope?

Stark concludes that Antioch was a city where at least half of the children died at birth or during infancy, "a city filled with hatred and fear rooted in intense ethnic antagonisms and exacerbated by a constant stream of strangers . . . a city where crime flourished and the streets were dangerous at night . . . above all, a city so repeatedly smashed by catastrophes that a resident could expect to be homeless from time to time, providing that he or she was among the survivors."[17]

Stark argues that the spread of the Jesus movement in the Roman Empire was not due to mass preaching, as we see with Peter in Jerusalem, but *due to its capacity to create a new culture, giving hope.* The followers of Jesus who first came to Antioch (Acts 11:20–21) brought with them a new society centered on Jesus. This breaks down divisions, heals, brings hope, and drives out despair, so a great many people in Antioch welcomed this as good news.

---

15. Stark, *Rise of Christianity*, 159.
16. Stark, *Rise of Christianity*, 159–60.
17. Stark, *Rise of Christianity*, 160–61.

27

The Gospel Reaches Antioch Syria
(Acts 11:19–30)

IN THE FOLLOWING PASSAGE Barnabas goes to Tarsus to find Saul. Since Saul also proclaimed Christ in the regions near Tarsus, it took considerable time and effort for Barnabas to locate him. This is suggested by the need for Barnabas to look for Saul and then finally find him (Acts 11:24–25).

Later I will write about my trip to Antioch, but now I share my trip to Tarsus, where Saul grew up and has returned. My daughters had not yet arrived in Turkey, so I now traveled alone with Refik, a young Turkish man who had lived with me and my wife while studying English at the University of Pennsylvania near us.

Refik was now married, and he and his wife were the best of hosts while I explored Tarsus and Antioch. My main objective for the first day was to visit the few existing ruins from first-century Tarsus and then drive northwest up the mountains to the famous Cilician Gates, which Paul went through on his second missionary journey (Acts 16:1).

Early in the morning, Refik and I headed east from his house in Mersin through the flat, fertile fields to nearby Tarsus, in the plains close to the Mediterranean Sea. From a glossy brochure I picked up when we entered Old Tarsus, I learned that not only Paul but also Julius Caesar, Cicero, Cleopatra, Mark Anthony, and many Roman philosophers had lived in or visited Tarsus.

Unfortunately, most of Roman Tarsus lies deep below the modern city, but a 200-foot (60 m) stretch of the Roman road was discovered in

1993, and I was ready to walk it. When we found the Roman road, I was surprised to see no one there. It was roped off with a sign forbidding us to enter. Refik said, "I guess we can't enter," but because the rope only partially covered the entrance, and there was no attendant, I convinced Refik we could step over the rope for a short visit. I had after all traveled all this way to walk the streets of Saul.

Compared to the extensive Roman ruins I would later visit, this was small, but since this was my first Roman road, I took it all in, walking all 200 feet of the road back and forth, then sat beside the road to imagine Barnabas walking it in his search for Paul.

From Tarsus we drove northwest to seek out the famous Cilician Gates. The road we drove was built over the same road Paul would later walk on his second mission trip from Antioch Syria, to Tarsus, then up through the Cilician Gates and into the mountains of central Turkey (Acts 15:40—16:1). I had downloaded images of the ancient Cilician Gates, and now my dream of seeing them was soon to come true.

The Cilician Gates had been cut into the mountains so that the armies of Alexander the Great and others could march through the mountains of Anatolia, pass through the Gates to Tarsus, and continue eastward. The pass is so narrow that only four soldiers (some say horses) walking abreast could pass through it at a time. And since the pass was also exceptionally steep, it provided a natural barrier for an army to pass unopposed.[1]

After fifteen minutes driving through the flat, fertile fields outside of Tarsus, we came into rolling hills covered with stones and shrubs. We then began a steady ascent on the steep, windy roads in the mountains topped with pine trees and snow-covered peaks above.

Enjoying the cool mountain air and the scenery, we wound our way past several sleepy mountain villages. Then in one village, we pulled over to check our map. A man hoeing a small garden near his modest house, with his children playing nearby, stopped to look up at me in the car in front of his house. I felt uncomfortable for invading his privacy, but Refik assured me he was used to people driving up here for picnics to escape the heat of the coastal plains below.

The way through the mountains became narrower and Refik, checking Google Maps on his phone, said the Cilician Gate was nearby. Soon we would pull off the highway and hike up to see the historic pass. Five minutes later we pulled over to the side of the highway on a busy overpass.

---

1. Alexandros, "Challenge of Crossing."

Refik said that this is where the Gates were. I looked out the window for the narrow pass I had seen images of on the internet. "This can't be it, Refik." He showed me his phone. We were parked on the overpass over what had once been the Cilician Gates, now dynamited away to make room first for a railroad and now for the highway.

These are the lessons from this story. If you want to walk where Paul walked in Tarsus, don't be afraid to step over the rope, and if you want to see the famous Cilician Gates, download images from the internet.

Figure 6: Cilician Gates before the Modern Highway. This photo by unknown author is licensed under CC BY-SA.

Paul knew the long history of cruel conquering armies passing through the gates. That got me thinking. When he later walked through the gates with Silas (Acts 15:41—16:1), did he stop and turn to him to say, "Because we pass through these gates with the message of peace, one day the nations will no longer pass through with their weapons"? Maybe he did.

UNNAMED DISCIPLES REACH ANTIOCH SYRIA (ACTS 11:19–24)

Stephen, though dead, continues to show his influence as a catalytic character in Acts. His teaching had led to his brutal death by stoning and resulted in all the disciples, except the apostles, fleeing Jerusalem. While many of the Hebrew-speaking disciples have now returned to Jerusalem, the Greek-speaking disciples associated with Stephen are labeled and remain a scattered people in exile from the land of Israel—but not from the kingdom of God they carry with them.

As they travel, most of them still only tell the good news to their fellow Jews. But now a few of them also begin to proclaim Christ to gentiles, here referred to as Greeks or Hellenists (Acts 11:20). These few unnamed disciples, originally from Cyprus and Cyrene (on the coast of present-day Libya), now travel as evangelists to Antioch. Most likely they knew Stephen and Philip and, emboldened by their examples, followed in their steps.

Since Antioch was the third-largest city in the Roman Empire, we now see a shift in Acts from the rural Galilean ministry of Jesus to the small urban Jerusalem movement of the apostles to a cosmopolitan mission in Antioch. Cities like Antioch, "where many people were already uprooted from previous centuries of traditions, tended to show greater openness to new ideas than the countryside, and first-century churches spread initially there (along trade routes) and usually only later to outlying villages."[2]

Strategically, God in his wisdom leads unnamed Greek-speaking disciples to Antioch (11:20–21), making it the city where disciples of different ethnicities gather as a family and learn to model God's will for all humanity to unite in Christ across racial and cultural differences.

It is not Peter or the other apostles still in Jerusalem or Saul, still in Tarsus, that the Lord uses to first reach large numbers of gentiles in a cosmopolitan city like Antioch but *a few unnamed disciples* who know the language and culture of Antioch, unnamed perhaps to encourage those of us who are not apostles to believe God can also use us to go and reach those who do not yet know him.

It is the hand of the Lord with them that causes many to believe. The mention of "a great number" (Acts 11:21), along with "a great many people" (Acts 11:24) brought to the Lord, recalls similar statements in the early chapters of Acts for the great many Jews who believed. What the Lord first did among the Jews, he now does among the gentiles!

News of a major work of God among gentiles in Antioch soon reaches the church in Jerusalem. They must have understood this as the Lord acting on what he had recently revealed to Peter, so they send Barnabas, a Greek-speaking disciple originally from Cyprus (Acts 4:36)

---

2. Keener, *Acts, Vol. 2*, 1833.

who was known "as a good man, full of the Holy Spirit and faith" (Acts 11:24). Barnabas was most likely sent by the apostles in Jerusalem to investigate the events in Antioch, but when he arrives, he immediately sees the evidence of God's Spirit at work and encourages the new believers to remain faithful to the Lord. With his vibrant walk with the Lord and his sensitivity to both Jewish and gentile culture, Barnabas was the right man to oversee this new development of Jews and gentiles meeting together as one family in the Lord.

A FOCUS ON HOUSE GATHERINGS

Up until the fourth century, when under the secure arm of Emperor Constantine, Christians constructed buildings for worship. The center of their life together was the home gatherings in small communities across their cities.

The multi-storied apartment buildings where they gathered contained apartments of different sizes (as I mentioned earlier). Most of them were the small one-room apartments of the predominantly poor on the top floors; the middle floors had medium-sized apartments for artisans and others financially better; and then the bottom, more secure floors had a very few spacious "exquisitely decorated, multi-roomed dwellings of the rich."[3] Ten to fifteen could squeeze into the smaller apartments and thirty to forty in the larger ones.

Almost all in the city lived close to one another in these apartment buildings. As the Jesus communities grew like the yeast, as Jesus said it would, and wealthier families embraced the faith, they would host a house church in their larger apartment. Neighbors watched with curiosity.

Why did they open their homes for meals to the poor from the shabby apartments on the top floors? It was as though they were a family. Slaves and freedmen, men and women and children, the rich and the poor, people of different color and cultures, *all gathering into the most intimate setting of the home.* This, too, made neighbors curious. Every Saturday evening or Sunday morning through the thin walls they could hear them singing, laughing, praying.

Who were these people?

---

3. Kreider, *Patient Ferment*, 79.

Every morning they were seen and heard going up and down the stairs (when they met for teaching and to pray before the workday), throughout the day (to bring food or clothing for the poor among them), and in the evenings (for meals). Unlike members of pagan associations, they always seemed to be together.[4] And they always seemed to leave their time together filled with joy and hope.

This movement of God's Spirit could not be hidden in these architectural islands of Antioch, these multi-storied apartment buildings where the disciples gathered. They were a light on a hill that could not be hidden; they were savory salt to their cities.

The people did not knock on their neighbors' doors to hand out booklets, but if they learned a neighbor was in need, they offered help. They prayed for healing for the sick, comforted those who mourned, gave what they could to the poor, and slowly more and more were joining them up and down the steps.

There were important advantages to meeting in homes that added to their growth. Because a shared meal centered on Jesus was central to their gathering, the home provided facilities for cooking, and since Jewish synagogues—permitted by Rome—often began in homes, this new, seemingly Jewish sect also meeting in homes would not have initially caused suspicion. Romans were always on the lookout for small associations that might be a cover for political activity, so meeting in homes initially provided legal covering for the Jesus gatherings.[5]

In addition, because they gathered in homes like the intimate family they were, their prayers and words of encouragement to one another were more personal, more to the point and thus more powerful. Since each one, no matter their station in life, had received a gift by the Spirit to encourage others, all participated and all felt valued.

Finally, the Jesus movement spread more rapidly by meeting in homes. Sociological studies show that "conversions" occur more rapidly through the web of close relationships.[6] Most often the nucleus of a house gathering was made up of the extended family, neighbors, and those with whom they shared something in common, such as their trade or ethnicity.

---

4. Kreider, *Patient Ferment*, 79.
5. Jeffers, *Greco-Roman World*, 72.
6. Keener, *Acts, Vol. 2*, 1895.

> The birth of a small church was not complex and costly. Paid professionals were not required. These small, simple communities were easy to reproduce. So, the Jesus movement spread slowly through familiar contacts from house to house, neighborhood to neighborhood, like the yeast Jesus said it would be.
>
> Did we lose something when Constantine allowed us to build our grand structures to meet in and attract others? Should we find our way back to the ways we have forgotten? It seems more than ever we need to find new ways to be the church people others will see and respect for what they see.

BARNABAS BRINGS SAUL TO ANTIOCH (ACTS 11:25—26)

As more people turn to the Lord, Barnabas realizes he needs assistance from a seasoned leader with a similar background to his and sees it in Saul. Barnabas helped welcome Saul to the believers in Jerusalem some ten years earlier, but soon Saul was forced to flee to Tarsus (Acts 9:26–30). Barnabas must have had some contact with Saul during this time, for he now travels to Tarsus searching the city until he finds him.

Since Saul had been chosen by the Lord to be his witness "before the gentiles and their kings and before the people of Israel" (Acts 9:15), he was surely overjoyed when Barnabas informed him of the Lord's work among the gentiles in Antioch. It doesn't seem Saul has been proclaiming Christ to gentiles (beyond those who attended the synagogues) for the past ten years. If he had, the news of it would have reached Jerusalem, as it did when Cornelius and his household believed, and now as great numbers of gentiles in Antioch turn to the Lord.

While Saul knew God had called him to proclaim the Lord among the gentiles, he did not know *when* the Lord would open the door to gentile ministry. Knowing how the call of Israel's prophets was fulfilled only over time,[7] Saul now sees this as his time.

When they come to Antioch, Saul and Barnabas teach and strengthen the disciples in the many multiethnic house gatherings for a year. Luke writes that in Antioch the disciples are first called Christians. Up until now, and even in the future, the Jewish disciples in Jerusalem and Judea

---

7. Keener, *Acts, Vol. 2*, 1680.

are called Nazarenes by others. That is, they are viewed as a Jewish sect following Jesus of Nazareth (Acts 24:5).

But these new, multiethnic communities in Antioch are a completely new phenomenon. The people of Antioch did not know what to make of this new kind of community composed of Jews and gentiles. The Jews they understood, for they had been found throughout the empire for centuries. But this new sect is made up of Jews and gentiles, gentiles who do not live by the Jewish ways. What's more alarming, these gentiles no longer worshiped the Roman gods but instead someone they call the Christ. They confess him as Lord, not Caesar, and build their communities on his teachings.

Not knowing how to classify this new sect, people in Antioch called them Christians, for they were people "belonging to, identified with, or adherents or followers of Christ."[8] Christ is the Greek word for Messiah, God's anointed King; thus, they were viewed as a people who pledged their loyalty to Christ their King.

The disciples did not choose to be called Christians (they took the name only much later in the second century). Opponents of the Jesus movement in Antioch came up with it to ridicule them. "Hey, have you heard of this new sect from the east who worships a man who was crucified? They say he is alive and give their undivided loyalty to him. Christ their crucified Lord, they claim." But "such mockery constituted the supreme irony,"[9] for Jesus became Lord only by his obedience to death by crucifixion.

For the next century and a half, the disciples continued to identify themselves as followers of Jesus, the Nazarenes, brothers and sisters, the family of God, and people of the Way (of Jesus).

Because so many in our culture who call themselves Christians fail to live by the teachings of the one they call Lord, more and more people prefer to identify themselves as followers of Jesus.

Christian, belonging to Christ, is a good name, but it needs to be explained and, most of all, lived.

FAMINE RELIEF (ACTS 11:27–30)

Now around this time, prophets from Jerusalem traveled to Antioch to speak words of encouragement to the growing family of disciples, but one

---

8. Witherington, *Acts of the Apostles*, 371.
9. Keener, *Acts, Vol. 2*, 1850.

of them, named Agabus, also predicted a severe famine over their known world. The disciples in Antioch gave generously to their Jewish brothers and sisters in Jerusalem and Judea.

We don't know why the believers in Judea were in greater need than those in Antioch, but their liberal gifts show that Barnabas and Saul had taught them Jesus' teachings about giving to those in need.

Think of the significance. The generous gifts from this young, largely gentile group of believers tangibly, powerfully illustrates that the Spirit has united them as one people with the Jewish church in Jerusalem. The initiative coming from them at an acute time of need would have a profound, perhaps even humbling effect on the now more established church in Judea. Their giving is an "important expression of solidarity defying conventional sociocultural boundaries"[10] creating a positive impression of the new sect in Antioch ridiculed as Christians.

---

10. Spencer, *Journeying Through Acts*, 132.

28

Herod Is Humbled
(Acts 12:1–25)

We read earlier of Peter's trip up to Caesarea, so I will not bore you with Herod's journey from Jerusalem to Caesarea in this story. The story is way too exciting to elaborate on the roads Herod took to Caesarea, yet we can assume that as a king, he rode in a chariot surrounded by soldiers, not by foot as Peter did.

This chapter elaborates on another prison break in Acts. This caused me to think about why Luke goes into such details about the rescues from prison and why he ends this chapter describing Herod's dramatic death.

Acts 11 ended with Saul and Barnabas teaching the disciples in Antioch, and chapter 13 begins with them in Antioch ready to be sent out by the Spirit on their first journey to the gentiles. Sandwiched between these two chapters we read in Acts 12 of King Herod's attempts to destroy the Jesus movement in Jerusalem.[1]

In that it would have been much smoother reading to omit the events of Acts 12, we must ask why Luke included it. One reason is that Luke uses the events of Peter's rescue in this chapter to transition from his leadership among the Jewish people in Acts 1–12 to Paul's ministry to the gentiles beginning in Acts 13. In Acts 12:17 we read that Peter left

---

1. Witherington, *Acts of the Apostles*, 383–84. This is not the Herod who took part in the trial of Jesus but a grandson of Herod the Great, who now rules over Judea, Galilee, Samaria, and the Transjordan. Educated in Rome and a friend of the third Roman emperor, Caligula, he helped Claudius, a schoolmate, to later become emperor.

Jerusalem and "went to another place." After this he is only mentioned once more in Acts, when he affirms Paul's ministry to the gentiles (Acts 15:7–11).

More important than the transitional function of this chapter (it could have been much shorter if that was Luke's only intention) is the reminder that the church in Jerusalem remained strong and under God's care when it was no longer the focus of the story. We see the strength of the Jerusalem church in how its leaders were ready to follow their Lord in suffering (even death), in the unity and fervent prayer of the disciples, and in their growth in numbers. At the end of the chapter we read, "But the word of God continued to advance and gain adherents" (Acts 12:24).

A final function of chapter 12 is its emphasis that Jesus is God's appointed Lord, not Herod or any other worldly ruler. We read how Herod accepts praise from an elated crowd, who shouts out that his is "the voice of a god, and not of a mortal" (Acts 12:22). For this and for his persecution of Jesus' people, the Lord takes the life of Herod.

This leaves me wondering. Why doesn't God take the lives of more demagogues who tarnish his name?

HEROD PUTS PETER IN PRISON (ACTS 12:1–5)

Except for Saul's brief visit to Jerusalem (Acts 9:26–30) and Peter's return there from Caesarea to report on the events at Cornelius' house (Acts 11:1–18), we have not read about the disciples in Jerusalem since the death of Stephen.

In the early chapters of Acts, it was mainly the leaders of Israel, the Sanhedrin, who tried to silence the disciples. Now we read that when "King Herod laid violent hands" upon some of the disciples and killed the apostle James with the sword, this pleased the people. For the first time in Acts, the people at large, who initially showed great favor to the disciples, join their leaders and turn against them.

We are not told of Herod's initial motives for persecuting the disciples, but we read that once he started and saw how it pleased the Jews, he intensified his efforts. As with most demagogues, he does not act out of conviction for what is right but for fame and power among the people.

First, Herod has James, the brother of John, killed with the sword. (This is the apostle James, not James the brother of Jesus, mentioned in Acts 12:27.) Then, when he sees that this pleases the Jews, he plans to execute Peter, the head leader. Perhaps he seeks to squelch the Jesus movement by eliminating their leadership, or perhaps he simply does whatever pleases the people.

There are parallels here between Pilate's actions against Jesus and Herod's actions against Peter. As Pilate had brought Jesus out to the people during the Passover, so now Herod intends to bring Peter "out to the people after the Passover" (Acts 12:4). By this, Luke again emphasizes that the disciples must be ready to suffer as their Lord to fulfill God's mission.

Luke also points out another parallel. Just as God rescued Jesus from death by resurrection, he rescues Peter so that he can continue to serve him. Luke makes no attempt to explain why James is killed and Peter is rescued. We leave such mysteries in the hands of God.

While Peter is in prison, we read that the disciples "prayed fervently to God for him" (Acts 12:5). But we will soon read that they were surprised when Peter suddenly appears in the middle of the night at the house where they prayed. They were praying for bold witness in death (they expected him to be killed as James was), and they prayed that he would know God's Presence, be strong, and glorify God in death as Stephen had.

We now read that *Peter was sound asleep,* chained up between two soldiers in his prison cell. Their prayer is answered. God is with Peter and provides him with a peaceful sleep.

THE LORD RESCUES PETER (ACTS 12:6–19)

Herod has learned of Peter's previous escape from prison (Acts 5:18) and takes all precautions to see that it will not happen again. Peter is securely contained by four soldiers rotating through the night for highest alertness. In the cell there are two soldiers, one on each side of Peter, who is bound in chains. And then outside the cell stand two other guards. This man will not escape again.

But Peter sleeps in the presence of his enemies. In fact, he is so sound asleep that the heavenly messenger God sends to deliver him must poke him in the side to wake him up. The last time a heavenly messenger directed Peter was through a vision (Acts 10:9–16). So, as the angel leads Peter out of prison, he thinks this, too, is a vision. When the angel departs once they are inside the city walls, Peter realizes that God has once again delivered him—this time from certain death by the sword or crucifixion.

As on his previous rescue from prison, Peter heads straight to the family of believers who are praying for him in the middle of the night in the house of a woman named Mary. Mary has a son named John Mark, introduced here to later reappear traveling with Saul and Barnabas (Acts 13:5, 13).

Luke again injects humor into the story. Peter must persist in knocking at the outer door of the house until the disciples finally believe it is him. It had been easier to escape from the hands of Herod than to enter the house where the disciples pray for him! As mentioned above, the disciples did not seem to believe the Lord would rescue Peter from death and thus do not anticipate seeing him again.

Some of the disciples act on the belief in a Jewish superstition that each person has a "heavenly" counterpart that can appear on earth. While Luke cites what is said, he does not necessarily support that this belief was common among all the disciples.[2]

When Peter enters, the house fills with shouts of praise. But Peter is in a hurry and quiets the disciples so that he can quickly report how the Lord has again delivered him. He is in a hurry to leave and put many miles between him and Jerusalem before Herod wakes up to discover he has again escaped.

We are not sure where Peter goes at first; Galilee, where he grew up and has family, is most likely. More important for the narrative of Acts, Peter will now increasingly travel to proclaim the gospel, leaving his residence in Jerusalem and position of leadership there.[3]

Before leaving, Peter directs the disciples to report his rescue to the other disciples in Jerusalem, especially to James. This is the first mention by name of this James, a brother of Jesus. Though not by name, he was previously mentioned along with his brothers in Acts 1 as belonging to the initial 120 disciples who met to pray after the ascension of Jesus (Acts 1:14–15).

James had not replaced Judas to become one of the twelve apostles because he had not believed his brother was the Messiah until Jesus appeared to him after his resurrection (1 Cor 15: 7), nor had he spent three years immersed in the life and teachings of Jesus as the twelve apostles had (Acts 1:21–22). But fourteen years have passed since Pentecost and James has devoted himself to the apostles' teachings about Jesus. He

---

2. Marshall, *Acts of the Apostles*, 210.
3. Peterson, *Acts of the Apostles*, 367.

became known as a man of "great piety." This, along with being a brother of Jesus, seems to have led to James becoming the leader of the Jesus community in Jerusalem when Peter now leaves.

Peter is far from Jerusalem when Herod wakes up, finds out he is missing, and searches all over Jerusalem to find him. A wiser and more humble man would have stopped to reflect on how Peter had once again been miraculously delivered from prison and consider believing in his message about Jesus. But Herod was not such a man. Peter's miraculous rescue was God's merciful work to wake Herod up and change his ways, but Herod ignored the hand of God and continued in his ways. Soon he would be thrown down from his throne. He now leaves Jerusalem to reside in Caesarea, where he will meet his fate.

Luke now ties the events of this chapter together. He links Herod's sudden death by the hand of the Lord to his accepting praise from the crowd, who cry out to him as a god. By implication he links Herod's death with his persecution of the disciples.

Herod is now at home in his palace in Caesarea, a largely gentile city and the seat of Roman government for Judea. We know that the gospel had reached Caesarea, first by Philip (Acts 8:40) and most recently by Peter (Acts 10:24–33). The gospel had also recently reached Phoenicia farther up the coast, with Tyre and Sidon as the main cities (Acts 11:19). Jesus is now worshiped as Lord in Caesarea, Tyre, and Sidon, but Herod seeks for himself what rightly belongs only to God and to his Messiah.

For an unspecified reason, Herod was angry and disputed with the people of Tyre and Sidon. Because of the economic power he held over them, they were forced to yield and seek reconciliation with him. Flattery would secure them the food they so desperately needed. So, a large contingency from Tyre and Sidon traveled down the coast to Caesarea and were granted audience with Herod to seek reconciliation. On a day appointed by Herod with an entourage of prominent guests, Herod entered the theater, which can hold four thousand, and took his seat on the platform to address his guests.

While Luke writes only that he wore royal robes, the Jewish historian Josephus writes that Herod's robe was made with silver, so that when the rays of the rising sun struck it, the people cried out, "We have reverenced you as a human being, but from now on we confess you to be more than mortal."[4]

---

4. Peterson, *Acts of the Apostles*, 369.

The worship of kings as gods was common among the nations in the ancient world by gentiles. But Herod is a Jew ruling in Israel and knows God alone is to be worshiped. For receiving this praise, Herod is immediately struck down by an angel of the Lord.

The angel of the Lord who struck Peter's side in prison to wake him up and rescue him now strikes the stomach of Herod (though not necessarily by visibly appearing).[5] Josephus, the Jewish historian, wrote that Herod was seized with violent internal pains, carried home, and died five days later to be "eaten by worms," a common idiom among ancient writers to describe a manner of death for those who most deserved it.[6],[7]

Luke concludes with a summary saying that the message about Jesus continued to advance (Acts 12:24). We again see that despite violent opposition from rulers such as King Herod, the risen Lord continues to advance the gospel of peace. Yes, there was intense suffering and the apostle James and others were put to death, but the Jesus community continued to grow.

Was this due in part because the people observed how the disciples responded to persecution without fear or retribution? Did they reflect on the connection between Herod's sudden death and how he persecuted the disciples?

Luke now picks up with Barnabas and Saul back in Antioch ready to be sent out on their first mission to the gentiles. They have returned to Antioch from Jerusalem, where they had given aid from Antioch to relieve the believers who would suffer from the famine.[8]

The compassion of the believers in Antioch to sacrificially provide food for the disciples suffering famine stands in sharp contrast to Herod's cruel restriction of food to the famished people of Tyre and Sidon.[9] Perhaps this also led to the growth of the gospel. Here is a different kind of kingdom at work than Herod's.

---

5. Peterson, *Acts of the Apostles*, 369.

6. Peterson, *Acts of the Apostles*, 370.

7. Peterson, *Acts of the Apostles*, 370. Herod's death could have been due to a perforated appendix, arsenic poisoning, or acute intestinal obstruction.

8. See Peterson, *Acts of the Apostles*, 371, for translating Acts 12:25a: "Barnabas and Saul returned, having fulfilled their service in Jerusalem."

9. Peterson, *Acts of the Apostles*, 371.

29

From Antioch to Cyprus
(Acts 13:1–12)

Refik, my host in Turkey, had to work all day, so I got up at 5:00 a.m. to take the four-hour bus trip to Antioch (today's Antakya). The road led southeast past Tarsus, winding by the Mediterranean Sea with mountains rising inland. I would return by bus at 11:00 p.m., making it a long day.

My visit to Antioch would be brief since ancient Antioch lay thirty-five feet under the modern city of Antakya. My main goal for the day was to visit the harbor where Paul and Barnabas set sail for Cyprus.

Most of the people on the bus were Turkish and likely traveled to Antakya for work or to visit family. We all caught up on the sleep we had missed from an early departure. When I woke up, I noticed an older woman in the seat in front of me glancing back at me. I had not uttered a word to reveal my nationality and could not understand why I was under such scrutiny. Then I realized I wore my "West Philly is the Best Philly" T-shirt.

Was this the woman whom the taxi driver who took me to Yellows had met in Philadelphia and almost married? Did she think I was him returning to look for her? I decided not to ask but did give her a very faint smile, after which she must have decided I was not Eli, her lost love she had met in Philadelphia.

Acts 13:4 says that when Paul and Barnabas left Antioch, they "went down to Seleucia (modern day Sammandag) about fifteen miles west-southwest, and from there sailed from to Cyprus."[1] I had learned from a Turkish archeologist visiting Philadelphia that they could have hiked the fifteen miles to the coast or taken a boat down the Orontes River, which flows through the heart of Antioch to the sea.

I didn't have time to hike, and since boats were no longer used on the river, I found a bus down to the sea. Ships from all over the Roman Empire sailed from the harbor at Seleucia, which was nestled between the mountains and from which on a clear day one could see Cyprus. From here Paul often sailed to and from his many journeys.

Despite the sewage that the Orontes River carried from Antioch to the sea, Paul and Barnabas likely took a boat down it to carry their belongings (the Scriptures, food, clothes, tents, etc.) to make for a faster, easier trip. Once they reached the sea, they would only walk a few miles north to the harbor of Seleucia, where they would wait for a ship to Cyprus, sixty miles west.

Seleucia was the overland end point of goods carried east on the great Silk Road to be shipped all over the Roman Empire and was one of the best and busiest harbors on the eastern Mediterranean.[2] The many ships that sailed from there did not leave according to a fixed timetable but according to the weather, finding an ideal cargo, and after the captain had made sacrifices to the sea gods.[3] So Saul and Barnabas needed to stay close to the harbor to listen for signals of a ship departing to Cyprus. If necessary, they would spend the night waiting in a tent made by Saul.

It was past noon and in the low nineties when my bus stopped by the Mediterranean Sea. Not a soul was to be seen. I asked, in two small beach hotels, where the Orontes flowed into the sea, but no one spoke English. I could see the mountains rising above ancient Seleucia to the north, so I reasoned the Orontes had to enter the sea somewhere to the south.

I became a lonely beach bum and headed south along the shore. Still, not a person to be seen to ask for my destination. Finally, after ten minutes, I spotted a lone fisherman a quarter of a mile ahead of me. I picked up my pace to catch up with him, partly to ask about the mouth of the river and partly for human contact. But he was leaving for the day, and as fast as I walked, he walked faster, leaving me still alone.

I plugged on, still hoping to see where Saul and Barnabas disembarked by the sea. Somewhat bored, I began taking pictures of the sea, the harbor,

1. Keener, *Acts, Vol. 2*, 1997.
2. Phillips, "Geographic Importance of Antioch" 270.
3. Keener, *Acts, Vol. 2*, 1998.

and the mountains that rose above them. Then I noticed a man, sitting on the back porch of his run-down beach house, observing me.

Was I a foreigner? Why was I walking alone fully clothed in the heat of the day taking pictures? Five minutes later several black sedans with tinted windows drove slowly by his house and quickly disappeared behind a high dune nearby.

I'm normally not paranoid, but I had to admit I looked suspicious. Would they believe my story? Why would anyone travel all the way here to a remote beach to see where two men sailed for Cyprus two thousand years ago? I checked for my passport and was relieved to grasp it in my pants pocket. I carried on. No one approached me, but I kept rehearsing my story.

I walked on and soon saw ahead of me what looked like a small stream winding through the sand into the sea. It seemed too small to be the Orontes. But as I followed it inland it broadened. This was it! This is where Saul and Barnabas disembarked to then walk north to sail from Seleucia.

For twenty minutes I walked up and around the Orontes, wading through its narrow flow by the sea, imagining the ships that once crowded the harbor. It was in the mid-nineties now, and I was tired, hot, and hungry. So instead of walking the few miles north to see the ruins of Seleucia, I decided to save them for a future trip.

As I walked along looking for the bus back to Antioch, the black sedans that had driven by thirty minutes earlier passed by me without incident. I guess we will never know if I was a person of suspicion, but the more I thought about it, the more I could see why I was a person of interest.

I caught the bus back to Antioch, ate a late lunch, and walked the narrow streets of old Antioch trying to imagine the life of the disciples in the ancient city. Then in the evening I boarded the bus back to Mersin. It had been a long day, but I will always be able to envision Saul's many journeys to and from Antioch by ship.

THE LORD SETS BARNABAS AND SAUL APART FOR MISSION (ACTS 13:1–3)

We can discern the wisdom of God in keeping Saul and Barnabas in Antioch for a year before they embarked on their first mission. They learned how to pastor and teach a growing community of multiethnic new disciples to work through issues of relating to one another as one family. The year also provided time for Saul and Barnabas to work together before beginning their long difficult mission. By not rushing off for mission but waiting for the Lord's timing, they would be much more effective.

By this time there were many small gatherings of believers in crowded apartments all over Antioch, each one a church, but collectively, underscoring their unity, they were "the church at Antioch."

Along with Barnabas and Saul there were three other prophets and teachers in Antioch: Simeon, who was called Niger, was likely from Africa in that Niger means "black";[4] Lucius, from Cyrene (North Africa), was likely among those Greek-speaking Jews who first spoke the word to gentiles in Antioch (Acts 11:20); and Manaen from Galilee, who had been a close friend of Herod Antipas, the ruler who tried to kill Jesus during his ministry in Galilee.

With Barnabas from Cyprus and Saul from Tarsus, *God brought together an ethnically diverse team of leaders in Antioch to meet the challenges of an ethnically diverse community of disciples.* The love and unity of the leaders provided a good example for the whole community of believers.

Because of my exposure to the leadership culture in North America, I have often pictured Saul as the proactive leader, always planning, always initiating mission. But we read that Barnabas and Saul only began their mission when the Holy Spirit spoke to the leaders collectively, saying, "Set apart for me Barnabas and Saul for the work to which I have called them" (Acts 13:2).

This does not mean that they had not been praying about traveling to reach other gentiles, but they did not go until the Spirit showed them the right time. *As we see throughout Acts, the risen Lord leads in mission. The leaders only acknowledge and act on what God has revealed to them.*

The text does not say *how* the Holy Spirit spoke to them. In that they were all prophets and sensitive to the leading of the Spirit, he could have spoken to them all collectively—or to one or several of them. Either way, they all agreed that the Lord had spoken.

As Jerusalem has been the center for reaching Jerusalem, Judea, and Samaria, now Antioch becomes the center for reaching both Jews and gentiles to the ends of the earth (Acts 1:8). And now Saul and Barnabas replace Peter and John as the principal pair, forging the way in gentile mission.[5] From Antioch, Barnabas and Saul will leave, and to Antioch

---

4. Peterson, *Acts of the Apostles*, 374.
5. Wall, "Acts of the Apostles," 188.

they will return (Acts 14:26–28). Luke will highlight the crucial events of their journey, which may have taken less than a year.[6]

A FOCUS ON TRAVEL BY SHIP

Travel by ship in the Mediterranean could be dangerous if you sailed on a small boat or in the winter months, when hazardous storms threatened everyone at sea. Because of the rough winter weather, ships were normally taken out of service between mid-November and mid-February.[7] In reading Acts, we will at times sense that Paul is waiting for spring before he sails.

If the winds were right, travel by ship was much faster than walking. A ship could cover about one hundred miles a day, while ordinary travelers like Saul and his companions walked at best twenty miles a day.[8] However, sailing into high winds when traveling west could take six times longer than when sailing east.[9] Paul may have chosen then to walk when traveling west.[10]

Since there were no passenger ships in antiquity, travelers would pay for passage on one the many merchant ships that covered the Mediterranean. The larger, more reliable ships that carried grain from Alexandria to Rome held "close to one thousand tons of grain and nearly that many passengers as well."[11] Smaller ships sailed close to the shoreline and pulled into port each night. Depending on his destination, Paul would sail on both large and small vessels.

There was generally no fixed schedule for when to sail. Winds and the weather were a major factor but also what sailors believed to be the whims of the gods. Sailors, like almost everyone else in the empire, were superstitious and would not sail on certain days or if the sacrifice the ship's captain made to their gods was unfavorable. This meant that Saul and Barnabas, like other passengers, would have to stay near the port, where they could hear the signal for departure.

---

6. Keener, *Acts, Vol. 2*, 2191.
7. Jeffers, *Greco-Roman World*, 37.
8. Jeffers, *Greco-Roman World*, 37.
9. Jeffers, *Greco-Roman World*, 38.
10. See, for example, Acts 15:41—16:1.
11. Witherington, *Acts of the Apostles*, 640.

If they needed to wait out a night and there was no lodging close to shore, Saul's tent would be useful.

Because the ships carried cargo below deck, passengers were forced to stay on deck, "sleeping in the open air or under a tent. They would travel with bags (*viduli*, or *manticae*) which would contain not only clothes but also cooking ware, food, bathing items, and sometimes bedding as well."[12]

CYPRUS (ACTS 13:4-12)

Barnabas and Saul now sailed the sixty miles to Cyprus. I like to imagine their joy of anticipation, knowing the Lord had called them, prepared them, and now sent them out by the Spirit to the nations, a mission unparalleled in history.

They likely sailed first to Cyprus because Barnabas had family and friends on the island. Barnabas was still the leader at this point, but in character with his humility he would soon recognize Saul as the leader when he sees Saul's strong apostolic gifting in an encounter with a false prophet in Paphos and when they sailed north to Asia Minor where Saul is more culturally at home than Barnabas.

Their ship docked at Salamis, the easternmost city of the island, where they remained at least a few weeks to proclaim the gospel in the several synagogues there. They then trekked west across the island "along the long but relatively recent Roman road on the southern coast from Salamis to Paphos."[13] The road was 115 miles long and would have taken only a week if they walked straight through to Paphos on the west coast of the island.

The road led them mainly through agrarian areas, and as they approached a city, they would see tombs at the side of the road. "Close to the gates of walled cities would be shrines, wells, and some shops whose odors kept them outside of the city, such as those of tanners and leatherworkers."[14]

---

12. Witherington, *Acts of the Apostles*, 639.
13. Keener, *Acts, Vol. 2*, 2006.
14. Keener, *Acts, Vol. 2*, 2007.

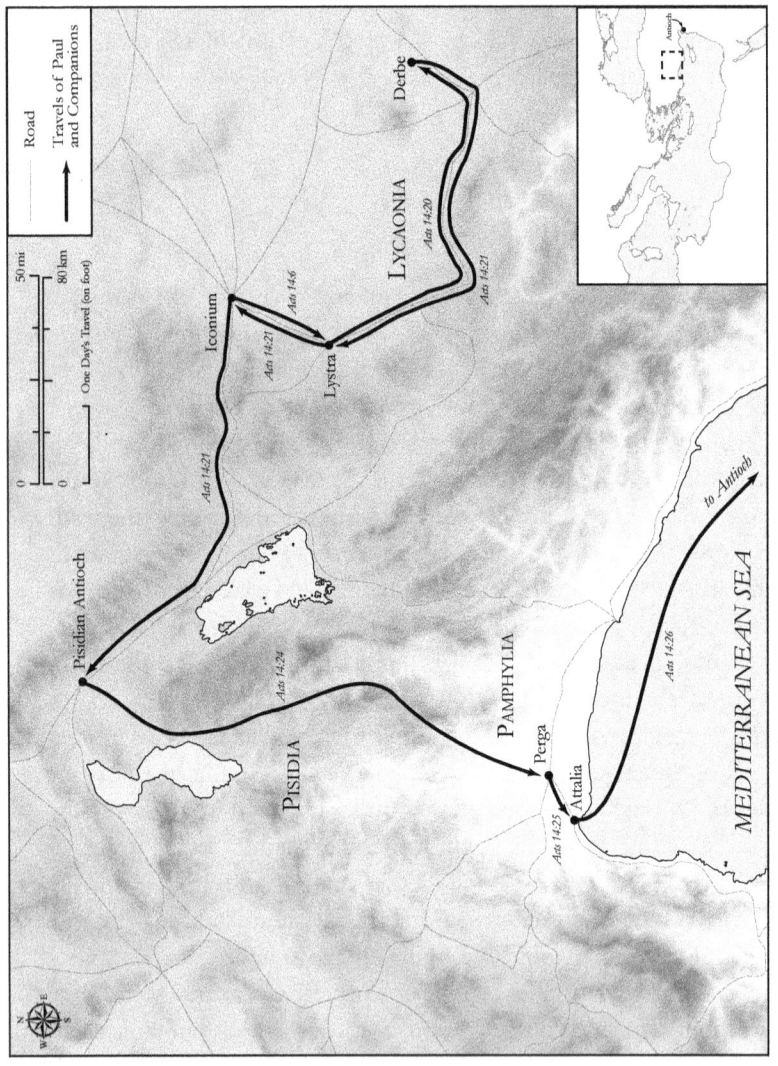

Figure 7: Paul's First Missionary Journey. Open Bible Maps.

Recalling that some men from Cyprus had gone to Antioch to tell the good news to gentiles (Acts 11:20), we are safe in assuming they had also proclaimed Jesus to the Jews on Cyprus. Barnabas and Saul would have stopped along the way to mainly strengthen the new disciples in their faith and visit Barnabas's family but keep moving in their mission to reach gentiles in more populated cities. This may be the reason Luke doesn't record their ministry across the island. We shouldn't assume it was because of little response, for Luke wants to highlight a power encounter Paul had with a Jewish magician in Paphos that led to the Roman governor of Cyprus (a gentile!) embracing the message of Jesus.

Paphos was said to be dedicated to the goddess Aphrodite, just as Athens was to Athena. Paul and Barnabas would have passed her temple by the sea in Old Paphos on their way to New Paphos, seven miles west, where our story takes place.

Believed to be born in sea foam created by the rocky coast, Aphrodite's statue was also believed to have fallen from heaven, where it was now placed in her temple as the most famous of deities in Cyprus. Both men and women made the annual seven-mile procession from Paphos to venerate Aphrodite in her temple. Her temple was said to even contain a sacred rock and a special court where rain would never fall. Luke's informed readers would have known the stories of Aphrodite and would have reflected on how the seeds of the gospel came to penetrate the dominant polytheistic culture in Paphos.[15]

Since the Jewish people were known in the Roman Empire for their depth of religious insight and wisdom,[16] we should not be surprised that the gentile Roman governor of all Cyprus, Sergius Paulus, employed a certain Bar-Jesus, a Jew, for counsel.

Bar-Jesus is described as both a magician and a Jewish false prophet. As a magician he "was a diviner who through various rituals claimed to be able to evoke the dead, including the shads or spirits of one's ancestors, and coupled with the word 'prophet' our text suggests that he claimed to be able to tell the future, perhaps through necromancy, perhaps through astrology or magic spells and rituals involving both."[17] The governor is listening to the wrong man for counsel, but he now summons the right men, Barnabas and Saul, to hear the word of the Lord. Traveling teachers gave orations so the governor, who is interested in Jewish—and generally

---

15. Keener, *Acts, Vol. 2*, 2007.
16. Witherington, *Acts of the Apostles*, 398.
17. Witherington, *Acts of the Apostles*, 396.

Eastern—religion, would want to listen to them if he had heard good reports about their visits in the synagogues in Paphos.[18]

Bar-Jesus opposes Saul and Barnabas because he knows that if Sergius Paulus receives their message, he will lose his livelihood and prestige as a man of spiritual power. Like Simon of Samaria (Acts 8:9–25), he is a man so filled with the powers of darkness, his very nature is to oppose the light and truth of the gospel.

Luke mentions at this point that Saul had another name, Paul, which he will use from now on because of his keen cultural sensitivity to his mission. Saul, a king of Israel and son of David, suited him well in his ministry among the Jewish people. But now that he will work more among gentiles, "Paul" fits better culturally, especially since in the Greco-Roman world, "Saul" (Saulos) referred to the seductive way of walking of a prostitute![19] Paul did not want his name to distract people from listening to his message. He had enough hardships in his ministry without his opponents yelling out in public, "Hey there's Saulos, still 'saulosing' around our streets."

The Holy Spirit fills Paul and Barnabas with power for their kingdom work. Bar-Jesus, by contrast, is "full of all deceit and villainy," an enemy of righteousness, and by his crooked ways seeks to keep the governor from the straight path of Jesus.

The scene is set for a power encounter. Paul, in the power of the Spirit, prophetically pronounces blindness on Bar-Jesus. The darkness that came over him may be a picture of how Bar-Jesus has kept the people in darkness.[20]

Paul's pronouncement of blindness recalls Peter's prophetic words of judgment on the false prophet, Simon of Samaria (Acts 8:20–24). As with Peter, so now with Paul, the Spirit of God advances the kingdom of God by empowering those he sends to defeat the forces of Satan (Luke 11:20). The kingdom does not advance without conflict but advance it does in the powerful name of the risen Lord Jesus.

While Paul had not been an apostate Jew as Bar-Jesus, he had been a vicious opponent of Jesus and was thus blinded by the Lord to contribute to his repentance. The Lord in his mercy transformed Saul. So, knowing the grace of God shown him, he may have hoped that Bar-Jesus' temporary blindness would lead him to see the truth of the risen Lord, but for

---

18. Keener, *Acts, Vol. 2*, 2008.
19. Leary, "Paul's Improper Name," 402.
20. Wall, *Acts of the Apostles*, 190.

now, the man who sought to guide the governor, Sergius Paulus, goes "about groping for someone to lead him by the hand" (Acts 13:11).

The story concludes with the outcome of the power encounter between two men who both claimed to have access to divine power and wisdom.[21] When the governor sees Bar-Jesus groping about blindly, reaching out for someone to lead him by the hand, and understands that this happened by the power of the risen Jesus (this seems to be the message about Jesus that astonished him), he believes the good news.

As the chief Roman official of Cyprus, Sergius Paulus's high social status would create a favorable climate for the faith to flourish in Paphos and across the island. His spacious living quarters would provide a place for the disciples to meet in Paphos. And his embracing the faith would have encouraged Paul and Barnabas that God would use them to reach gentiles in other urban centers of the empire.[22]

Sergius Paulus had wide family connections in Antioch Pisidia in central Turkey. So, when Paul and Barnabas sailed from Paphos's busy harbor to Asia Minor, they would at once travel through the interior to Antioch Pisidia, where they anticipated a good reception based on a letter of recommendation they likely carried with them from Sergius.[23]

A FOCUS ON TRAVEL BY LAND IN THE ROMAN EMPIRE

It is estimated that Paul's journeys in Acts alone covered at least twelve thousand miles (twenty thousand kilometers), and by our standards, "travel was arduous, miserable and long."[24] Paul's mission made him a traveler, and he was admired for both his fitness and courage as a traveler.

Reading Acts illustrates the importance of travel for fulfilling the command of Jesus to proclaim the good news to all nations (Acts 1:8). In fact, Luke organizes his narrative on the movement of the gospel from Jerusalem to Rome. While Acts is not a travel narrative

---

21. Witherington, *Acts of the Apostles*, 402.

22. Keener, *Acts, Vol. 2*, 2008. In that Acts ends with Paul in a Roman prison in Rome, Luke will show throughout Acts that the Roman authorities did not oppose Paul's message but at times embraced it, as with Sergius Paulus.

23. Witherington, *Acts of the Apostles*, 403.

24. Jeffers, *Greco-Roman World*, 35.

per se, first-century readers knew the hardships and dangers of travel and, like many today, read such stories with suspense.[25]

Many of Luke's original readers would have been able to visualize Paul's travels in Acts—possibly by personal experience but most often through shared knowledge. This means, for example, when Luke quickly mentions that Paul and Barnabas "went on from Perga to Antioch in Pisidia" (Acts 13:14a), his readers could envision their week-long walk north through the mountains to Antioch.

Just as we in America can visualize college students taking a road trip from New York to San Francisco—driving the interstate, pulling off the road at rest areas and restaurants, and looking for lodging at a motel or campground—Luke's readers could visualize the roads Paul and Barnabas walked and where they found lodging and food. We can read Acts with better understanding and suspense if we know how people traveled the Roman Empire.

As ordinary travelers Paul and Barnabas likely walked fifteen to twenty miles a day.[26] On this first journey, when they are often soon chased out of town, they spent more time walking than in ministry.[27]

Since I like to hike and camp, I have had to resist the temptation to romanticize Paul hiking through the mountains and sleeping in a tent by a warm fire. Paul didn't hike; he walked. He walked because that was how you got to where you wanted to go unless a ship could get you there faster.

I had traveled to Turkey to get a better feel for the terrain and the distances Paul walked. As I walked and read Acts, questions kept popping up, driving me to dig deep for answers. What were the roads like? Were they safe? Who else traveled them? What did Paul and his companions talk about while walking eight to ten hours a day, day after day? Where did they spend their nights and find food between cities? Here are some answers I found.

Roman roads were well designed and paved with large stones "to withstand the wear of hobnail boots and loaded wagons."[28] Superior to most roads in Europe until 1850, many of them are still there.[29] "Ro-

---

25. Keener, *Acts, Vol. 1*, 583.
26. Keener, *Acts, Vol. 1*, 597.
27. Jeffers, *Greco-Roman World.*, 36.
28. Jeffers, *Greco-Roman World*, 35.
29. Keener, *Acts, Vol. 1*, 586.

man roads were often initially military constructions ... designed for marching men to walk abreast, and the main ones carried wheeled vehicles ... They were ditched on either side and, at least near frontiers, the undergrowth was cleared for some distance on each side to deter ambushes."[30]

When military vehicles and merchants with their carts occupied the main road, pedestrians like Paul and Barnabas were forced to walk on an uneven two-foot-wide path to the side of the road. "Persons traveling long distances, such as the apostles, would carry a sack with food, a change of clothes and perhaps the tools of their trade. They would buy food in towns or from farmers along the way."[31] Paul carried his tools for making tents and other items from leather.

While travel on the main roads was relatively safe due to the presence of Roman soldiers, in the mountains, which Paul and Barnabas entered at least twice on this first journey, bands of highway men were common, and danger from robbers was always present.[32] While the wealthy could enjoy the safety of traveling in large and well-guarded caravans, the unguarded poor, like Paul and Barnabas, were easy prey.[33]

Paul later writes of his travels at this time, "I have traveled many weary miles. I have faced danger from flooded rivers and from robbers ... I have lived with weariness and pain and sleepless nights. Often, I have been hungry and thirsty and have gone without food. Often, I have shivered with cold, without enough clothing to keep me warm" (2 Cor 11:26–27 NLT).

The Romans believed that the gods—especially the god Hermes, deity of travelers—would protect them when traveling. At regular intervals of the road, Paul and Barnabas would have come across sacred monuments devoted to Hermes and other gods, reminding travelers to pray to them for protection. Paul and Barnabas likely looked away and prayed psalms of ascent that Jews prayed on pilgrimages to Jerusalem.

---

30. Clow, *St. Paul Trail*, 44.
31. Jeffers, *Greco-Roman World*, 36.
32. Keener, *Acts, Vol. 1*, 587.
33. Keener, *Acts, Vol. 1*, 585.

Travelers sought good companions for conversation on the road, and Paul and Barnabas found that in each other. They had been sent out by the Spirit as a team and their life with God and much else was in common. We easily forget that they walked together all day and at times day after day. What would they talk about? They probably talked about everyday matters such as the night's sleep, how they were feeling, the scenery, and where they could purchase food and lodge for the night. We can assume they spent good parts of the day encouraging each other, praying, singing songs of praise, discussing Scripture, and processing the events from the previous city.

They were not alone on the road. They shared the road and likely conversation at times with merchants, slaves with messages to deliver from their master, Roman soldiers, entertainers, and wealthy tourists.[34] "Other travelers included touring companies of actors, athletes and pilgrims headed to a religious festival or shrine and wandering philosophers."[35]

How would others size up Paul and Barnabas? Possibly as traveling sages, pilgrims, and possibly artisans, since Paul carried the tools of his leather trade. Once they learned of Paul and Barnabas's mission and message, it was harder to classify them. Jewish philosophers? Proponents of a new Jewish sect? There were likely many occasions for sharing the word on the road that Luke simply didn't have space to record on his scroll.

But where would they spend the nights? As a hiker and camper, I liked to envision them sleeping by a fire in a tent Paul had made, but it is doubtful they would carry a heavy leather tent day after day across the mountains, and it certainly would not be safe for sleeping in.

Once they had made disciples in a town, they could stay with them. But at this point on this journey there were none. So, they could stay in towns which afforded "a greater variety of restaurants, baths, and accommodations."[36] Yet the towns on the way up to Antioch were off the main road. So, the choice at this point seems to be to stay in an inn along the road.

Inns were spaced out along Roman roads based on how far people could travel in a day. There were larger inns for eating, many

---

34. Keener, *Acts, Vol. 1*, 588.
35. Jeffers, *Greco-Roman World*, 36.
36. Keener, *Acts, Vol. 1*, 587–88.

rooms for sleeping every eighteen to twenty-three miles, and smaller stations every ten miles, where one could find a bed and something to eat.[37]

But staying at inns could be a challenge for Paul and Barnabas. There simply may not be space available since inns were reserved first for those who traveled in the service of the empire—soldiers, dispatchers of government business, and the like. In addition, the owners charged exorbitant prices. There was a more spiritual challenge for Saul and Barnabas as devout Jews. Inns provided prostitutes, leading the innkeepers to be classified as pimps.[38] The inns doubled as brothels, "with sexual partners available, especially in the rooms."[39] So, would a devout Jew like Paul have stayed at an inn? What do you think?

Paul was a devout Jew but also a man now possessed by the Spirit of Jesus. Since he knew that many of the prostitutes may have been "throwaway babies raised as slaves"[40] and learned of the abuse they now received from the owners of the inns, the compassion of Christ for "prostitutes and sinners" must have moved him to not look away in disgust but to show compassion as he could.

So, I suggest that instead of hiking many miles out of their way to a town off the main road, Paul and Barnabas stayed in the inns. That's what I think.

37. Keener, *Acts, Vol. 1*, 587.
38. Keener, *Acts, Vol. 2*, 2415.
39. Keener, *Acts, Vol. 2*, 2416.
40. Keener, *Acts, Vol. 2*, 2416.

30

Paul's Gospel Sermon in Antioch Pisidia
(Acts 13:13–41)

THE DAY AFTER TRAVELING to Antioch I flew to Antalya (Attalia in Paul's day—Acts 14:26), which Paul and Barnabas sailed into from Cyprus after thirty hours out at sea. I would be alone until two of my daughters (Sonja and Daniela) joined me to travel north through the Turkish mountains to Antioch Pisidia.

Until they arrived, I spent time at the harbor Paul and Barnabas sailed into before walking or taking a small boat eight miles inland up to Perga (Acts 13:13). The ancient harbor they sailed from still sits nestled between two ridges jutting out into the sea.

For months I had eagerly studied maps to hike part of the Saint Paul Trail straight up the mountains to Antioch. While most scholars believe Paul and Barnabas likely walked around the mountains on their way up to Antioch, it seems they hiked straight down them on their way back to Perga (Acts 14:24–25). While traveling in a different direction, I would be hiking the same terrain as they did.

My daughters, Sonja and Daniela, joined me now, and after breakfast we loaded a rental car and slowly wormed our way out of the narrow, windy streets of the Old City. In thirty minutes, we were out of the city, and an hour later we were leaving the coastal plains to enter the mountains.

We found lodging in rooms with a view across a small meadow by a river winding its way along the foot of the mountains. Next to the river, Daniela spotted people walking a trail. It was the Roman road!

The following morning, we laced our hiking boots and packed a lunch and our trusted guidebook to hike the Saint Paul Trail. This part of the trail was especially difficult due to the steep mountain slopes and the precipitous gorge of the deep canyon.

Both Sonja and Daniela had braided their hair that morning and often stopped to pick wildflowers to artistically arrange in each other's hair. Watching them became the favorite memory of my trip.

We began our hike on the Roman road with the deep gorge to our left and the steep mountains rising directly beside us to our right. We soon came across a Greek inscription cut into the wall of the mountain rock with a niche for offerings to the gods for protection when traveling this way. The trail soon left the flat river valley straight up the mountains. We understood why the inscription was there.

Our trusty guidebook warned that the trail was faint on this stretch. We followed its switchbacks for an hour, but then the trail vanished. I pulled out the guidebook, sat on a rock, and read it one more time. "The faint path leaves the dried-up stream (which we never saw), then resumes zigzagging to a low stone wall, then turns slightly left to a shepherd's hut and the ruins of a fortification on the pass."[1]

How hard could it be to find a stone wall, a shepherd's hut, and the ruins of a stone fortification? We decided to split up and go separate directions to find the trail. No success. At times when I can't fit in the last piece of a puzzle, I become convinced that the manufacturers made the last piece wrong on purpose. Now I was convinced that someone had taken down the wall, the hut, and the fortification to build a house in the village—or that our guidebook had thrown in a few extra challenges to test our determination.

Esuga once shared with me some good African wisdom he had learned from his mother: "Don't let anyone rob you of your joy." Path or no path, I was out for a good hike with my daughters, and I was determined to enjoy it. So, with no path, we hiked straight up the mountain and found a spot with expansive views of the mountains and valleys beyond to enjoy our lunch.

---

1. Clow, *St. Paul Trail*, 65.

After lunch Daniela, one never to give up, decided to explore ahead. Ten minutes later she returned to tell us she had spotted the mark for Saint Paul Trail on a rock, the ruins of the fortification, and the pass through the mountains beyond. Should we press on? It would take another hour and a half to reach the summit, and it had started to rain. We decided against it.

The guidebook had warned of sudden rain and snow in the mountains at this time of the year, so I came prepared. I had carried my two-person tent all over Israel and Turkey so I could protect my daughters in case of cold beating rain on such an occasion as this.

The day had begun so warm and sunny, so I had left the tent in the trunk of the car. No choice but to head straight back down the mountain, slipping and sliding our way to the Roman road by the river.

That night I stood out on our balcony and looked toward the mountains through a pitch-black sky. And I thought of the incredible condition and courage Paul and Barnabas had to walk out there day after day. And I thought of them sleeping out there. Paul wouldn't have forgotten his tent.

A FOCUS ON ANTIOCH PISIDIA

Antioch was a Roman colony by the time of Paul's visit, providing its citizens with equal legal status to citizens in Rome. Its architecture and sculptures were breathtaking, on a par with those in Rome, so that it became recognized as a miniature Rome.[2] Built on seven hills in a mountainous region like Rome also contributed to Antioch being thought of as a little Rome.

The fertile countryside surrounding Antioch and its location on the Via Sebaste made Antioch relatively prosperous as an important commercial center in the region. A wall surrounded the 115 acres of the city proper with the greater area consisting of 540 square miles, making it large for a city in the hill country.

Recognizing its importance as a fortress city on the border with good views to the north, south, and west, Roman soldiers had been settled there to keep the surrounding mountainous area under

---

2. Pearson, "Antioch," 32.

Roman control.³ Antioch was also the home of a good many first-century senators and other high-ranking Romans.⁴

"As elsewhere in the Empire, residents of Antioch worshipped multiple deities. Yet two objects of worship thoroughly dominated their attention."⁵ The first was the city's patron deity, the god Men. Worshipers of this cult ascended a steep hill to his temple for an hour's climb just south of Antioch.⁶ Reliefs and coins typically portrayed Men "wearing a Phrygian cap and cloak, with a crescent moon behind his shoulders, carrying a pinecone and often a cock."⁷

The worship of Augustus and his family was more important to the many Roman citizens in Antioch. "The city center was dominated by a vast complex of buildings focused on the imperial cult."⁸ The temple, built to the emperor, dominated the city high on a hill at the end of a long colonnaded street and could be seen for miles when approaching the city on the Via Sebaste. "The imperial cult, with its civic celebrations on special days and months (cf. Gal 4:10), regulated much public life in Antioch."⁹

Because Antioch was a Roman colony, and most of its citizens were proud Romans, they were "eager to demonstrate their loyalty in the city's imperial temple."¹⁰ With the temple only recently completed around the time of Paul's arrival to the city, religious fervor for the emperor must have run high.

Augustus had inscribed on the public buildings in Antioch and elsewhere in the empire significant portions of "the remarkable work Res Gestae, 'Matters Accomplished,' to point out who was in charge and the 'religious' implications of the new imperial reality. Caesar and Rome were the central focus of worship, a worship that would bind together the city and the region and give it security by linking it so obviously to its ultimate patron."¹¹

3. Jeffers, *Greco-Roman World*, 276.
4. Wright, *Paul*, 117.
5. Keener, *Acts, Vol. 2*, 2041.
6. Keener, *Acts, Vol. 2*, 2041
7. Keener, *Acts, Vol. 2*, 2041
8. Wright, *Paul*, 117.
9. Keener, *Acts, Vol. 2*, 2042.
10. Keener, *Acts, Vol. 2*, 2042.
11. Wright, *Paul*, 118.

> Paul entered a city built by Rome on a road built by Rome where most of the citizens are fiercely loyal to Rome and worship the emperor as a god, but he knows he carries with him the seed of the gospel that will grow and one day displace emperor worship. He will proclaim Jesus as Lord of all and Savior to all who seek him. As the Prince of Peace, he will unite all who turn to him. Paul knows that proclaiming this gospel will be a direct challenge to emperor worship and will be dangerous. For this reason, Paul will not directly speak out in the marketplace against emperor worship, but eventually Rome will understand the implications of Paul's challenge for all peoples to give their allegiance to Jesus alone as Lord, and it will cost him his life in Rome on a cross built by Rome.

CONTINUING TO ANTIOCH

After our short adventure hiking the Roman road, we drove north to Antioch. The road followed the valleys between the mountains, passing farms and a few villages where we at times received curious stares. We pressed on until we reached the plateau of rolling hills outside of Antioch. All hikers know the relief of sighting level ground after hours hiking up and down mountains. After walking twenty miles a day for six days, Paul and Barnabas would have been relieved to spot level terrain.

While we drove up to the ruins of Antioch from the south, Paul and Barnabas approached the city on the Via Sebaste from the northwest. Even though the city looked like it was built on a plateau, it was built on seven hills, like Rome.[12] Walking the 12-foot-wide (3.5 m), well-paved road built for military vehicles, Paul and Barnabas would have seen from miles away the recently completed temple dedicated to the worship of the emperor elevated on the then highest hill of the city.[13] What went through their minds when they first saw the temple?

We parked our car at the southern entrance of ancient Antioch. Sonja, always the artist, grabbed a coffee and parked herself on a bench in a nearby garden to sketch sites from the trip while Daniela and I explored the ruins of Antioch.

12. Keener, *Acts, Vol. 2*, 2038.
13. Keener, *Acts, Vol. 2*, 2042.

As we entered the southern gate, we immediately came to the ruins of small shops lining each side of the street. The shops would have been covered with leather canopies to shield workers and customers from sun and rain. As a potter I always look up other potters selling their ceramic pieces at craft fairs, so I imagined Paul stopping to converse with artisans like himself who made leather products. Later in Acts, after Paul stayed in a city for several years, he set up shop on a street such as this beside other artisans (Acts 18:1–3).

Figure 8: Shop Area in Antioch Pisidia.
This photo by unknown author is licensed under CC BY-SA.

Daniela and I hurried up the hill near the western gate that Paul and Barnabas had entered. Near it we found the ruins of the fourth-century church built over the synagogue where Paul had proclaimed the good news (Acts 13:14).

The synagogue, elevated on one of Antioch's seven hills, was easy for Paul and Barnabas to locate when they entered the city at the western gate. Luke writes that Paul's first message in the synagogue stirred so much interest that on "the next Sabbath almost the whole city gathered to hear the word of the Lord" (Acts 13:44).

While Daniela went on to see the aqueduct outside the city, I stood at what would have been the entrance to the synagogue and imagined the hundreds upon hundreds of people approaching the synagogue, crowding into it and standing outside eager to learn more about Jesus, the promised Messiah.

From the synagogue I hurried south down the main street, past the ruins of Roman baths and the Palestra to the temple built to the emperor Augustus. It was built on a hill at the very opposite side of the city from the synagogue, just as the Jewish people would have liked it.

Here temple sacrifices were made to the emperor, worshiping him as Lord and Savior, the source of peace for the empire. I was keen to visit the temple to the emperor knowing that the true Lord and Savior, the Prince of Peace, upended the myth of peace by military might.

Like the ancients, I approached the temple walking up a lengthy staircase, which led to the temple court. The temple itself came into view at the far end of a large courtyard with splendid two-story colonnades surrounding it. The temple itself was small, but its setting was constructed to cause awe and mystery for worshipers.

In front of the temple were the remains of a large stone altar where priests sacrificed animals to the emperor. I carefully walked up the twelve steep stairs of the temple and looked down into the remains of the temple. Only dirt and broken stones.

I thought again of how Jesus had become our source for peace, not the military might of Rome's emperors. But then I thought how many Christians today still put their faith in their governments and military might to make the world a better place for them rather than trusting in the Ruler of all and his way of making peace. And I was sad.

While Paul and Barnabas would have had no reason to go near the emperor's temple, they could not have missed its towering presence in Antioch and seen it as a constant reminder of why the Spirit of Jesus had sent them out on mission.

JOHN MARK LEAVES THE TEAM (ACTS 13:13–15)

When the mission team came to Perga in Pamphylia, a region more familiar to Paul, he is the natural person to lead. Not only is he the more experienced traveler, having grown up in Tarsus of Cilicia and having spent the ten years before his year in Antioch Syria more exposed to gentile culture, but he also knows the language and customs of the land better than Barnabas.

Before they leave for Antioch, Luke injects that when they came to Perga, John left them and returned to Jerusalem. This is the John Mark that Luke has already mentioned twice. Who was he and why did he travel with Paul and Barnabas? More important, why did he suddenly leave the team, and what impact did that have on Paul and Barnabas?

John Mark was first mentioned as the son of a widow named Mary, and he belonged to the strong community of disciples who met in their house in Jerusalem (Acts 12:12). He was a devout young disciple and *a cousin of Barnabas* (Col 4:10). These may be the reasons that Barnabas (who first led the team), and Paul brought John Mark back with them from Jerusalem to help in their work at Antioch Syria and now to assist them on their mission (Acts 12:25).

He is also mentioned assisting them in Cyprus (Acts 13:5) as an apprentice in their work. As a younger apprentice, John Mark was a good traveling companion, helping to carry extra luggage, helping with travel arrangements, purchasing food and other supplies, and generally assisting in the ministry.[14]

We do not know why he left (or deserted them to use Paul's words in Acts 15:38), but it was not for a legitimate reason such as a serious illness. The verb used for his departing is often used for "leaving due to fear."[15] Paul experienced it as desertion. To abandon a mentor was an expression of unfaithfulness. True friends remained loyal even in adversity.[16]

Later Barnabas would want to give Mark another chance and took him with him on a second journey, but Paul still would not be ready (Acts 15:37–38).

Paul and Barnabas now traveled alone, likely with initial disappointment in feeling deserted, and headed north to Antioch Pisidia. Once they arrived, they found housing and on the following Sabbath went to the synagogue where the Jewish population of the city gathered.

---

14. Wright, *Paul*, 116.
15. Keener, *Acts, Vol. 2*, 2031.
16. Keener, *Acts, Vol. 2*, 2031.

A FOCUS ON THE SYNAGOGUES

Paul made it his practice in every city to first go to his Jewish brethren and teach in their synagogues. While synagogues could be found in public buildings, like many Roman associations, they were most often located in houses with the normal layout and façade of private homes.[17] They consisted of a simple room with "stone benches along the walls . . . reserved for dignitaries. The general congregation may have sat on mats or carpets."[18]

Since only ten adult Jewish men were required for a synagogue, they could be relatively small, connected communities. In cities with larger Jewish populations such as Rome and Antioch Syria, there may have been up to a dozen or more synagogues. As Jewish communities grew both in size and wealth, they may also have met in larger public buildings.[19]

Synagogues functioned primarily as places of prayer and instruction in the Scriptures. In addition, funds were collected in synagogues to set aside for poorer members. Legal rulings were made there by the synagogue elders. New arrivals to a city would seek out the synagogue to find fellowship to connect with those of the same trade. This is how Paul likely met Priscilla and Aquila, who also worked with leather (Acts 18:2).

Because any competent person could be called upon to address the assembly, as a Jewish man educated in Jerusalem, it was natural for Paul to be called upon to deliver a word of exhortation in Antioch (Acts 13:15).

Paul did not "infiltrate" synagogues as a "Christian" to steal sheep from the Jews. Paul was a Jew through and through and went to other Jews to share with them the fulfillment of *their* Scriptures by *their* Messiah. Despite rejection and persecution in city after city from his fellow Jews, Paul continued to go to them first because salvation was promised first of all to them.

At the same time Paul realized the strategic importance of the synagogue for spreading the good news. For centuries the Jewish people had been scattered everywhere across the empire so that in

---

17. Yamauchi, "Synagogues," 1149.
18. Yamauchi, "Synagogues," 1146.
19. Jeffers, *Greco-Roman World*, 216.

the first century, 4 to 6 million Jews of nearly every social class lived in the diaspora, with only 2.5 million in Palestine.[20] In this we see the hand of God preparing the nations to receive his salvation. Paul saw God's wisdom and acted upon it.

When the synagogue officials learned (by their clothing and accent?) that Paul and Barnabas, learned men, had spent much time in Jerusalem, they invited them to give a message of encouragement. Paul welcomed the opportunity, but to their surprise, his address became more than the normal moral exhortation they expected.

PAUL'S MESSAGE (ACTS 13:16–41)

This is the first of Paul's gospel messages recorded in Acts and well worth careful reading. While it may seem long and involved, you will be able to understand much of it from your careful reading of Peter's sermons. In my comments I will limit myself to unique points in Paul's message.

Luke includes the most important details of Paul's message so that we know what Paul said later when Luke writes of what Paul said when he visited synagogues throughout the empire. In addition to the message, Luke also records here, in more detail, Paul's practice of first going to the Jewish community in each city he visited and the reaction he received from them. When most of the Jewish people rejected the message of Jesus as their Messiah, Paul then went to the gentiles, who were more receptive.

As a Jew addressing his fellow Jews, Paul's message at Antioch was similar in many ways to Peter's messages. He showed how the message of Jesus is rooted in God's promises to Israel. Paul did not preach a new faith but a fulfilled faith, the fulfillment of God's plan for Israel and all humanity.

Though Paul, like Peter and Stephen, began by emphasizing God's choice of Israel (Acts 13:17–20), he quickly moved on to God's promises to King David of a descendent who would receive an eternal kingdom. The leading point of Paul's speech (Acts 13:21–24) became *"the descendant of David, Israel's Savior, has come and now reigns as Lord over God's kingdom!"*

All Jews knew that their hope for God's eternal kingdom on earth hinged on the coming of their Messiah, a descendant of David, coming to rescue them. What they did not expect was for their Messiah to be

---

20. Jeffers, *Greco-Roman World*, 218.

crucified on a Roman cross. For this reason, Paul would first emphasize how the death of Jesus the Messiah was God's plan for defeating the real enemies of God's will on earth, the forces of evil all around us and the darkness within us that we are not able to overcome on our own. Only after the Messiah's victory over sin did he enter his reign as Lord over God's kingdom.

Paul first spoke in detail of the death of Jesus (alluded to five times in Acts 13:27–29), then the resurrection of Jesus to reign over God's kingdom (Acts 13:30–37) before returning to the death of Jesus to explain its meaning (Acts 13:38–39).

The Death of Jesus (Acts 13:27–29, 38–39)

Paul began by linking the salvation God promised Israel to Jesus' death and resurrection (Acts 13:26). Like Peter, he emphasized that though the residents and leaders of Jerusalem took the lead in having Jesus crucified, they unknowingly carried out God's plan. Now Paul explains the meaning of Jesus' death.

In verse 29 Paul says Jesus was taken "down from the tree," not the cross as we would expect. His choice of the word tree recalls Deut 21:22–23, where we read that anyone hung on a tree was under God's curse. This means that Jesus, the righteous One who lived without sin, carried the curse of all our sins on the cross so that we could be forgiven. Thus, like Peter, Paul said, "through this man forgiveness of sins is proclaimed" (Acts 13:38).

Paul then added a second important result of Jesus' death not taught by Peter or anyone else in Acts. He said, "By this Jesus everyone who believes is set free from all those sins from which you could not be freed by the law of Moses" (Acts 13:39). There is a setting free from sin by the death of Jesus. His death for us not only provides forgiveness for sin but also frees us from the power of sin, so that by God's Spirit we can obey God in a way never possible by following the law of Moses (see Rom 8:1–4).

Paul's emphasis on freedom from living by the law of Moses would cause fierce reactions from the more conservative disciples in Jerusalem, "the circumcised party" (Acts 11:2–3), when they learned of it.

The Resurrection and Installation of Jesus as Lord (Acts 13:30–37)

Paul then showed how the salvation promised to Israel had been fulfilled by God's raising Jesus from the dead to make him Lord over his kingdom (Acts 13:32–33). The promise of salvation is tied to Ps 2, which all Jews knew spoke of God's promising a kingdom over all the earth to a descendent of David. Peter had made it clear in his message at Pentecost that Jesus was installed as Lord over God's kingdom when he was raised from the dead (Acts 2:36). Paul taught the same good news: the king God promised to Israel now reigns as Lord at God's right hand.

The resurrection of Jesus and his installation as Lord at God's right hand are linked in Acts. Jesus' resurrection in Acts is a code word for why he was raised: to be made Lord over all. At his exaltation to God's Presence, sharing God's glory, Jesus entered the full experience of his messianic destiny. It was then that he fulfilled "the holy promises made to David" (Acts 13:34) of providing the longed-for salvation.

For support, Paul quotes Ps 2:7—"You are my Son; today I have begotten you"—as a prediction that the messianic son of David would be installed as King over the ends of the earth. Paul, along with Peter and the first disciples, believed that Jesus was "begotten" in the royal sense of being installed as Lord or King over God's kingdom. "Begotten" in the ancient Near East was used for "a god" adopting a person to rule as his King on earth.

Thus, Ps 2 refers to the day when David's descendant is coronated as King and "designated or recognized to be God's son."[21] Jesus was already the promised Messiah at his birth, but he only began his official rule as Messiah over God's kingdom at his exaltation (Acts 2:26).

This is what Paul writes in Romans when he says that Jesus was declared (or, appointed) "to be the Son of God with power" at his resurrection (Rom 1:2–3). Jesus became the Son of God *with new resurrection power as he entered his kingly reign becoming Lord of all.*

---

21. Witherington, *Acts of the Apostles*, 412.

31

The Response in Antioch
(Acts 13:42–52)

AFTER PAUL WARNED HIS listeners to not ignore God's saving work through Jesus (Acts 13:41), the people urged him to return the next Sabbath and continue teaching. It seems many Jews, along with gentiles devoted to Judaism, had already accepted the message, for as they left the synagogue and walked with Paul and Barnabas through the city, they were encouraged to continue in the gracious work of God.

It is safe to assume Paul and Barnabas met with these new disciples and their relatives throughout the week, teaching and encouraging them, and from this, Paul's teaching spread throughout the week in all Antioch. For we read that the following Sabbath nearly the whole city gathered to hear him teach the message about Jesus.

When unbelieving Jews saw the large crowd packed into the synagogue to listen to Paul, they were filled with jealousy. Their jealousy reminds us of the Sanhedrin's jealousy of Jesus and then the apostles when the crowds flocked to hear them in the temple. Jealousy at the success of others is a common human failing, even for religious leaders.[1]

They charged Paul with teaching blasphemy, just as Stephen had been charged. The charge of blasphemy was likely due to believing Paul taught a cheap, watered-down message to gentiles, centered on allegiance to Jesus rather than following the Jewish law. The leaders of the synagogue had labored hard to convince gentiles attending the synagogue

---

1. Peterson, *Acts of the Apostles*, 397.

to be circumcised, renounce their own ethnic identity, and live like the Jewish people. Now Paul and Barnabas show up in Antioch undermining their efforts.[2]

We then read of what becomes *a pattern in Acts*. Because the promises of salvation were given to Israel, the gospel is always offered first to them, but when (as we read now) most of the Jewish people reject it, Paul and Barnabas turn to the gentiles. The Lord has called Paul to take the good news also to gentiles, for it has always been his intention to make his salvation known among the nations (Acts 13:47).

When the gentiles in Antioch heard that they could receive eternal (salvation) by turning to Jesus, they were filled with joy and praised God. In sharp contrast, unbelieving Jews incited civic leaders in Antioch against Paul and Barnabas. These leaders drove them from the region after less than two weeks in the city. They must leave the new disciples for now, but they are not alone, for God's Spirit remains and lives in them, filling them with joy.

Before continuing with the next leg of their journey, I want to share why the Jews and gentiles who did not believe responded as they did to Paul's message.[3]

First, why did most of Paul's fellow Jews reject the gospel? Paul had violently persecuted the Jesus movement, so he must have known that many Jews would also oppose it, even with violence. There were several reasons for their opposition. To begin with, "Nobody had ever heard of a *crucified* Messiah."[4] The Messiah was expected to conquer Israel's enemies, not be crucified by them.

In addition, the Jewish people could not ever imagine that the greater part of them would not be part of God's kingdom. Yet Paul warns that if they do not turn to Jesus to be rescued, they will be excluded from the kingdom promised for them.

If this was not enough to get Paul and Barnabas driven out of city after city, Paul also teaches that because of Jesus, gentiles can be equal members in God's kingdom—and without following the Jewish law! If he were truly a devout Jewish teacher, how could he violate the Jewish law by bringing Jews and gentiles together into the same house, eating and worshiping together as equal members of God's new community?[5]

2. Keener, *Acts, Vol. 2*, 2095.
3. Much of the following is taken from Wright, *Paul*, 2008.
4. Wright, *Paul*, 120.
5. Wright, *Paul*, 120.

What would be the challenges for unbelieving gentiles? It must have seemed strange to them that the God of the Jews demanded their allegiance to a Jewish man from the remote part of the empire, a man crucified by their authorities, a man Paul claims was raised from the dead, to be made Lord over all things!

Paul did not simply say Jesus is a Jewish King over the nation of Israel. That they could accept. Paul proclaimed Jesus was to be worshiped as Lord over all the nations of the earth. This meant that gentiles must abandon idol worship, which held the Roman Empire together. Even worse, "Paul was deliberately finding ways to make the point: there is one 'Lord,' one Kyrios, and it isn't Caesar."[6]

Wright points out that announcing Jesus as Lord was not a religious statement inviting gentiles to a new religious experience among many in the empire. *Confessing Jesus is Lord was (and always is!) not only a spiritual claim but also a political and social claim.*[7]

Challenging gentiles to give their sole allegiance to Jesus as their Lord was *a political statement* because that meant they would no longer worship Caesar as Lord and Savior of the empire. The gospel was not political in the sense that the Way of Jesus was made law and forced on others. However, it was political in the sense that wholehearted allegiance is given to Jesus and his teaching, even if that means disobeying Caesar!

Paul now knew that Jesus would not reign from Jerusalem as Israel's King. Instead, until he returns to make all things right, the reign of the Messiah is established among the nations as his Spirit works in and through small house communities of Jews and gentiles meeting together as one family to find ways among their neighbors to live the Way of the kingdom. So, announcing Jesus is Lord was also *a social statement* as Paul sought to establish a new kind of society right at the heart of the existing systems.[8]

Even though Paul did not encourage disciples to tear down statues of Caesar, gentiles knew that these "strange new subversive teachings . . . might upset the delicate social and cultural status quo" in their cities.[9] The Jewish people had the privilege, unique in the empire, of not being required to worship the Roman gods. But what would happen if large numbers of gentiles ask for the same exemption? This could lead to

---

6. Wright, *Paul*, 112.
7. Wright, *Paul*, 106.
8. Wright, *Paul*, 106.
9. Wright, *Paul*, 121.

real civic upheaval because the worship of the Roman gods, and Caesar was the glue that held the empire together.

I've often wondered what went through Paul's mind when he walked into a Roman city such as Antioch to proclaim the good news. In time he became prepared for the reactions he would receive, and they did not daunt him, for in every city he saw the Spirit of God transform hearts through the message of Christ crucified, and he believed he carried with him the life and message that would slowly transform societies and one day cover the earth. Whether he was driven out of town, jailed, or stoned, Paul always got up, put on his sandals, and walked to the next city.

He and Barnabas now walk southeast for four days on the Via Sebaste to Iconium. It is closer to Paul's home province of Cilicia but separated "by the difficult passage across the Taurus mountains."[10]

---

10. Keener, *Acts, Vol. 2*, 2115. The Via Sebaste had been built some 50 years earlier so that ruts in the road, caused by wagons transporting the Roman military, or carts pulling the goods of merchants, were now noticeable. The Via Sebaste made a major loop from Perge in the south where Paul and Barnabas began their journey up to Antioch in the north before continuing south as they now walk to Iconium, Lystra and on. The Via Sebaste was the only major road through the central mountains of Turkey.

32

To Iconium, Lystra, and Derbe
(Acts 14:1–20)

WHEN PAUL AND BARNABAS visit Lystra, they encounter an idolatry found all over the empire. Paul challenges the idol worshipers to "turn from these worthless things to the living God" (Acts 14:15). While most in the modern world do not make idols out of wood or stone to set up as shrines in their homes, still, since idol worship has been prevalent throughout the history of humankind, we can assume its "unseen" practice even today.

If an idol is anything we rely on, or give our lives to for ultimate meaning, for prosperity, for power, for guidance, for security, for peace about our future (see these functions of idol worship in Roman religion), then we can identify the unseen idolatry that permeates our modern world.

We can also take our lead in identifying our unseen idols from Jesus, who said we cannot serve both God and wealth (Luke 16:13) (the word "serve" suggests idolatry), and later Paul, who wrote that greed is idolatry (Col 3:5). If our hearts are consumed with greed, the insatiable pursuit of material gain (money, land, or possessions); status; or power, then there is no room for God or for fulfilling his will to help others.

Some suggested questions to help identify our potential unseen idols:

- What do we trust in to hold our life together?
- What do we build our lives on?

- What do we trust in for our security both now and in the future?
- How do we seek guidance through life?
- Do we put our trust in a political ideology, a strong military, and a strong economy for our prosperity and peace of mind?

TO ICONIUM (14:1–7)[1]

Luke begins by saying "the same things occurred in Iconium" (present-day Konya) that had just happened in Antioch (Acts 14:1). As he writes about the continued outward expansion of the gospel, "he draws parallels and makes connections with previous narratives, but also highlights the distinctive features relevant to each new context."[2] There is no need for unnecessary repetition.

As for the parallels, Paul and Barnabas first go to the Jewish synagogue in Iconium and proclaim the message of life, just as they had in Antioch, and we can assume Paul spoke a message like that in Antioch, for he received a similar response. Though many Jews and gentiles believed, unbelieving Jews stirred up opposition to the extent that the whole city was divided. Those are the parallels.

As to the distinctive features of their work in Iconium, there is the minor point that they were able to stay longer in Iconium than in Antioch (Acts 14:3). A second added feature is that the Lord granted "signs and wonders to be done through them" (Acts 14:3). Did this contribute to their being able to spend considerable time there? Signs and wonders were done through Paul wherever he went, and Luke may only remind us of them here.

By far the most distinctive feature of their time in Iconium is *the escalation of violence* against them. Now *both Jews and gentiles,* along with the local authorities, sought to stone Paul and Barnabas to death. They had been driven out of Antioch, but now in Iconium they are forced to

---

1. After visiting Antioch, Sonja and Daniela were weary of Roman ruins and wanted to spend their last few days in Istanbul. I had originally planned to drive on alone to see Iconium, Lystra, and Derbe but had grown weary of traveling and wanted to spend all my remaining time with my daughters. Still, I include some interesting details about these towns in my comments.

2. Peterson, *Acts of the Apostles*, 401.

flee for their lives. This is at least the third attempt on Paul's life so far (Acts 9:23–25, 29–30).[3]

The increased persecution seems only to increase their boldness and resolve in proclaiming the good news of Jesus. Jesus had told Paul he would suffer greatly in taking the gospel to the gentiles (Acts 9:16), so they were not surprised. They do not flee Iconium due to cowardice but to continue to proclaim the good news.

TO LYSTRA (ACTS 14:8–20)

Paul and Barnabas flee Iconium first to go to Lystra, a town in the new political district of Lyconia where they cannot be charged by local officials for anything done in Antioch or Iconium. Lystra was only twenty to twenty-five miles southwest of Iconium, but the walking would have been difficult due to the cold, poorly watered plateaus devoid of trees.[4] As they approached Lystra from the hills to the north, they would have welcomed the sight of it elevated on a higher hill yet.[5]

Augustus founded Lystra as a sister colony to Antioch with about a thousand Roman colonists to guard the Via Sebaste highway.[6] A more prominent native element remained in the hills alongside the Roman colonists. We will see that this led to difficulties in communicating the gospel in Lystra, for few people there knew Greek (which Paul spoke), and Paul's Latin was not yet adequate to speak with the Roman colonists. Of course, his knowledge of the native Lycaonian language was nonexistent.[7]

Just when we think the story might start repeating itself, with Paul going to another synagogue to address the Jews, we read that he speaks in the marketplace to gentile countryfolk. Apparently Lystra did not have the ten Jewish men required to form a synagogue. The events in Lystra are distinct in other ways.

Paul has recently proclaimed the gospel to Jews in Antioch by reveiwing Israel's history, showing how Jesus has fulfilled the promises to

---

3. As we continue in Acts, we will see that Paul made it his practice to stay longer in a city to build up those who came to faith. But on this first journey his stays were cut short due to persecution.
4. Keener, *Acts, Vol. 2*, 2128.
5. Keener, *Acts, Vol. 2*, 2129.
6. Keener, *Acts, Vol. 2*, 2128.
7. Keener, *Acts, Vol. 2*, 2145.

Israel. Now Paul must address gentiles with no knowledge of that history; thus he skillfully adapts his approach. Another difference in the events at Lystra is the mass confusion that erupts when Paul shares the gospel in this remote, interior region where few people were proficient in Greek. Finally, many native people in backwater Lystra show themselves to be gullible, fickle, and superstitious.

While the events in Lystra differ from those in Antioch and Iconium, Luke begins by drawing a parallel between the healing of a man crippled from birth by Paul and the healing of the lame beggar by Peter in early Acts (Acts 3:1–10). This healing not only illustrates the signs and wonders done through Paul and Barnabas (Acts 14:3), but more significantly it emphasizes that just as the exalted Lord attested the witness of Peter and the apostles with signs and wonders among the Jews, so now he attests the witness of Paul and Barnabas with signs and wonders among the gentiles.

Since there was no synagogue in Lystra, Paul speaks to a small crowd out in the marketplace, perhaps near the city gate, where people would gather and a crippled man was likely to beg.[8] Likely speaking in Greek through an interpreter, it seems Paul has had time to speak of Jesus and his power to save and to heal. As a man, crippled from birth, sits and listens, the Spirit enables Paul to see that he has faith to be healed. When the man is healed, he jumps up and moves about, gathering an even larger crowd, much like what had happened when the lame beggar was healed by Peter in the temple.

Witnessing the healing of the crippled man they knew so well and listening to Paul, the chief speaker, speak fluently in Greek, the crowd concludes that he is the god Hermes, "chief in speech among the deities, . . . the chief messenger of the gods, . . . a deity of crafty and eloquent speech."[9] Barnabas, they conclude, must then be Zeus, for the two were often paired and worshiped together throughout Asia Minor, especially in the region of Lystra.[10]

Convinced that Barnabas is the god Zeus and Paul the god Hermes, the crowd cries out, "The gods have come down to us in human form!" (Acts 14:11). But something more significant than the healing of the crippled man and Paul's fluent Greek led them to believe Paul and Barnabas were gods. A local legend, widely known even outside the region, lived

8. Keener, *Acts, Vol. 2*, 2154.
9. Keener, *Acts, Vol. 2*, 2151.
10. Keener, *Acts, Vol. 2*, 2150.

in the collective psyche of the native people of Lystra. "The Latin poet Ovid . . . had earlier recorded the legend of a visit by the supreme God Jupiter (Zeus to the Greeks) and his son Mercury (Hermes) to this area, disguised as mortals and seeking lodging. But according to the legend, a majority of the people did not receive Zeus and Hermes who promptly destroyed their houses."[11]

Coupling this legend with the miraculous healing and Paul's powerful speech led the superstitious Lacaonians to conclude that the gods Zeus and Hermes had returned to their city in human form. This time they would welcome them and worship them with sacrifices in order to not again meet their wrath.

As they shout out in their native language (which Paul and Barnabas do not understand), "The gods have come down to us in human form," someone apparently runs to the priest of Zeus, who has a temple dedicated to him just outside the city gates, for the priest soon arrives with oxen, an expensive and thus important sacrifice. The crowd is ready to sacrifice to Paul and Barnabas as the great gods Zeus and Hermes!

Those who have experienced the mass confusion of a crowd speaking different languages can sympathize with the panic and confusion Paul and Barnabas must have felt. Finally, when someone in the crowd explains to them in Greek what is about to happen, they tear their clothes, symbolizing that the greatest of all blasphemies is about to occur. Imagine the horror that went through the heads of these two devout monotheistic Jewish apostles when they realized they were about to be worshiped and sacrificed to as gods!

They try as best they can to communicate that they are normal human beings. They are not gods but have come to share the good news of salvation that comes by turning from lifeless, powerless idols ("worthless things") to the true living God.

Paul then shows his ability to adapt how he communicated the gospel to diverse audiences. He provides us with a good example of knowing both the gospel message and the audience so well that we can find common ground for spiritual conversations.

Reviewing the history of Israel to show its fulfillment in Jesus would only confuse those who did not know it, and speaking of Jesus first required belief in "the living God, who made the heaven and the earth and the sea and all that is in them" (Acts 14:15). So, Paul begins with God

---

11. Peterson, *Acts of the Apostles*, 408.

and how he has revealed his goodness and care for all humanity in his creation. He continues saying that up until this point in history, God has "allowed all the (gentile) nations to follow their own ways" (Acts 14:16). Paul will later address gentiles in Athens in a similar way, saying, "While God has overlooked the times of human ignorance, now he commands all people everywhere to repent . . . (Acts 17:30)." But what does Paul mean by God previously allowing gentiles to follow their own ways and overlooking their ignorance?

Up until this time God has been more specifically engaged with the people of Israel, appearing to their ancestors, giving them his law, caring for them in their land, and promising them salvation at the end of the ages.

While God revealed his existence and goodness through creation to all the nations, he was not as actively engaged with them as with Israel.[12] In Romans we read gentiles were responsible for the revelation of God's existence and goodness seen in his creation (Rom 1:19–20), but they were not held accountable for all God had revealed only to his people Israel.[13]

Now a new time had come when God sent his disciples to all peoples with the full and complete revelation of salvation through Jesus. Thus, the time of ignorance had come to an end "so far as those who hear the gospel are concerned."[14]

The gentiles in Antioch, Iconium, and now Lystra, who have witnessed the power of God through their miracles, listened to Paul and Barnabas speak of the power of God's Spirit of salvation through Jesus and witnessed lives transformed by their message, no longer having any excuse for their ignorance.

Paul tried as best he could in the mass confusion to tell the crowd (presumably with the help of someone who knew some Greek) to turn to the living God and would have wanted to continue to tell them the story of Jesus as he had in the marketplace (Acts 14:9), but the deep-rooted superstitions of the crowd kept them from listening to Paul. They keep pressing on with their attempts to sacrifice to him and Barnabas as the gods Hermes and Zeus.

Then suddenly, unbelieving Jews from Antioch and Iconium finally found Paul in Lystra and wanted to carry out their earlier failed attempt to stone him to death. Since they knew the culture, and some of them

---

12. Bock, *Acts*, 478.
13. Marshall, *Acts of the Apostles*, 239.
14. Marshall, *Acts of the Apostles*, 290.

from nearby Iconium knew the native language, they had a clear advantage and could win the crowd over to their side.

They convinced the fickle, superstitious crowd, claiming these foreigners had not come to town as gods but as magicians (their explanation for the healing of the crippled man). They are not gods. They seek to turn you away from your gods! Paul and Barnabas could have also been accused of not serving the Jewish God but rather of serving the dark spiritual forces to gain power over the town.

It is so pitiful to see unbelieving Jews join forces with pagan idol worshipers to persecute fellow Jews. It is equally pitiful to see the fickle crowd so quickly turn from sacrificing to Paul and Barnabas as gods to stoning Paul to supposed death. Urban mobs were all over the empire, so it is not surprising to see one quickly formed for vengeance against Paul for feeling deceived.[15]

Once the mob returned to town supposing Paul to be dead, a few disciples gather around him and pray for him to be healed. The Lord had worked a remarkable miracle through Paul when he came to Lystra. Now he works one on Paul's broken and bruised body, answering the prayers of these young disciples, strong in faith! Paul is healed and with the help of the disciples gets up to return in secret to Lystra to spend the night in the house of a disciple.

Because the walk back to Iconium took a day, his persecutors from Antioch and Iconium likely also spent the night in Lystra, but believing Paul was dead, they would not have been looking for him. Because the mob action they incited was illegal, they might not have wanted to risk it again in the same town, even if they had learned he was alive.[16]

Paul's return to the town shows he would not act cowardly and abandon the disciples. His miraculous rescue and courageous example to return to them would strengthen them to also endure persecutions for Christ, and their care and prayers for him contributed to his continued recovery so he could leave for Derbe the next day. Later, Paul would remind those very disciples that the scars on his body from this stoning show that he belongs to Jesus (Gal 6:17).

Paul was in his mid-thirties, strong and fit, but no one's body is strong enough to recover so quickly from the battering of stones his body received. The power of God restored him.

---

15. Keener, *Acts, Vol. 2*, 2173.
16. Keener, *Acts, Vol. 2*, 2177.

The following day Paul does what he always does. Just like when Jesus was driven from a village, he got up and went to the next one to proclaim the arrival of God's kingdom. A year or so later Paul would return to Lystra and find a young disciple named Timothy, whom he would take with him on his second journey (Acts 16:1–3).

Hermes was not only the deity of eloquent speech but also the patron god for travelers with cultic sites and monuments lining the Roman roads.[17] After the events in Lystra, what do you think Paul may have said to Barnabas when they passed the first cultic site dedicated to Hermes on the road to Derbe? "Good travelers! I am Hermes your god, here to protect you as you travel this road to carry out your business."

A FOCUS ON ROMAN RELIGION

Proclaiming Jesus as Lord in the first twelve chapters of Acts took place in the context of listeners who believed in the one God of Israel. Now that the gospel penetrates the Roman world with its worship everywhere of gods and the emperor, an understanding of Roman religion will help us understand the world into which Paul now walks.

N. T. Wright says that "the gods were everywhere and involved in everything. In the ancient world, whether you were at home, on the street, attending festivals great and small; or at moments of crisis or joy (weddings, funerals, setting off on a journey), the gods would be there to be acknowledged, appeased, pleased, or placated."[18]

Polytheism thus was the dominant culture. People's beliefs and feelings "involving deities pervaded people's daily lives and habits; their experience seemed continuous and second nature." To give up the gods meant to abandon an entire worldview and all that was familiar.[19]

The head male of a home was considered the priest of the household and "performed rituals of worship and sacrifice to several (often unnamed) deities who were believed to be watching over the house and its inhabitants."[20] Many apartments had altars to their gods, and

---

17. Keener, *Acts, Vol. 2*, 2152.
18. Wright, *Paul*, 111.
19. Keener, *Acts, Vol. 3*, 2163.
20. Papandrea, *Week in the Life of Rome*, 71.

privately owned houses had niches built into the walls for statues of the household gods.[21] One can understand why a Jew would not want to enter the home of a gentile.

Yet the Romans did not approach their multitude of gods out of what we call personal devotion; it was more to be a good citizen (since the state was inseparable from religious observance) and to perform rituals for the god's protection.[22]

Virtually everyone appeased and placated the gods by performing elaborate, well-developed *rituals*. "Greeks or Romans could believe whatever they liked, so long as they performed the rituals properly."[23] *Prayer* did not flow from a heart of devotion to a deity as much as reciting fixed formulas to coerce the deity.

The Romans were so "obsessed with performing the rituals in a certain, precise way . . . that one wrong syllable or gesture could invalidate the prayer."[24] The gods must be pleased with the right ritual and sacrifice to ensure their approval so that one could prosper.

"Although many Romans were suspicious of religions based on personal devotion, they did have their own brand of personal belief, which mostly had to do with what we would call the occult—astrology, horoscopes, fortunetelling, and magic."[25]

Magic is a means to influence the events of life by the supernatural (that is, the occult). The premise of magic was that occult formulas and rites would effectively compel spiritual forces to act.[26] Among the aims of magic were healing, gaining power and wealth, and averting evil by using amulets. Elaborate invocations were made to the gods using their many names and "mysterious and most likely meaningless strings of syllables that were presumed to be powerful, foreign incantations."[27]

Divination, the belief that the will of the gods could be determined by observing everyday events and phenomena, was also a widespread belief. By divination people sought to determine the

---

21. Papandrea, *Week in the Life of Rome*, 71.
22. Papandrea, *Week in the Life of Rome*, 71.
23. Jeffers, *Greco-Roman World*, 90.
24. Jeffers, *Greco-Roman World*, 90.
25. Papandrea, *Week in the Life of Rome*, 72.
26. Croy, "Religion, Personal," 928.
27. Croy, "Religion, Personal," 929.

causes that displeased the gods and to interpret signs sent by them. Public diviners sought to proclaim the gods' approval or displeasure by observing the flight of birds, the entrails of sacrificed animals, and even an innocent sneeze.[28]

Astrology, "the observation of celestial phenomena for the purpose of predicting human events,"[29] was used to determine the will of the gods. It was based on the presumption that because the sun and the moon affect life on earth, then all other heavenly bodies must affect life on earth. Astrology became a sophisticated art that gained widespread popularity among all social classes, but the fixed nature of the stars led to a fatalistic outlook on life. Since the course of the stars was determined, it was believed all life on earth was also determined.[30]

In addition to placating the gods and practicing the occult, all but Jews were required to worship the emperor. The reminder to worship the emperor was seen everywhere on Roman coins and inscriptions on public buildings and statues. Temples for emperor worship were built in prominent places in most cities and were used for "sacrificing a bull or offering incense to the emperor's image."[31] Some of the idols Paul called the gentiles to turn from "would have been statues of Caesar or members of his family."[32]

Emperor worship had been developed by Rome to establish their hold over the empire and test the people's loyalty to them.[33] By ascribing divinity to the emperor, Rome made the state inseparable from religion. The people were taught that loyalty to the emperor was essential to maintain the well-being of the empire.

Because almost all people believed in the multitude of gods, Rome did not require them to worship only the emperor.[34] Even though the Jews felt the enormous social pressure to sacrifice to the emperor, they were granted a special exemption because Judaism was an ancient established religion.

28. Croy, "Religion, Personal," 928.
29. Croy, "Religion, Personal," 930.
30. Croy, "Religion, Personal," 930.
31. Jeffers, *Greco-Roman World*, 102.
32. Wright, *Paul*, 111.
33. Jeffers, *Greco-Roman World*, 101.
34. Jeffers, *Greco-Roman World*, 101.

In the years covered in Acts (AD 30–63) the disciples were generally seen as a small Jewish sect, meeting in houses like the Jews. Thus, they too were able to avoid the suspicion of being disloyal to Rome by not worshiping the emperor. While Paul calls people to turn from worshiping idols, we do not read of him publicly challenging emperor worship. Still, proclaiming Jesus as the one Lord and Savior became an indirect challenge to worshiping the emperor.

In time the Jesus movement was viewed as distinct from Judaism. Once it "was recognized as a *novelty* and not a long-standing ancient religion of a particular people, it was in trouble."[35] To make matters worse, deification of the emperor was developed to Nero being addressed as *lord* (AD 54–68), then Vespasian and his son Titus as *savior* (AD 67–79), and finally Domitian demanding that he be addressed as *lord and god* (AD 81–96).[36] These developments led to increased pressure and persecution of the disciples for not worshiping the emperor.

Eventually Rome came to understand the implications of Paul's challenging people all over the empire to confess Jesus alone as Lord and Savior. How could he proclaim undivided loyalty and devotion to Jesus as Lord without being disloyal to Rome, for devotion to the emperor holds the empire together?

Understanding the nature of Roman religion and the fear people had of their capricious gods helps us understand some of the factors that made the good news so attractive to them. There was no exact and demanding religious ritual. People gathered in homes to spontaneously worship the living Spirit. Their worship "did not require temples, costly animal sacrifices, priests—the very essence of much ancient religion. It could meet in homes, and its rituals were flexible."[37]

Ironically, some of these very characteristics which made the Jesus movement so attractive were lost several centuries later when Christianity was endorsed by the emperor Constantine and took "on the very properties of other ancient religions with priests, temples, sacrifices, and the like."[38]

---

35. Jeffers, *Greco-Roman World*, cited in Witherington, *Acts of the Apostles*, 544.
36. Jeffers, *Greco-Roman World*, 101.
37. Witherington, *Acts of the Apostles*, 398.
38. Witherington, *Acts of the Apostles*, 398. Italics mine.

33

The Return to Antioch Syria
(Acts 14:21–28)

EARLIER I WROTE ON the social and economic makeup of Antioch Syria. What I write now is more of a physical description of Perga and the typical Greco-Roman cities Paul visited. I hope it will be useful as you read on in Acts, following his travels to Philippi, Corinth, and other cities.[1]

My guess is that you, like me, don't recall reading about Perga in the New Testament. It is only mentioned twice here in Acts (Acts 13:14; 14:25), with the brief comment that Paul and Barnabas "preached the word in Perga."

Because Perga was a well-excavated Roman city near my hotel and its large theater could seat between thirteen thousand and fifteen thousand, making it a major city in the region,[2] I decided to spend the day exploring its ruins.

I took a train outside of the city and then caught a taxi to a dirt road in the countryside a mile south of Perga. A lone traveler on the country road up to Perga, I walked by farms and orchards, taking in the scenery, scents of the countryside, and the Presence of God. A strange sensation gradually came over me as I walked on the remote road. I sensed I was in a different culture, a different time.

---

1. Except where I quote other sources, the following is based on observations I made when exploring Perga and from Jeffers, *Greco-Roman World*.
2. Keener, *Acts*, Vol. 2, 2029.

Figure 8: Aerial View of Perga.
Source: Unknown Author is licensed under CC BY-SA-NC.

The road continued winding upward until I spotted Perga at a distance with its massive, buttressed walls and watchtowers at each corner and on both sides of the city gates. Tombs lined each side of the road near the city. As I came closer to the gate, I saw religious shrines and smelled the putrid odors of shops not allowed within the city walls.

I came to water wells for weary travelers and their animals just outside the gate. I couldn't shake my loneliness, longing for human interaction, and the strange sensation that now fully enveloped me. So, I approached two kind-looking men in their mid-thirties drinking from one of the wells. They appeared worn out from their travels. One of them bore cuts and bruises on his face and arms.

Sensing my loneliness, they offered me conversation and a drink of water. When I shared my interest in exploring Perga, they told me they had briefly visited here a year earlier and had just returned after a strenuous week walking through the central mountains from Antioch. The man with the bruised face said they had been beaten and robbed twice by bandits, once nearly drowned crossing a river, and had been forced to sleep out in the cold two nights. I told them I had recently hiked those same mountains with my daughters but got lost looking for the Saint Paul Trail. This was met with a puzzled silence.

Because they seemed kind and trustworthy and had spent a few days in Perga, I was bold enough to ask if they could spare a few hours to explain the layout of the city to me. In return I offered to help carry their luggage to the harbor when they sailed to Antioch and treat them to Turkish coffee and Turkish delight. This, too, was met with puzzled silence, but they were happy to show me around Perga. We entered through the main city gate that had recently opened at sunrise. Farmers and shepherds from the countryside crowded through the gate on their carts pulled by mules to sell their produce in the city for the day and buy specialty products found only in the city's market.³

We began the walk down the sixty-five-foot-wide main avenue running north to south through the city. Colonnaded on each side, the main avenue itself showed Perga to be a city of significant size and resources.⁴

The man with the bruises explained that like most Greco-Roman cities, Perga was built on a well-planned grid, with streets crossing at right angles to the main street. He said this made it easier to learn your way around and was especially useful when you needed to get out of town quickly, as he often did. Most of the side streets and alleys were dirt, making for careful running in event of recent rain.

As in other Greco-Roman cities, we would find in Perga prominent, public landmarks such as temples, a forum or two, amphitheaters, streets, market buildings, the senate house, basilicas, sports parks, gymnasia, and baths. These public places typically took up a fourth of the land in the city.

We then came to two tall oval towers built by the Greeks several centuries earlier as part of the city's defense. According to my guidebook, this was the most magnificent and oldest entrance of the city.

Directly behind the towers we entered a courtyard covered with marble slabs and decorated with niches and Corinthian columns. In each niche was a statue of a god or goddess, and on an arched gateway beyond the courtyard were statues of the emperors with their wives. They told me Greek and Roman gods, along with the emperor, were worshiped everywhere.

We continued up the main street to the Agora, the city's central marketplace and civic center. There we bought ointment for the bruised man's wounds and supplies for their trip back to Antioch. The streets and shops and small fountain squares were packed with people everywhere I looked.

The men explained that days in the warm, dry climate of the Mediterranean were largely spent outdoors. The apartments of most people were tiny, poorly lit, and drafty, mainly places to sleep and perhaps cook a meal on a small brazier by a window.⁵ So, the poor spent the day in

---

3. Jeffers, *Greco-Roman World*, 48. Only 10 percent of the empire's population lived in its thousand or so cities at this time.

4. Keener, *Acts, Vol. 2*, 2029.

5. Jeffers, *Greco-Roman World*, 57.

public places and hurried home before dark to avoid getting robbed, for the streets were pitch-dark after the sun set, creating dark corners for robbers to hide.

The smell of the city overwhelmed me. The stench of sewage, rotting garbage, urine, smoke, un-refrigerated fish and meat, and the body odor of the crowd overtook the occasional sweet smell of baking bread. And it was loud! People were competing over prices and politics in Latin, Greek, and other languages.[6]

Still, the covered street of the agora, lined with colonnades on each side, was a pleasant sight. The colonnades had been built at the expense of a local aristocrat to procure his honor and show off his wealth. Shrines and temples to the gods surrounded the agora.

The agora was lined with shops, each twenty-three feet (seven meters) deep. While shops selling necessities such as food and clothing were scattered all over the city, here clustered together were shops for merchants and artisans with the same trade or craft. The front part of the shops was used for sales, and in the back, I saw bags and crates for storage and equipment used to produce the goods. Shop owners often lived in the corner of their shops.

We looked for the street with shops for leatherworkers, since one of the men worked with leather and wanted to learn more about establishing himself in a city in the future. They explained that unlike where I seemed to come from, in Greco-Roman cities merchants and artisans with the same trade or craft clustered together and used their trade to name the street where they worked.

Working alongside each other benefited everyone. "They helped each other get raw materials, share water resources, helped new arrivals get started and talked about common interests,"[7] and everyone knew where to go if they wanted to buy a tent, the tentmaker said.

As we continued north on the main avenue, I noticed wagon ruts in the stone pavement made several thousand years earlier and felt connected to ancient history. Down the middle of the impressive avenue flowed a six-foot wide channel of fresh water fed by springs higher north in the hills. The city's main source of water, the channel was diverted to the Roman baths and was also used by shops on the street. The sound of cool, flowing water during the hot Mediterranean summers refreshed the shoppers.

---

6. Jeffers, *Greco-Roman World*, 61.

7. Jeffers, *Greco-Roman World*, 54.

The avenue curved slightly before it ended at an immense fountain at the foot of the acropolis, which towered over the city. In front of the fountain was a statue of Kestrus, the deity of the local river, reclining. The gods were everywhere.

We left reclining Kestrus to take a side street to the gymnasium, where Perga's youth trained for track events and the independently wealthy exercised.[8] Dedicated to the Emperor Claudius (AD 41–54), my guides told me it was recently built. "The gymnasium was essentially a courtyard surrounded by a colonnade. Most athletic events occurred in the open-air courtyard. Rooms under the colonnade were used to instruct children in all areas of education and for bathing."[9] I was tempted to jog around the track, but the men were in a hurry and suggested we visit the stadium outside the city walls.

Here at the stadium the Roman games were held. "The games were intimately connected with Roman religion, and priests frequently directed the games. Admission to the public games was free to Roman citizens. Slaves and noncitizens were not allowed to attend."[10] The stadium was huge—over 1,000 feet long (334 meters) and over 100 feet wide (34 meters). Eleven rows of stone benches encircled the courtyard, seating twelve thousand spectators. Below the benches were seventy vaulted chambers used for entering the stadium, for dressing rooms for the athletes, and for stores for the spectators.

We walked up to the last row of benches. I stood to take it all in. I noticed an arena at the far end that was separated with a wall from the rest of the stadium. I asked what it was for. Sadly, they said wild beasts were released there from adjoining vaults to prey upon their helpless victims. And here gladiators, almost always slaves who became professional fighters, drew huge crowds as they fought each other or wild beasts. "The blood, the odors and the threat of death gave the games a unique excitement for Romans."

I asked if they had time to visit the theater outside the city gates. But they were in a hurry to get down to the harbor and wait for a ship to sail back to Antioch. I reminded them of my offer to help carry their luggage, but they said I looked tired and might slow them down.

I expressed my thanks and hope to see them again in the future. I continued alone. It was only then that I realized how hot, hungry, and thirsty

8. Jeffers, *Greco-Roman World*, 29.
9. Jeffers, *Greco-Roman World*, 29.
10. Jeffers, *Greco-Roman World*, 32.

I was. I felt dizzy and dreary as I walked back to the entrance of Perga. There I found a small shop selling sandwiches, Turkish coffee, and Turkish delight. After eating I felt like a new man coming out of a strange dream.

All other tourists had left by the time I entered the theater near closing time. Performances were of two kinds: comedies with stereotyped characters and "a clown burlesque made up of songs and crude jokes laced with sexual comments. Open sexual expression was a widespread theme in plays, dances and art, and in the private lives of Rome's leaders."[11]

Down by the stage I found a frieze of Dionysus, the god of the grape harvest, wine-making and wine, fertility, orchards and fruit, vegetation, insanity, ritual madness, religious ecstasy, festivity, and theater in ancient Greek religion and myth. I wondered what kind of people worshiped a god like Dionysus.

Time was short so I rushed up the aisle past forty-four rows of seats to the top. Looking down, I took in the sheer size of the theater, imagining the thirteen thousand to fifteen thousand people seated here to watch a performance far below.

A shout startled me. The attendant far below was waving his hands and yelling that the theater was now closing. The steps were steep and short, so I walked with care down to him, thanked him for his patience, exited the theater and then Perga.

Outside the gate a taxi driver offered me a ride. I decided to walk the dirt road back to catch the train into the city. It had been a good day but a long day, and I had much to process.

TO DERBE THEN RETURN TO ANTIOCH

After severe suffering in Lystra, Paul and Barnabas are now out on the road to Derbe, sixty miles southeast of Lystra. Unlike Antioch, Iconium, and Lystra, Derbe was off the main highway, the Via Sebaste. Located along a difficult dirt road to travel on, Derbe was less advanced than the other cities they had visited.[12] One naturally wonders why they went there.

Perhaps after Paul's near death in Lystra they wanted to get off the main road, far from those who sought to stone Paul to death. From Derbe they could have continued east to Paul's hometown of Tarsus (about a week's walk away) and from there continued to Antioch Syria, where they

---

11. Jeffers, *Greco-Roman World*, 33.
12. Keener, *Acts, Vol. 2*, 2178.

had been sent out. This would have been the easiest way to end their travels. Instead, after many became disciples in Derbe, they head straight back northwest to Lystra, Iconium, and Antioch, making for a much longer and potentially dangerous trip! Since many became disciples in Derbe, they may have spent weeks there, allowing time for things to calm down in the cities to which they returned, and they did not now visit the synagogues in these cities.

Returning to Lystra, Iconium, and Antioch could be dangerous, and they had to be careful. So why did they retrace their steps into potential danger, making for a much longer journey back to Antioch Syria, when they had a much shorter and safer trip back from Derbe? In short, the answer is their love and concern for the disciples, young in faith. They knew they also would suffer persecution and could waver in their new faith. So, driven by love, Paul and Barnabas returned to strengthen and encourage them to persevere in suffering. Paul told them, "It is through many persecutions that we must enter the kingdom of God" (Acts 14:22). His words carried much weight, for they could see the scars and bruises on his body from the stoning in Lystra, yet he risked new danger by returning to encourage them.

As Paul and Barnabas met with the disciples, they prayed for discernment in appointing leaders who would shepherd them after they left. Above all, the Lord will shepherd them, so with prayer and fasting they entrusted them to his care.

Now they must leave to begin their long journey back to Antioch Syria before winter sets in. Walking through the snow-covered mountains would be treacherous, and ships would cease to sail.

After months of planning to hike the Saint Paul Trail straight through the mountains of central Turkey, I was disappointed when I later read that most scholars believe Paul and Barnabas had likely taken the Via Sebaste northwest around the mountains. But then I was saved by a footnote I found on the next to the last page of volume two in Craig Keener's mammoth commentary of Acts.[13] It said they likely took the central and faster route down the mountains from Antioch to Derbe. For Luke writes that *they passed through Pisidia in the interior* down to the coastal region of Pamphylia (Acts 14:24).

Because there was not a Roman road straight to the harbor at Attalia, they arrived on one that went to Perga, eight miles inland. In their

---

13. Keener, *Acts. Vol. 2.*

haste to get to Antioch, they had not stayed in Perga when they first arrived from Cyprus (Acts 13:13–14), but now with increased confidence in speaking to gentiles, they stayed and proclaimed the word in the largely gentile city.

Then they headed down to the harbor in Attalia to sail directly back to Antioch Syria instead of retracing their journey to Cyprus.

We can imagine their joy, gratitude to God, sense of accomplishment, and the sense of safety they felt as they sailed back to their brothers and sisters in Antioch, who had sent them out on their mission. With God's care and empowerment, the mission has been completed (Acts 14:26). The good news of Jesus has now penetrated deeply into a few important gentile cities in the Roman Empire.

Thirteen to fourteen years earlier, on his way to Damascus, Paul was changed forever by the Lord, who had chosen him to take the good news to the gentiles (Acts 9:15). Now after many years of preparation and seemingly little success, he has seen substantial fruit and gained a taste for mission throughout the empire.

This has been God's work, worked out through Paul and Barnabas. For we read that God had "opened a door *of faith* for the gentiles" (Acts 14:27). Salvation *by faith alone* has been proclaimed throughout the journey (Acts 13:8, 12, 39, 41, 48; 14:1, 9, 22–23) and is now emphasized again at its conclusion, when Paul and Barnabas report to the church how God had opened a door of faith for the gentiles (Acts 14:27).

The emphasis on God welcoming gentiles into his family through faith, apart from the Jewish law, prepares us for the resistance Paul would soon meet for teaching this.[14]

All seems well as Paul and Barnabas rejoice in God's grace to the gentiles and settle in to strengthen the disciples in Antioch. Then, after a time, some conservative Jewish disciples from Jerusalem showed up in Antioch, threatening to unravel all that God had accomplished among the gentiles.

---

14. Peterson, *Acts of the Apostles*, 416.

34

Debate and a Decision About the Gentiles

(Acts 15:1–21)

THE NIGHT BEFORE FLYING home, Daniela, Sonja, and I enjoyed a pleasant meal together in Istanbul. While waiting for our food, they asked me how they would answer their friends back in New York and San Francisco for why they had traveled through remote mountains of central Turkey just to walk Roman roads and see Roman ruins. Why follow Paul's journeys?

Their question prompted me to reflect on Paul's unique vision and why he suffered and fought for it when challenged by others. What did he see that others initially did not? What was the one unifying vision he carried in his heart and mind as he trudged through the Turkish mountains? I answered my daughters something like this.

At this time Paul was unique in understanding that the death of Jesus demolished the barriers between all people groups and that the Spirit of God had united all who put their trust in Jesus into one people, a new creation unparalleled in human history. What we take for granted now was then a revolutionary new way of ordering society.

I am especially indebted to N. T. Wright's insights on Paul's vision and refer to him for your insight and inspiration. Wright points out that while the Greco-Roman world had its guilds and societies, one had to pay to belong to them, and membership was limited to the right people. "In the ancient Near East *the idea of a single community across the traditional boundaries of culture, gender, and ethnic and social groupings was unheard of.* Unthinkable, in fact."[1]

God has now created a new kind of community across all traditional boundaries that society sets up, and it's free to belong to! He has created it through Jesus and the Spirit. Its identity is formed by belonging to Jesus and thus each other; its life is shaped by the cross of Jesus; and its allegiance is to Jesus alone as Lord. *"These communities, small at first but growing, were an experiment in a way of being human, of being human together, that had never been tried in the world before."*[2]

Paul saw that "God was creating a new world order, a new social and cultural reality, where all people of the Messiah were welcome on equal terms."[3] Paul later writes, "In this new life it doesn't matter if you are a Jew or a gentile, circumcised or uncircumcised, barbaric, uncivilized, slave or free. Christ is all that matters, and he lives in all of us" (Col 3:11).

It baffled the gentile and the Jewish mind when they saw this mysterious mosaic of people going through their apartment buildings to gather in homes as one family united in love for one another and their neighbors.

This new community was not only an enigma to the gentile world; it also threatened the Jewish way of being. "The vibrant and excited group of Jesus-followers in Antioch (and other cities) was doing something radically countercultural. Nobody else in the ancient world was trying to live in a house where the old walls were being taken down. Nobody else was experimenting with a whole new way of being human."[4]

But at this time Paul uniquely saw God's vision for creating a new humanity in our divided world in Christ alone. He saw that God was breaking down old hostilities between ethnic and social groupings to unite all peoples in Christ. With singular vision he labored and suffered, traveling the Roman Empire, forming small cells with the DNA of God's new society in homes with Jew and gentiles.

N. T. Wright suggests that we try to think of a world where music has never existed. But then one day music enters our world, unleashing a new joy and a new way of communicating. If we can try to imagine that,

---

1. Wright, *Paul*, 91. Italics mine.
2. Wright, *Paul*, 112. Italics mine.
3. Wright, *Paul*, 134.
4. Wright, *Paul*, 91.

says Wright, "then we may have a sense of the crazy magnitude of Paul's vocation."[5]

This was what I tried to communicate with Sonja and Daniela our last night in Turkey. And with Wright's help I've wanted to share my immense admiration for Paul's keen mind and undaunted courage as he tirelessly travels to labor and watch the Spirit of God make the vision of God a reality.

Paul's insistence on entering communities of faith by allegiance to Christ alone, without living under the Jewish law, explains why he is so intense when he soon writes Galatians, and it helps us understand what he fights for when he now travels to Antioch for Jerusalem. The following focus explains why so many Jewish believers fought Paul's vision.

A FOCUS ON THE BACKGROUND TO THE JERUSALEM DEBATE

We can better appreciate the intense debate that now takes place among the disciples at the Council in Jerusalem by the rise in Jewish nationalism at this time.[6] The rise in Jewish nationalism was a response to an increase of anti-Semitism from the Roman government.

Caligula, the Roman Emperor in the years preceding the Jerusalem Council (AD 37–41), had created new policies to restrict the Jews and even permitted violent, unrestrained anti-Semitism in Alexandria, the second-largest city in the empire, where 150,000 Jews lived.[7] Because he believed the Jewish people disdained him, he ordered a statue of himself as a god to be constructed in the holy of holies of the temple in Jerusalem.

While the statue was never built, if it had been, the Jewish people throughout the empire would have risen in revolt. Just the possibility of the emperor worshiped as a god in the temple became deeply ingrained in the Jewish psyche. All this led to "a crisis of fierce religious nationalism."[8] Based on their interpretation of the prophet

---

5. Wright, *Paul*, 109.

6. Israel has been keen to maintain their national identity in the land since their return from exile in Babylon, but now in a time of crisis, it is especially on the rise.

7. Jeffers, *Greco-Roman World*, 275.

8. Barnett, *Jesus and the Rise*, 242.

Daniel, the Roman Empire was the gentile beast that would make war against the nation of Israel.

All this meant Jews everywhere must unite against the beast of Rome so that God would demolish it and establish his kingdom on earth for Israel.

Compromise with the pagan gentile idolaters was out of the question. This was a time of testing for all Jews to be loyal to their God *by faithfully following the law* he gave them through Moses. They must not compromise as they did in the past by making concessions with the pagan world. They must unite and be loyal to God by following his law and keeping separate from the immoral gentile idol-worshipers.

In this context, the disciples could easily be seen as pro-gentile and therefore disloyal to Israel. By welcoming gentiles among them, they appeared to be friendly with the enemy, "seen as traitors to the nation's holy cause."[9]

At this already highly charged time, Paul and Barnabas went out to "immoral, idol worshipping" gentiles in central Turkey, proclaiming the good news that they could be equal members of God's family without living under the Jewish law! With fuel added to the fire under the banner of Jewish nationalism, conservative disciples from the Pharisaic party in Jerusalem insisted Paul and Barnabas's teaching to the gentiles was non-Jewish and must be stopped.

All this helps us understand the intense social and religious pressure the all-Jewish Jesus movement in Jerusalem felt at this time. Other Jews in Israel believed they were "allied with a supposedly Jesus-related movement, out in far-flung lands, teaching Jews that they didn't have to obey the Torah!"[10] Soon Jews "would find themselves indistinguishable from pagans. Here in Jerusalem all loyal Jews knew that the pagans were the enemy whom God would overthrow, just as he overthrew Pharaoh's armies in the Red Sea. But out there in the Diaspora this new movement was, it seemed, treating pagans as equal partners."[11]

---

9. Barnett, *Jesus and the Rise*, 242.
10. Wright, *Paul*, 140.
11. Wright, *Paul*, 140.

"The word on the street in Jerusalem, then, would have been that these Jesus-followers were not really loyal Jews."[12] Already viewing the Jesus sect with suspicion, *many in Jerusalem would be on the lookout for any further signs of disloyalty to the Jewish cause.*

This general background before the Jerusalem Council helps us understand the intense pressure the disciples in Jerusalem felt to not appear friendly with the gentiles.

Then came *three crucial events* shortly before the Council, adding to the tension. We learn of these events, events filled with confusion, disappointment, slander, and tense encounters, from Galatians, which Paul had written before the Council in Jerusalem.

First, we learn that Peter went to Antioch after Paul and Barnabas had returned from their mission to Turkey (Acts 14:28). When Peter came, he joined the gentile disciples in their homes for meals and participated in the joint Jewish/gentile worship in their house churches.

But then when certain disciples came to Antioch from Jerusalem, claiming (falsely) that James had sent them to separate the Jewish and gentile disciples into different fellowships unless the gentiles were circumcised and followed the law of Moses, Peter caved in due to fear. Paul wrote, "When they arrived, he began to draw back and separate himself from the Gentiles because he was afraid of those who belonged to the circumcised group" (Gal 2:12).

Sadly, when Peter, the lead apostle, separates himself from the gentile believers, all the other Jewish disciples in Antioch (including Barnabas!) follow his lead!

Paul, now alone, knew what was at stake and what he had to do. However awkward, however difficult, he knew he had to confront Peter face-to-face in the presence of the other disciples and put a stop to separating what Jesus had united. Paul had witnessed God pouring out his Spirit on gentile believers, and that meant "everything had changed. A new world had been launched."[13] So Paul says to Peter, "Since you, a Jew by birth, have discarded the Jewish laws and are living like a Gentile, why are you trying to make these Gentiles obey the Jewish laws you abandoned?" (Gal 2:14 NLT).

12. Wright, *Paul,* 140.
13. Wright, *Paul,* 146.

Then, *a second disturbing event* occurred. Some more conservative Jewish disciples from Jerusalem (like those who had caused the disturbance in Antioch) traveled all the way to central Turkey, to the Jewish/gentile churches birthed through Paul and Barnabas's recent labors there. They also falsely claimed that James had sent them to tell the Jewish believers to stop meeting with gentile believers unless they were circumcised and lived by the Jewish law (Acts 11:18).

When Paul learns of this, he is furious and writes the churches the letter we call Galatians. This is *the third significant event* before the Jerusalem Council. While Paul's logic in Galatians can be very Jewish and very involved, we can understand his main point knowing he writes it to answer one primary question: *Are gentiles required to become Jewish and live by the law of Moses in order to be saved and belong to God's family?*

In answering this question Paul makes two central points—one about the significance of Jesus' death on a cross and the other about the significance of God's Spirit dwelling also in gentile believers.

In short, Paul argues that the death of the Messiah has put an end to the law, and it is the law which defines Israel as Israel and defines gentiles as outsiders. We know that by his death Jesus took upon himself the curse for our wrongdoings so that we can be made right with God. But I had never thought about how his death abolished the law, freeing gentiles from having to live it. So, I met with my friend Steve, who teaches the New Testament at a local seminary, and asked him for help.

He helped me understand Paul's logic this way. Paul knew that the Torah (i.e., the Mosaic law) pronounced the curse of death and exclusion from Israel on those who disobey it and the blessings of life (salvation) to those who obey it. Steeped in the Scriptures, Paul knew that Israel had never lived by the Torah; thus, it had only brought them under God's judgment. This is one reason Jewish believers should not argue so vehemently for gentiles to live by the law. If they couldn't, how could they demand others to?

But Steve explained that Paul makes an even more profound case for the finality of living by the Torah. Jesus died a shameful death on a cross (or a tree). *But according to the law his death was a curse and meant exclusion from Israel* (Deut 21:22–23). Thus, by dying on a tree, Jesus died under the curse of the Torah, so it seemed he was cut off from Israel and the blessings of God forever. So it seemed. But then to the surprise of the disciples, God raised Jesus from the dead, vindicating him from the penalty and curse of the law.

Thus, God blesses with life, resurrection life, a man cursed by the law and hung on a tree. *This must mean that the law is not the all-defining eternal power Israel believed it was.* While it had an important part in Israel's youth as a tutor, it was never intended to be permanent.

So, what does this mean for gentiles (and for Jews!) not having to live by the law? *Since God delivered Jesus from death and blessed him with resurrection life apart from the Torah, gentiles too can be blessed by their union with him without becoming Jewish and living by the law.* With Jesus, the time for the Torah came to an end. The people of God are no longer defined by the law but by union with Christ and obedience to him by the Spirit.[14]

This leads us to what Paul says about *the Spirit and his second main argument* in Galatians to those who insist gentiles must live by the law to be saved and have fellowship with Jewish believers.

Paul's first reminds the Galatians that they received the Spirit when they believed, not after first becoming Jewish and living by the law. He writes, "Did you receive the Spirit by doing the works of the law or by believing what you heard . . . Well then, does God supply you with the Spirit and work miracles among you by your doing the works of the law, or by your believing what you heard?" (Gal 3:2, 5). Quite clear. *The blessings of salvation come through the Spirit to anyone who gives allegiance to (believes in) Christ apart from the law.*

Then towards the end of Galatians, Paul makes a second point about the Spirit and the law. The Jewish people had always believed obedience to the law of Moses was the only way to keep pure and separate from the idolatry and immorality prevalent in the gentile nations around them. So, it is natural that they would want to know how Paul's teaching would keep gentile believers from continuing to live as gentiles if they do not live by the law.

Paul's answer is the indwelling Spirit! The Spirit not only inspires worship of the one true God but also empowers the gentiles to live pure lives. In fact, the new obedience created by the Spirit far exceeds the previous obedience by Paul and any other "righteous Jew"

---

14. Steve Taylor, correspondence with author, Apr. 6, 2022.

who lived by the law, for the law with its 613 commandments not only cannot give us power to obey it: it also cannot cover every possible circumstance of life for the will of God, his mercy, and justice to be expressed. Only love, Spirit-filled, Spirit-led love throughout the day, can do that.

Paul emphasizes that the whole law (i.e., the law considered as a unit, or the spirit and intent of the law)[15] is summed up with the single commandment to love. Love is the very heart and essence of the law.

Thus, by expressing love through the Spirit to all who cross our path every hour of every day, we *can fulfill the very essence of the law.* (See Gal 5:13–14 and Rom 8:3–4.)

Now that we know more about the pressures the Jewish disciples felt at this time to show themselves to be loyal Jews and live by the law and distance themselves from gentile disciples who didn't, and Paul's understanding that to do so would be to abandon Christ and the gospel, we can better understand what is at stake at the Jerusalem Council.

DEBATE AND DISSENSION IN ANTIOCH (ACTS 15:1–5)

Paul and Barnabas rejoiced in God's work among the gentiles from their mission to central Turkey and in Antioch Syria (Acts 14:28). But then some disciples from Jerusalem who belong to the strict party of the Pharisees showed up in Antioch, threatening to undo it all. They claimed that James (the brother of Jesus, who now leads the church in Jerusalem) had sent them to bring order to the churches in Antioch (Acts 15:24).

Bypassing Paul, Barnabas, and other leaders in Antioch, they secretly infiltrated the gatherings of Jewish and gentile disciples to insist that they stop meeting together unless the gentiles are circumcised and begin to live by the law of Moses (Acts 15:1, 5; Gal 2:4). The gatherings crossing cultures composed by God to mirror his intent for uniting all humanity are told to separate into Jewish and gentile churches.

They also teach the gentile believers that they have been deceived by Paul. They cannot be accepted by God unless they take the identifying

---

15. Fung, *Epistle to the Galatians*, 345.

mark of circumcision (their faith and baptism into Christ is not sufficient!) and live like Jews, according to the laws and customs of Moses.

To say the least, this was deeply unsettling to Paul. He feared that if the false brothers succeeded in their attempt, all he had suffered to make Christ known among the gentiles would be in vain (Gal 2:2). Imagine what this did to the joy, unity, and freedom of the disciples. They had worked to understand each other and live in the unity of the Spirit, only to be told they must now separate.

If you can imagine that, then you can begin to imagine how Paul and Barnabas responded when they learned these men were in Antioch. Locating them led to "no small dissension and debate with them" (Acts 15:2). Paul and Barnabas likely told them how they had seen the Spirit come to dwell in the gentiles when they turned to Christ, and Paul likely shared some of what he had recently written in Galatians. But none of this seemed to soften the hardline stance of the Pharisaic disciples. So, the disciples collectively appointed Paul, Barnabas, and a few other leaders to go to Jerusalem to settle the issue. As they passed through Phoenicia and Samaria, the Jews there responded with joy at the conversion of the gentiles. Will the Jewish believers in Jerusalem?

Once they reached Jerusalem they were welcomed by the apostles, elders, and the other disciples. But when they shared all that God had done through them among the gentiles (Acts 15:4), some from the group of strict Pharisaic believers (who had likely sent the men to Antioch) stood up and again insisted that gentiles who wanted to be accepted by God and belong to his people, the Jewish family of believers, must live by the Jewish law.

By this time both Peter and Barnabas have worked out the conflict with Paul when he called them out for separating themselves from their gentile brothers and sisters (Gal 2:11–14). But we do not know how the other leaders in Jerusalem, now led by the more conservative James, would respond. Would there be two Jesus movements? One exclusively for Jews and another for gentiles? Will Christ be divided? This is what is at stake.

After much debate arriving at no clear consensus (Acts 15:6, 7), Peter stands to state his view.

PETER SPEAKS (ACTS 15:6-11)

Paul and Barnabas have already made their case (Acts 15:2, 4). The hardliners don't recognize their calling or message and dismiss their arguments. But Peter they know well, since until recently he had led the believers in Jerusalem. Peter spoke powerfully in support of Paul's work and his teaching to the gentiles with four convincing arguments.

First, he reminded them that God called him to speak the message of Jesus to the gentiles when he went to Cornelius's house. Their shared salvation with Jewish believers did not originate with Paul or himself. It was God's choice (Acts 15:7). Then he pointed out that God gave evidence of their faith by giving them the Spirit just as he did with the Jewish believers at Pentecost (Acts 15:8). Third, he said God *cleansed their hearts by faith in Christ* (Acts 15:9), just as he does with Jewish hearts (Acts 15:11). Thus, God makes no distinction between them and Jewish believers. Finally, perhaps looking at the hardcore Pharisaic believers who are confident of their purity before God by living by the law, Peter asked why they want to place the demands of the law on the necks of the gentile believers when God clearly hasn't. If they were all honest, they would have to admit that neither they nor any Jew had ever been able to live by the law fully and faithfully.

All those gathered kept silent, weighing Peter's convincing words. Then they listened to Barnabas and Paul again. I can see the scowling faces of the Pharisaic disciples when they stood to speak.

BARNABAS AND PAUL SPEAK (ACTS 15:12)

Barnabas and Paul had no need to repeat Peter's points, so they only reported "all the signs and wonders that God had done through them among the Gentiles" (Acts 15:12). What is their point in emphasizing the miracles God did among the gentiles? Surely God's intention was to show his love and power among them so that they would believe! Perhaps Paul added what he had written in Galatians. God worked miracles among the gentiles and gave them his Spirit—not after they first obeyed the law of Moses but only because of their allegiance to Christ (Gal 3:5).

JAMES SPEAKS (ACTS 15:13-21)

James, the brother of Jesus, now speaks. Speaking last suggests his primacy among the leaders.[16] Luke briefly introduced James when Peter left Jerusalem some four to five years ago (Acts 12:17) and now enters him into his account again as the recognized leader of the church in Jerusalem. James is not just another speaker at the Council but is portrayed more as a judge or authority figure who will give a final ruling to settle the debate.[17]

The hardliners had claimed they had been sent by James to Antioch to demand that the gentiles live by the Jewish law in order to have full membership in God's family. But while James did send the Pharisaic group of disciples on a fact-finding mission to Antioch, he did not send them with orders to separate the Jews from the gentiles and demand that all gentiles be circumcised and live by the laws of Moses.

Still, because James sent the more conservative Pharisaic disciples to Antioch, it seems he has more conservative leanings than Peter and Paul. What will he say? The Pharisaic disciples hope he will use his authority to overrule Peter and Paul.

But to the relief of Peter, Paul, and Barnabas and to the dismay of the hardliners, James affirms his full agreement with Peter's position. Unlike Peter and Paul, James has not had firsthand experience witnessing gentiles believe and receive the Spirit, but he knows the Scriptures and using their authority quotes from the prophet Amos to support that what Peter, Paul, and others have witnessed is what God had planned for the last days when he came to restore his people, Israel.

Amos says that God will come to "rebuild the dwelling of David ... so that all other peoples may seek the Lord ... even all the Gentiles over whom my name has been called" (Acts 15:16–17). On the day of Pentecost, God began to rebuild his people Israel by fulfilling his promises to them. But then Amos adds that God will rebuild Israel *so that the gentiles may seek the Lord and belong to him.*

From the beginning God chose Israel so that through her the nations would also know him. Now, at last, after repeated failures, Israel becomes God's agent to bless the nations! First, Philip to the Ethiopian eunuch, then Peter to Cornelius and his household, then unnamed Greek-speaking disciples to gentiles in Antioch, and finally, Paul and

---

16. Peterson, *Acts of the Apostles*, 429.
17. Witherington, *Acts of the Apostles*, 457.

Barnabas to gentiles in Central Anatolia (Turkey). All were Jews, Jews who had been "rebuilt" and then had taken God's salvation to gentiles. This should not surprise those who know the Scriptures, for it has always been part of God's eternal purpose.[18]

The question of gentiles receiving the same salvation as Jews by allegiance to Christ alone apart from the law is settled, but there remains the practical issue of how Jews and gentiles relate to one another with their deeply ingrained cultural differences.[19]

The decision James delivers (by the Holy Spirit) seeks to answer this question.

JAMES GIVES A RULING (ACTS 15:19–21)

James reaches the decision that gentile disciples will only be required to abstain from practices among the gentiles that are associated, directly or indirectly, with idol worship in pagan temples. Ben Witherington argues convincingly that the four prohibitions given in Acts 15:20 are not isolated commandments from the law (Lev 17–18) but are all related to attending pagan temples.[20]

One example is to abstain from going to a pagan temple to eat meat that has been sacrificed to idols. The only time and place where poor, working-class gentiles could eat meat would be at a public celebration such as a feast in a pagan temple.[21] Thus, this would be a sacrifice of love to their Jewish brothers and sisters.

Even though gentile believers no longer worshiped idols, they still might be tempted to go to a pagan temple to eat meat (from a strangled animal still containing blood) and be tempted to have fornication with a temple prostitute. All four prohibitions are thus related to the specific social setting of frequenting a pagan temple.[22]

Gentile believers might claim their freedom in Christ to attend temple celebrations only to eat the meat, but their Jewish brothers and sisters and their Jewish neighbors would not know that. Israel had worshiped idols time and again in their history and faced severe judgement because

---

18. Peterson, *Acts of the Apostles*, 432.
19. Peterson, *Acts of the Apostles*, 432.
20. Witherington, *Acts of the Apostles*, 464–65. The four prohibitions are (1) things polluted by idols, (2) fornication, (3) whatever is strangled, and (4) blood.
21. Witherington, *Acts of the Apostles*, 461.
22. Witherington, *Acts of the Apostles*, 461.

of it. At this crucial time, all agreed—they do not want gentile believers to practice anything that might lead them back to idol worship.

Gentile believers are to follow these few instructions for the sake of witness to the Jewish people, who would struggle to meet with anyone who had visited a pagan temple, where idols are worshiped and people engage in temple prostitution. Frequenting pagan temples would both weaken their witness to unbelieving gentiles and could tempt weaker believers into idolatry and immorality.[23]

THE DECISION IS DELIVERED (ACTS 15:22–35)

To implement the decision, the believers in Jerusalem unanimously agreed to select two prophets from among them, Judas and Silas, to travel with Paul and Barnabas to Antioch and verbally confirm the contents of the letter they carried. The letter speaks of "our beloved Barnabas and Paul, who have risked their lives for the sake of our Lord Jesus Christ" (Acts 15:25–26). In this way James and the Jerusalem believers affirm their full support and admiration for Paul's work among the gentiles.

The letter also says "it has seemed good to the Holy Spirit and to us" to impose only the essential commands to not frequent pagan temples with all that is practiced there (Acts 15:28). The Spirit of God who initiated mission to the gentiles now leads in the decision to fully welcome them without living by the law.[24]

The letter is addressed to all the gentile disciples in Antioch and Syria and Cilicia.[25] It assures them that the men who have unsettled their minds by insisting they live by the Jewish law have not been sent by James for that reason. Their gentile brothers and sisters are not to be burdened by following the Jewish law but are only to abstain from the prohibitions related to idol worship and pagan temples.

Paul and Barnabas, along with Judas and Silas, traveled back to Antioch. After the tense debates in Jerusalem, they must have traveled with joy and a renewed passion for their mission among the gentiles. They looked forward to bringing peace to their gentile brothers and sisters who had been disturbed by the Pharisaic disciples from Jerusalem.

---

23. Paul will later address the related but separate issue of eating meat sacrificed at a pagan temple but purchased at a market (1 Cor 8; 10:23–33, 14–15).

24. Keener, *Acts, Vol. 2*, 2291.

25. From Antioch, the administrative capital of united Syria and Cilicia, the gospel had now reached gentiles in those provinces.

When they arrived and brought the disciples together to read the letter from Jerusalem, all rejoiced (Acts 15:31). Joy comes from freedom when the burden of law is lifted.

Judas and Silas stayed in Antioch for a time to encourage and strengthen the believers. The presence of these Jewish brothers, prophets from Jerusalem, was a tangible testimony of their unity centered on Christ, not the law. After a time, Judas and Silas are sent back to Jerusalem in peace, peace in their unity as brothers and sisters and peace from the Judaizers and their demands to live under the law.

Paul and Barnabas remained a short time in Antioch, their home church and base for mission. Soon they would travel again to proclaim the word of the Lord among the gentiles (Acts 15:36). Until then, they taught the word of the Lord in Antioch with others. Luke implied that opposition to the gospel of grace has again been met; thus, the church continued to grow in peace.

Paul, especially, had fought long and hard for one family of believers centered on Christ, not Jewish law. His labors had not been in vain. Now with the Jerusalem Church behind him, he could continue in peace with the call the Lord had given him.[26]

---

26. Paul will later experience conflict again with Jewish believers zealous for the law in Jerusalem. When he arrives in Jerusalem, he is warmly welcomed by many of the disciples, James, and the elders. But then the latter warn him, "You see, brother, how many thousands of believers there are among the Jews, and they are all zealous for the law. They have been told about you that you teach all the Jews living among the Gentiles to forsake Moses, and that you tell them not to circumcise their children or observe the customs" (Acts 21:20–21).

35

The Gospel and the Story of the Bible

As WE READ HOW the good news about Jesus spread through the disciples by the Spirit's power, we feel drawn into the story, wanting to be part of a community of believers who follow in their steps.

I feel this book would end abruptly (somewhat as Acts 28) if I did not say something more about how we can continue the story of Acts. To continue the story of Acts, the message proclaimed must be so deeply ingrained in us that we can tell it with ease and explore ways to live it in our neighborhoods and cross-culturally among the nations.

In the introduction to this book, I mentioned two crucial questions that consumed my thinking for many years: what is the gospel, and what is the nature of the church and its mission on earth?

I now return to these questions to develop thoughts written earlier in the book with suggestions for how we can make them part of our lives. In this chapter I outline how the gospel completes God's aims for humanity from the very beginning.

I clearly recall sitting at home in my recliner on a brisk fall Saturday morning reading through the Gospel of Luke. I came to an abrupt stop at the end of Luke 4. There Jesus said, "I must proclaim the good news of the kingdom of God to other cities also; *for I was sent for this purpose* (Luke 4:43, italics mine).

I was sixty years old and had spent my life studying and teaching the New Testament, but that morning I had to admit that I did not know what Jesus meant by *the good news of the kingdom of God. Yet this was the message God sent Jesus to proclaim!*

I tended, like many I guess, to read into Jesus' message of the kingdom of God his death for our sins to make us right with God. Of course, Jesus had not yet spoken of his death and wouldn't for quite a while.

Reading Luke, I observed how those who first heard Jesus' message, saw it expressed in his compassionate deeds, experienced it with his healing touch, and were so moved that they praised God in song, dance, and poetry expressing their joy. Whether they were buying food at the market, working out in the fields, eating a meal with Jesus, or at a place of prayer, they would stop to praise God and tell others of what they encountered with Jesus.

I often ask myself if the reason we do not respond with a similar joy and excitement is that we don't fully grasp the good news of the kingdom of God that Jesus was sent to proclaim. If we did, perhaps we, too, would begin to sing and dance and write poetry. Perhaps we, too, would find ways to share it with those around us. Perhaps the world around us, too, would change more and more.

That Saturday morning, I realized how deeply ingrained popular presentations of the gospel were planted in my mind and in our culture, so much so that I read the Bible through their lens, not seeing what it said. When I came to Luke 4:43 that morning, I realized I must change. I knew I must devote myself to an extended time of prayer and study to learn the gospel of the kingdom God sent Jesus to proclaim.

I got to work. I knew the background for Jesus' message of the kingdom of God was rooted in the many prophecies of the Messiah, a son of David, who was promised an eternal kingdom over which to reign. So, I spent six months reading through the Old Testament prophets summarizing what they said about the nature of the coming kingdom. Only then did I begin to see how it was fulfilled in Christ.

At this time, I also noticed articles each month in *Christianity Today* by Scot McKnight. He wrote passionately about what he called "the full, robust gospel message of Jesus," explaining what Jesus meant by the good news of the kingdom of God and showing how our popular view of the gospel was too small.

In time he wrote a book entitled *The King Jesus Gospel*, with a question in bold print on the dust jacket: "Is the gospel you've been taught the gospel Jesus taught?"[1] We can ask as he does: is it the same message that Peter and Paul taught in Acts and in their letters?

The question before us—the question the authors of the New Testament answer—is, How does Jesus complete the story of the Bible? How do the six crucial truths of the gospel Peter proclaimed at Pentecost (see examples in chapter five) proclaimed about him (the gospel message) fulfill the promises and plan of God we read of in the Old Testament?

To answer this, we must go all the way back to Gen 1, where we read of God's reasons for creating humans.

THE OLD TESTAMENT BACKGROUND TO THE GOSPEL

I like to say that God created all things out of the overflow of his being: his light (glory), his love, and his laughter (or joy, if you like). The beauty and glory of God were everywhere displayed in his creation. Then in the center God placed humankind, created in his image, to rule over it and to enjoy it in his Presence.

Scholars like to point out that the creation account in Gen 1 parallels, yet counters in important ways, creation accounts of ancient Near Eastern religions. In these accounts the stone image (idol) of a king was placed in the kingdom's temples. The king was said to be the image, an idol of the god, over whose kingdom he ruled.

The biblical account of creation depicts *the whole earth as God's cosmic temple*, his dwelling place. And here he places humankind, created in his image, at the very center in the garden. "While pagan temples held lifeless images at the center, God put his own holy living image in the middle of his cosmic temple of creation. The holiest place in this cosmic temple was the Garden where God began to dwell with his people."[2]

> Then God said, "Let us make man in our image, after our likeness. And let them have dominion over the fish of the sea and over the birds of the heavens and over the livestock and over all the earth and over every creeping thing that creeps on the earth."
>
> So, God created man in his own image, in the image of God he created him; male and female he created them.
>
> And God blessed them. And God said to them, "Be fruitful and multiply and fill the earth and subdue it, and have dominion over the fish of the sea and over the birds of the heavens

---

1. McKnight, *King Jesus Gospel*, dust jacket.
2. Hood, *Imitating God*, 42.

and over every living thing that moves on the earth." Genesis 1:26-28

God created us in his likeness to fill the earth as his living images:

1. To collectively rule for him as *kings* over the earth. As God's vice-regents we were to care for the earth according to his good and righteous will. *This was our royal calling.*

2. To radiate his character to one another so that we would live and rule over the earth according to his will. *This was our prophetic calling.*

3. Finally, God created us to mediate his Presence to one another. We were created as *reflective beings,* and what we reflect shows what we ultimately give our lives to. In the beginning it was God in the beauty of his creation.[3] *This was our priestly purpose.*

"Every aspect of human identity, destiny and mission finds its genesis here in the Bible's opening chapter: humans are God's royal representatives, imaging the one true God as we rule over the world he created."[4]

God created us to enjoy his Presence in the beauty of his creation, to rule for him over his creation according to his good will, and to reflect his being to one another as his image-bearers. This was God's good will for us, and this was our good. This is what it meant to be fully alive as humans: enjoying God, enjoying one another, and enjoying the richness of God's world.

But something went wrong. . . .

HUMANITY USURPS THEIR ROLE

As the Genesis account teaches, we took on the role of rebels, seeking to control our destiny and rule over God's world the way we wanted. We defaced God's image in us, alienated ourselves from God, and strayed from our calling on earth. So, we deconstructed the world as it was meant to be. Instead of loving and imaging God to one another, instead of caring for God's creation and one another, we began to love ourselves and exploit God's creation for our own gain.

---

3. Beale, *We Become What We Worship*, 22, quoted in Hood, *Imitating God*, 44.
4. Hood, *Imitating God*, 20.

Turning from God, we sought to be humans in our own way. We tend to devote ourselves to what we want out of life. We tend to think we know best how life works, not considering what God says.

Our broken relationships, conflicts, quarrels, and the world's never-ending wars are largely due to wanting our own way. While we may praise the independent human spirit, we don't know what it means to be human, so we fail to fully live as human beings.

Yet, deep within us we know something is wrong, something is missing. Someone is missing. We are restless and keep longing, keep searching, not knowing for what. We keep filling the hole in our souls with whatever we set our eyes on, for we are not drinking from the well God has provided.

GOD CHOOSES ISRAEL TO BE HIS IMAGE-BEARERS ON EARTH

God, the Gracious One, patiently works to restore us to his image and our full humanity to rule over his creation. "The mission of Adam and Eve and humanity—numerical and geographic expansion, worship in the presence of God, rule over God's world in his authority—is also given to Israel, Abraham's family, as the people through whom the nations of the world would find blessing and the presence of God."[5] God made them his sons, his image-bearers, *giving them* the *same tasks he gave to the first humans.*

God gave them *a land,* representative of all the earth. He came to dwell among them in their *temple,* representative of Eden. He gave them the *law* to live by his will on earth. In short, Israel was to reflect the character and Presence of God to each other and to the nations. They were to be a kingdom of royal priests to the nations.

Israel was chosen as an instrument to a much greater end than itself, to be a light to the nations of God's will on earth. But the Old Testament account shows how Israel with almost all her kings, prophets, and priests leading the way, failed at their calling just like the first humans.

Not only did they not fulfill their tasks as image-bearers, but instead they often worshiped the idols, the images of the gods also worshiped by the nations they were chosen to bless. "They never even entertained,

---

5. Hood, *Imitating God,* 45.

except in brief poetic moments in prophets like Isaiah, governing the world on God's behalf."[6]

The mission of God remained unfulfilled until he narrowed it down to one human being.

GOD CHOOSES A SON OF DAVID TO FULFILL HIS MISSION

God, the Gracious One, still patiently worked to restore humans to their calling. Despite Israel's failure, he promised them he would give a descendant of their King David an eternal kingdom to rule over. In time this King became identified with the Messiah, who would defeat the powers of evil on earth and rule over God's kingdom with justice and righteousness. The descendant of David is, of course, Jesus, the promised Messiah, who now rules in God's Presence over all creation as his vice-regent.

When we read about Jesus, his message of the kingdom of God, and his mission to make it once again flourish on earth, it is important to remember that *God has never changed his original plan for humans to thrive by reflecting his likeness and ruling over the earth for him.* "The great drama in Scripture resolves around the question, when will humans be the rulers God intended them to be?"[7]

Jesus is not only proclaimed as Lord and Messiah in the New Testament but as the one true image of God.[8] In the man Jesus we finally see the image of God fully restored in a human being. In Jesus we see "man as man was meant to be."[9]

Paul writes he is "the image of God" so that we see "the glory of God in the face of Jesus Christ," and as we see the glory of the Lord Jesus, we "are being transformed into the same image from one degree of glory to another" (2 Cor 3:18; 4:4–6). Jesus is the image of God, and as we become more and more like him, we, too, reflect God's image on earth, as in the beginning.

As God was pleased to first dwell in the garden among humans then dwell among Israel in their temple, so now *all the fullness of God came*

---

6. McKnight, *King Jesus Gospel*, 150.
7. Hood, *Imitating God*, 63.
8. McKnight, *King Jesus Gospel*, 139.
9. Williams, *Far as the Curse Is Found*, cited in Hood, *Imitating God*, 62.

to dwell (temple) in Jesus, most likely at his baptism, when the Spirit was given to him without measure (Col 1:19; John 3:34).

Paul writes that even now, "the whole fullness of deity dwells bodily" after Jesus' resurrection and exaltation to the right hand of God (Col 2:9). Then he quickly adds that believers have come to fullness in him, the head over all things (Col 2:10). The image of God, the reign of God, is first seen in Jesus and then in us.

Jesus was the second Adam. Adam as Adam was meant to be, and Israel as Israel was meant to be. Bearing the very likeness of God on earth, Jesus restores the image of God on earth so that we also "bear the image of the man from heaven" and so be like God (1 Cor 15:49).

As a prophet Jesus teaches God's will and proclaims the arrival of God's kingdom to earth. *As a priest* God came to dwell uniquely in Jesus so that he revealed the holiness of God, became a holy sacrifice for sins, and now appeals to God on our behalf. Because of his humble obedience to God, Jesus was *exalted as Lord to rule* over God's creation (Phil 2:5–11).

Finally, what God created humanity to be is now fully realized in Jesus. "What the apostles were telling us is that the assignment God gave Adam, the assignment transferred to Abraham, Israel, and Moses, and then to David has now been transferred to and perfectly fulfilled by Jesus."[10]

Jesus "does for humans what Israel was supposed to do for them, *and thereby launches God's project of new creation, the new world over which he already reigns as king.* This is the great narrative, the true Pauline Adam-and-Christ story, and we need to learn how to tell it and live it."[11]

God's purposes have been fulfilled in the perfect man, Jesus (Heb 5:8–9), but what about the rest of humanity? How can we reflect God's image on earth? How can we live fully as a new humanity, carrying out the tasks God gave us as his image-bearers?

Something drastic must happen, for we still live as rebels, building our alternative kingdoms on earth. A death, a cleansing, and a rebirth with power are necessary if we are to join Jesus in showing the world what God is like and how he wants us to live on earth.

This is where in the story of the Bible we pick up *the six facets of the gospel, the six key events in Christ's life proclaimed in Acts* (described in the following section). Together they make up the gospel of the kingdom proclaimed first by Jesus, then by Peter and Paul.[12]

---

10. McKnight, *King Jesus Gospel*, 139.
11. Wright, "Paul's Use of Adam," quoted in Walton, *Lost World*, 57.
12. See chapter five, "Peter's Sermon at Pentecost," for further explanation.

JOINED TO JESUS AS A NEW HUMANITY

Crucial as it is, the gospel does not begin and end with the death of Jesus. It begins with *the Spirit-empowered life of Jesus*, who "went about doing good and healing all who were oppressed by the devil, for God was with him" (Acts 10:38). The Spirit-empowered deeds of Jesus in restoring the sick, the possessed, the sinner, and the oppressed show us God's will to restore broken humanity and what the image of God is to look like in humanity. *This is the first key event in the story of Jesus, the gospel.*

The life of Jesus climaxes with *his death, the second and a most central event in the story of Jesus*. By his death Jesus cleanses us, makes us holy in order that God may once again dwell in and among us. And by his death Jesus breaks the power of sin over us so that we can become like him, living images of God filling the earth everywhere for all to see.

The grave could not hold Jesus. *God raised him from the dead, a third crucial event in the gospel story*. Jesus rose from the dead as the Firstborn of a new humanity, a new creation. The resurrection proved that Jesus was God's chosen Messiah and that his life and teachings were God's way to remake a broken world.

When Jesus is exalted by God to rule as Lord, he is then qualified[13] *to receive the Spirit from the Father more fully than at his baptism. Now saturated with the Spirit (1 Cor 15:45), he pours out Spirit on his disciples, the fourth event in the story of Jesus (Acts 2:33)*. By the Spirit, God comes to dwell in and among us, as he had in the beginning.

The Spirit works deeply in our hearts to transform us into the image of God (2 Cor 3:17–18; 4:4). We may not always recognize it, but the Spirit works quietly in us each day to make us like God—through trials, prayer, words of Scripture, the example of others, and all of life's circumstances.

We have now come to one of the most important questions we can ask: what does it look like to be God's image in the world? It looks like Jesus! He was the first human to fully live in perfect godlikeness on earth. We are called to be imitators of Jesus and so fill the world again with the image of God.

The most important way we can grow into God's likeness is to saturate ourselves with the life and teachings of Jesus recorded in the Gospels. To believe in Jesus means to be his disciple. And to be a disciple at the time of Jesus meant to give complete allegiance to one's rabbi, observing

---

13. McKnight, *King Jesus Gospel*, 121.

how he lived, learning his teachings by heart in order to be like him and spread his message beyond one's community.

This is why the apostles emphasize the Spirit-filled life of Christ as part of the gospel (the first truth of the gospel). *The risen Lord Jesus gives us the Spirit so that we will live the life he lived by the Spirit.* In the Gospels we read of Jesus' humility; the selfless pouring out of his life in love for others; his suffering to fulfill the purposes of God; his anointing by God to rescue and restore the ostracized, the lost, the lonely, and the lowly.

He loved the alien, the sinner, and sought out the most vulnerable. He rejected the temptations of the devil to establish an alternative kingdom to God's. In all this and so much more he revealed what God is like. To see him is to see God, he boldly claimed. Jesus restored the image of God on earth.

His life is to be our life, his story our story, his image our image. This is the point of gospel; this is the goal of our salvation.

The core of godlikeness is found in the Sermon on the Mount, where Jesus teaches us to love, pray for, and actively do good to even our enemies (Matt 5:43–48; Luke 6:27–36). Instead of paying back those who have hurt us, breaking off contact with them, we seek to break the cycle of enmity by praying for them, finding ways to do them good and so make peace as best we can.

Such unnatural, supernatural responses of generous love are what Jesus means when he says *we are to be perfect as our heavenly Father is perfect* (Matt 5:48). This does not mean moral perfection, but it does mean we grow and grow so that our lives become characterized by generous undeserved love to others, even our enemies. In this way, as sons, we image our Father, who shows undeserved love to the ungrateful and wicked (Luke 6:35–36).

Learning from Jesus, Paul also emphasizes practicing Christ's kind of love to grow into God's image. He says, "Be imitators of God, as beloved children, and live in love as Christ loved us and gave himself up for us . . ." (Eph 5:1–2).

For me this is the hardest part of following Jesus, but I work at it because I know it is the world's, my world's, greatest need. When I find myself weary and in conflict with others, I often cry out to the Lord for strength to love as he loves, and he always gives me the strength to love.

We are to "bear the weight of others' errors, absorbing blows, turning cheeks, forgiving grievances, surrendering bitterness and vengeance."[14] Such unnatural, supernatural generous love reflects the heart of God, radiates his image to the world, and helps remake the world.

Then the gospel teaches that when God exalted Jesus to his Presence, he made Jesus Lord over all. Jesus received a new status, the honored position of Lord over all at his exaltation. He did not simply return to his pre-incarnation position. This is *the fifth major event in the story of Jesus*. When God exalted Jesus to his right hand as Lord, we "finally had the king the earth needed."[15]

Beginning with Gen 1, the Scriptures anticipate humans once again ruling for God on earth. Now the apostles proclaim that a descendent of King David, that is, one of his flesh and blood, rules in God's Presence as his Vice Regent on earth.

Jesus succeeded where all others failed. Paul writes that Jesus is the second Adam, a man from heaven who at his resurrection became "a life-giving Spirit," anointed to breathe God's new creation into his followers (1 Cor 15:45–47). The new creation is birthed through the new man, the man Jesus Christ our Lord, the firstborn of a restored humanity.

God has enthroned Jesus to be Lord as "the true human who perfectly bore the divine presence and carried out the divine will."[16] Again, it is important to embrace the full humanity of Jesus. I emphasize Jesus' humanity because many have so emphasized deity that they have neglected his humanity.

But the gospel doesn't work, God's way of restoring humans to his image to rule on earth doesn't work, with a Jesus who walks a foot above the earth. Jesus is "the man of heaven" (1 Cor 15: 47–48) yet fully human as Messiah and Lord, leading the way as the firstborn of a new humanity.

Jason Hood underscores the importance of Jesus' humanity in fulfilling other titles used for him. "If the significance of Jesus' humanity is often not appreciated, his status as a human king is also underplayed. Terms like *Messiah* (Christ), *Lord*, and *Son of God* tend to be used without regard for the royal status those terms originally carried."[17]

Jesus is exalted as Lord to God's right hand as the man Jesus of Nazareth, attested by God (Acts 2:22). Jesus became fully human and forever

---

14. Beale, *We Become What We Worship*, 22, quoted in Hood, *Imitating God*, 44.
15. McKnight, *King Jesus Gospel*, 152.
16. Hood, *Imitating God*, 118.
17. Hood, *Imitating God*, 62.

remains fully human (now with a glorified, resurrected body) at God's right hand. When Jesus is enthroned, what is new "is not that God is on the throne in a new way, but that a human is finally enthroned with him."[18]

The gospel teaches that God will send Jesus back *to justly judge the world, the final and future event of the gospel.* Paul told those gathered to hear his message in Athens that God "has set a day when he will judge the world with justice by the man he has appointed" (Acts 17:31).

This is good news, the gospel. It is good news because our risen Lord will banish all evil, all cruelty, all oppression, and all injustice from the world so that everywhere we will see and experience God's love, God's joy, and God's peace. Only then will the earth be fully and forever restored, filled with the glory of God from sea to sea. Only then will humans rule with Jesus over the earth for God.

The last chapter of the Bible describes the climax of history with a restored humanity on a new earth. We read that Jesus has made us "to be a kingdom and priests serving God" and reigning on earth (Rev 5:10). We read that when we see the face of God, we will then fully reflect his image for his name, that his image will be placed on our foreheads. And so, we will live with God and the Lamb in the beauty of a restored earth (Rev 22:1–4).

Everywhere we look we will experience only light, love, and joy in God and the Lamb and in each other in the beauty of God's new creation.

As said earlier, Luke ended Acts somewhat abruptly, with the expectation that the disciples would continue the mission of God. What he has written in his Gospel and now Acts has equipped them to do so. I hope that what I have written on Acts will be of benefit for your journey. I now offer a few brief additional suggestions.

For those of us who have been taught a reduced gospel focused mainly on Jesus' death for our sins, easy to explain in a few minutes, the six truths of the full gospel may seem like too much to learn and share. But I assure you, it is not. In fact, understanding the full story of the gospel has made it much easier for me to talk about Jesus—and much more often.

Previously I thought I had to have (or force!) an opportunity to talk about our sin, our separation from God, and Jesus as our Savior. That was awkward, even scary, to say to someone at work, a neighbor, or someone sitting next to me at a coffee shop. No wonder there is so much fear in witnessing.

18. Hood, *Imitating God*, 63.

Then I learned while reading Scot McKnight's book *The King Jesus Gospel* that whenever I say something about Jesus, I witness about him. For Jesus is the gospel. Obviously, there will be much more to share and discuss, just as with Jesus when he proclaimed the good news about himself and the kingdom of God.

I go to the same coffee shop in my neighborhood every day to write. Often someone next to me will ask what I'm writing about. I love that question! Most often I say that while I am uncomfortable with much organized Christianity (most people are where I live) I am fascinated with Jesus and try the best I can to follow his teachings. This puts Jesus at the center, his whole life, and eliminates the need to defend Christianity. It's not the whole story of the gospel, but it often leads to further conversations.[19]

Knowing that *I am always an image-bearer* also emboldens me as a witness. Paul speaks of us as the aroma of Christ and a message from God not written in print but the Spirit (2 Cor 2:14—3:3). In most circumstances in our culture, it can be wise to first let others see God in you before you speak of him.

My philosophy of witnessing has become quite simple. I first ask the Spirit each morning to awaken my heart to the love and Presence of God and to be obedient to him, drinking throughout the day from the fountain of love. Then, when I walk out the door, I know something of God's life and love (his image!) will be seen in me, and I'm eager to talk about him. I have also cut back on church activities so that I can spend more time around those who do not yet know God.

To this I also suggest learning the six truths of the gospel and discussing them with another believer. This gives more confidence and helps you to speak naturally. Normally, we will say something about the beauty of Jesus and then, depending on the response, continue with what is most natural.

Whatever the response, the person will know you love Jesus, and the Spirit will stir up what they may have left or what they are looking for.

---

19. Writing about Jesus in coffee shops the past fourteen years has opened countless natural conversations to talk about him. So, whatever your occupation, I encourage you to take a pen and pad with the New Testament to your local coffee shop and take notes as you read about Jesus in Mark, the shortest gospel. Then when someone asks you what you do, you can say, "I'm a student or a teacher or a musician, and while I'm uncomfortable with much organized Christianity, I'm fascinated with Jesus and trying to learn more about him." This has worked for me, and I believe it can for you. Give it a try for a few months. I guarantee you that the Lord will honor your faith.

No word about the Lord is ever in vain. And they will be watching you! Ready to talk again another time.

As I learned the story of the full, robust gospel, I began to see how radically different it was from what Christianity means to most Christians. I was a believer and loved God, but I began to see that there was so much more to being a disciple of Jesus. This was like an awakening.

I journaled the full, robust gospel:

- Builds on the story of *the entire Bible.*
- *Speaks to all areas of our damaged world,* not just our sin problem.
- Because it speaks to all areas of our broken world, it is relevant to *all of life.*
- Because it is relevant to all of life, *it speaks to the longings of people.*
- It thus becomes *a point of contact in conversation.* We can ask, What do you think is wrong with our world? What can we do about it?
- By making it clear that we are not trying to convert people to the Christian religion but inviting them to life with Jesus in the kingdom of God, *we disarm and defuse possible criticisms.*
- *The church then is seen as relevant to impacting society.*
- The full, robust gospel *begins to feel like good news,* something worth laying down our lives for.
- *It emboldens our witness as we talk about Jesus* and life with him in the kingdom of God, not only salvation from our sins.
- We are called to take up, with Jesus leading the way, the assignments God gave to Adam and Eve.
- *We begin to long for the reappearing of Jesus,* our King, to make all things new.

Appendix 1

The Danger of Mixing Culture with the Gospel

WHEN ESUGA AND I visited a Jewish souvenir shop in Old Jerusalem we had an engaging conversation with the owner, who frequently met with Christian leaders visiting Israel. Towards the end of our conversation, he made a comment I could not forget, a comment that made me think about Paul and the relevance of Acts.

While he expressed an openness to the ethical teachings of Jesus, he quickly dismissed Paul's teaching. Since more customers were pouring into the shop and we left Jerusalem the next day, I was never able to ask him what he didn't like about Paul. But my guess was that it was Paul's teaching that gentiles did not have to adopt Jewish culture based on their law and traditions in order to know Israel's God.

Why do I bring this up now at the end of this book? Think of where our world would be now if gentiles throughout the world had been forced to live by the laws and traditions of Israel to be saved. Given the deeply entrenched idolatry in the Roman Empire, the monotheism and obedience to the Way of Jesus would not have spread as it did. And, of course, it was Paul who led the charge in freeing life with God through Jesus from the requirements of adopting Jewish culture.

The problem Paul faced has continued even into our very own culture. *For whenever there is a dominant culture that embraces the gospel, the tendency is to blend that culture's preferences and values into what it means to follow Jesus. And when we do that, we limit the gospel mainly to those who favor our subculture's preferences and values!*

This is a bit tricky. Believers are called to live and speak the gospel into their culture with prayers that the gospel will change their culture's beliefs and values for the better. And patriotism, loving the culture we grow up in, is good and normal, but we must be careful not to assume that because the majority in our nation identify themselves as Christians that we have the privileged position to make our culture the official culture of the country.

Russell Moore points out that some would argue much of white American evangelicalism is built more on culture than the Bible. It was "built from the beginning on nationalism, racism, militarism, misogyny, populism, or right-wing politics."[1] Over this was glued the veneer of "biblical" beliefs and practices.

This may be an overstatement, but there is more truth to it than we would like to admit. As Moore points out, "*Most people are shaped by cultures and subcultures, not by theological abstracts.*"[2] People raise their hand to be born again, but rather than having their hearts and minds transformed by the teaching of Jesus and the apostles, they continue to conform uncritically to the ideas of the country they grew up in (Rom 12:2).

American exceptionalism, the belief that America is a nation uniquely chosen and favored by God, is deeply woven into the fabric of the American psyche and influences our politics and our views of other ethnicities and cultures and shapes what we call Christianity.

American exceptionalism is the mother of Christian nationalism. In its stricter meaning, Christian nationalism is the belief that our country should be *defined as* a Christian nation and that *the government should promote our Christian culture*. More and more religious and political leaders are embracing Christian nationalism, with six in ten Christians now saying we should be a Christian nation. While they may not all hold to the stricter meaning of legislating Christian morality and Christians holding a privileged position in our country, Christian nationalists are on the rise.

While we lament the secular trend in our nation, the answer is not to legislate morality, or even to establish it by force as was attempted on

---

1. Moore, *Losing Our Religion*, 14.
2. Moore, *Losing Our Religion*, 14. Italics mine.

January 6, 2021. In general, this has been the practice of Islam in the past and the more militant Islamists in the present. But Jesus calls us to lay down our swords and persuade others with love, even to the point of suffering.

As Russell Moore points out, "Christian nationalism cannot turn back secularism, because it is just another form of it,"[3] for it fights the powers of this world with their own weapons rather than Christ's.

Distinguishing the gospel of Jesus from popular Christian culture has been especially relevant to my wife and me as we have engaged in respectful witness with Muslims the past fifteen years. Very early in our work we learned from a seasoned leader why many Muslims find it difficult to hear the pure good news about Jesus. He illustrated his point with a set of boxes stacked inside each other like Russian babushka dolls. What, he asked, do Muslims see when we invite them to become Christians? They may first see a box painted with an American flag on it as God's favored nation. Inside that box they may find a box painted with Israel's flag alongside the Bible. Then inside that box they may find one with Jesus standing among the all-white founders of America with his hand on our constitution. Still deeper they finally find a box with Jesus painted on it. But his robe is an American flag. They conclude that Jesus is an American God and close their ears to our witness.

Sadly, dangerously, wedding our Christian culture to the gospel can keep people from seeing the beauty of Jesus and his gospel.

---

3. Moore, *Losing Our Religion*, 14, 120.

Appendix 2

Paul, the Artisan, Working with Leather

YOUNG PAUL'S FAMILY MAY have owned a large textile business in Tarsus which also made products from leather as part of the family business. He likely learned to work with leather from his father in his youth in Tarsus and was able to make not only tents but also shoes, awnings, and other items from leather.[1] His father taught him "how to cut the leather pieces so that their placement would take advantage of the natural strengths of the leather and thus best withstand strains and pulling. An apprentice like Paul would have also learned how to sew these leather pieces together."[2]

As a potter who works with clay, I am fascinated with Paul working with leather. And as a hiker, I like to think that he made the bag he carried his clothes in when traveling and the tent he may have had to sleep in at times. I imagine sitting in his shop under a leather awning he has made to protect him and his customers from the blazing Mediterranean sun.

While some shops, like sculptors and metalsmiths, were "dirty, noisy and potentially dangerous," as a leather worker, Paul's "shop was more like a shoemaker's, which could be quiet and allow extensive conversation (with customers and other shop workers) without distracting one from one's work."[3]

---

1. Keener, *Acts, Vol. 3*, 2734.
2. Hock, *Social Context of Paul's Ministry*, quoted by Keener, *Acts*, 2730.
3. Keener, *Acts*, 2735.

While he works on an order, he talks of life, philosophies, and especially the Messiah of God coming in the man Jesus. People would ask questions: Where are you from? Why are you laboring in the sun making tents if you are from Tarsus? Shouldn't you be teaching somewhere? Paul shares he will teach tonight. Some will come and listen, and inroads are made to the Gentile community.

The basic tools for working with leather were "oil and blacking or the leather; knives, awls, and sharpening stones; a table and stool," along with benches for customers.[4] When on the move Paul normally walked twenty miles a day, and as all hikers know, he would not have wanted to carry any extra weight while trekking the mountains of Asia Minor. But since working with leather was his main source of support (along with gifts from "churches") and he could set up shop in almost any city, he likely took his most valuable, lighter tools with him on his travels.

When he arrived at a city, he could then purchase the leather and tools necessary for his work. Soldiers were everywhere and always in need of shoes and tents for travel. And sailors needed tents for lodging until their ship left port and the wealthy purchased tents for shade on ships and while visiting festivals.[5]

---

4. Keener, *Acts*, 2736.
5. Keener, *Acts*, 2734.

Bibliography

Alexandros, Megas. "The Challenge of Crossing the Cilician Gates." Megas Alexandros (blog). Jun. 9, 2016. https://makedonia-alexandros.blogspot.com/search?q=Cilician+gate.
Barnett, Paul. *Jesus and the Rise of Early Christianity*. Downers Grove, IL: InterVarsity, 1999.
Beale, Greg. *We Become What We Worship: A Biblical Theology of Idolatry*. Downers Grove, IL: InterVarsity Academic, 2008.
Beers, Holly. *A Week in the Life of a Greco-Roman Woman*. Downers Grove, IL: InterVarsity, 2019.
Beitzel, Barry J., ed. *Lexham Geographic Commentary on Acts Through Revelation*. Bellingham, WA: Lexham, 2019.
Blenkinsopp, Joseph, et al. *The New Interpreter's Bible*. Nashville: Abingdon, 2002.
Bock, Darrell L. *Acts*. Grand Rapids: Baker Academic, 2007.
Clow, Kate. *The St. Paul Trail*. Istanbul: Upcountry, 2013.
Croy, N. Clayton. "Religion, Personal." In *Dictionary of New Testament Background*, edited by Craig A. Evans and Stanley E. Porter, Jr., 926–31. Downers Grove, IL: InterVarsity, 2000.
DeSilva, David, A. *A Week in the Life of Ephesus*. Downers Grove, IL: InterVarsity, 2020.
Duddleston, Jim. *Why Jesus the Messiah*. Philadelphia: James Duddleston, 2017.
Evans, Craig A., and Stanley E. Porter, Jr., eds. *Dictionary of New Testament Background*. Downers Grove, IL: InterVarsity, 2000.
Eybeschutz, Jonathan. *Ya'arot Devash, Vol. 1*. https://www.hebrewbooks.org/32683.
Franklin, Eric *Christ the Lord: A Study in the Purpose and Theology of Luke-Acts*. London: SPCK, 1975.
Frost, Michael, and Alan Hirsch. *The Shape of Things to Come*. Grand Rapids: Baker, 2013.
Fudge, Edward William, and Robert A. Peterson. *Two Views of Hell: A Biblical and Theological Dialogue*. Downers Grove, IL: InterVarsity, 2000.
Fung, Ronald Y. K. *The Epistle to the Galatians*. Grand Rapids: Eerdmans, 1988.
Garrett, Susan R. *The Demise of the Devil: Magic and the Demonic in Luke's Writings*. Minneapolis: Fortress, 1989.
Gaventa, B. R. *The Acts of the Apostles: New Testament Commentaries*. Nashville: Abington, 2003.

Green, Joel B., et al. *Dictionary of Jesus and the Gospels: A Compendium of Contemporary Biblical Scholarship.* Downers Grove, IL: InterVarsity, 1992.
Hale, John R. *Classical Archeology of Ancient Greece and Rome.* Chantilly, VA: Great Courses, 2006.
Hays, Richard B. *The Moral Vision of the New Testament.* San Francisco: HarperCollins, 1996.
Hock, Ronald F. *The Social Context of Paul's Ministry: Tentmaking and Apostleship.* Philadelphia: Fortress, 1980.
Hood, Jason B. *Imitating God in Christ.* Downers Grove, IL: InterVarsity, 2013.
Jeffers, James S. *The Greco-Roman World of the New Testament Era.* Downers Grove, IL: InterVarsity, 1999.
Johnson, L. T. *The Acts of the Apostles.* Collegeville, MN: Liturgical, 1992.
Keener, Craig. *Acts: An Exegetical Commentary, Vol. 1.* Grand Rapids: Baker Academic, 2012.
———. *Acts: An Exegetical Commentary, Vol. 2.* Grand Rapids: Baker Academic, 2013.
———. *Acts: An Exegetical Commentary, Vol. 3.* Grand Rapids: Baker Academic, 2014.
Krayer, Patrick. "Moving Beyond: Frontier Missions in Our Post-Colonial World." Unpublished article.
Kreider, Allan. *The Patient Ferment of the Early Church.* Grand Rapids: Baker Academic, 2016.
Ladd, George Eldon, *A Theology of the New Testament.* Grand Rapids: Eerdmans, 1975.
Leary, T. J. "Paul's Improper Name." *New Testament Studies* 3 (1992) 467–69. Cited in Ben Witherington III, *The Acts of the Apostles: A Socio-Rhetorical Commentary.* Grand Rapids, MI: Wm. B. Eerdmans, 1998, 402.
Leith, John H., ed. *Creeds of the Churches.* Atlanta: John Knox, 1963.
Magness, Jodi. *The Holy Land Revealed.* Chantilly, VA: Great Courses, 2010.
Marshall, I. Howard. *The Acts of the Apostles.* Grand Rapids: Tyndale, 1980.
McKnight, Scot. *The King Jesus Gospel.* Grand Rapids: Zondervan, 2011.
McRay, J. R. "Caesaria Maritima." In *Dictionary of New Testament Background*, edited by Craig A. Evans and Stanley E. Porter, Jr., 176–77. Downers Grove, IL: InterVarsity, 2000.
Moore, Roger. *Losing Our Religion: An Altar Call for Evangelical Christians.* New York: Sentinel, 2023.
Murphy-O'Connor, Jerome. *St. Paul's Ephesus: Texts and Archaeology.* Collegeville, MN: Liturgical, 2008.
Ogilvie, R. M. *The Romans and Their Gods.* New York: Norton, 1981.
Papandrea, James, L. *A Week in the Life of Rome.* Downers Grove, IL: InterVarsity, 2019.
Pearson, B. W. R. "Antioch Pisidia." In *Dictionary of New Testament Background*, edited by Craig A. Evans and Stanley E. Porter, Jr., 31–34. Downers Grove, IL: InterVarsity, 2000.
Peterson, David. *The Acts of the Apostles.* Grand Rapids: Eerdmans, 2009.
Phillips, Elaine A. "The Geographic Importance of Antioch on the Orontes." In *Lexham Geographic Commentary on Acts Through Revelation*, edited by Barry J. Beitzel, 94–104. Bellingham, WA: Lexham, 2019.
Polhill, J.P. *The Acts of the Apostles.* Grand Rapids: Eerdmans, 2009.
Rowe, C. Kevin. *World Upside Down.* New York: Oxford University Press, 2009.

Schnabel, Eckhard J. "The Topography of Jerusalem in the Book of Acts." In *Lexham Geographic Commentary on Acts Through Revelations*, edited by Barry J. Beitzel, 19–41. Bellingham, WA: Lexham, 2019.

Spencer, F. Scott. *Journeying Through Acts: A Literary Cultural Reading*. Grand Rapids: Baker Academic, 2010.

Stark, Rodney. *The Rise of Christianity*. Princeton, NJ: Princeton University Press. 1996.

Stassen, Glen H., and David P. Gushee. *Kingdom Ethics: Following Jesus in Contemporary Context*. Downers Grove, IL: InterVarsity. 2003.

Stott, John. *The Message of Acts: To the Ends of the Earth*. BST: Bible Speaks Today. Downers Grove, IL: InterVarsity, 1990.

Stutzman, Linford. *Sailing Acts*. Intercourse, PA: Good Books, 2006.

Tannehill, Robert C. *The Narrative Unity of Luke-Acts: A Literary Interpretation*. Minneapolis: Fortress, 1990.

Thompson, Alan J. *The Acts of the Risen Lord*. Downers Grove, IL: InterVarsity, 2011.

Twelftree, G. H. "Sanhedrin." In *Dictionary of Jesus and the Gospels: A Compendium of Contemporary Biblical Scholarship*, edited by Joel B. Green, et al., 728–32. Downers Grove, IL: InterVarsity, 1992.

Wall, Robert W. "The Acts of the Apostles." In *The New Interpreter's Bible, Vol. 10*, edited by Joseph Blenkinsopp, et al., 3–368. Nashville: Abingdon, 2002.

Walton, John H. *The Lost World of Adam and Eve*. Downers Grove, IL: InterVarsity Academic, 2015.

Wangerin, Walter, Jr. *The Book of God*. Grand Rapids: Zondervan, 1996.

Weitzel, Barry J., ed. *Lexham Geographic Commentary on Acts Through Revelations*. Bellingham, WA: Lexham, 2019.

Wilkens, Steve, and Mark L. Stanford. *Hidden Worldviews: Eight Cultural Stories That Shape Our Lives*. Downers Grove, IL: InterVarsity, 2009.

Williams, Michael D. *Far as the Curse Is Found: The Covenant Story of Redemption*. Phillipsburg, NJ: Presbyterian and Reformed, 2005.

Witherington, Ben, III. *The Acts of the Apostles: A Socio-Rhetorical Commentary*. Grand Rapids: Eerdmans, 1998.

———. *New Testament History: A Narrative Account*. Grand Rapids: Baker, 2001.

———. *A Week in the Fall of Jerusalem*. Downers Grove, IL: InterVarsity, 2017.

———. *A Week in the Life of Corinth*. Downers Grove, IL: InterVarsity, 2012.

Wright, N. T. *Acts for Everyone, Part 1*. Louisville: Westminster John Knox, 2008.

———. *Acts for Everyone, Part 2*. Louisville: Westminster John Knox, 2008.

———. *Paul: A Biography*. New York: Harper One, 2018.

———. "Excursus on Paul's Use of Adam." In *The Lost World of Adam and Eve* by John H. Walton, 170–80. Downers Grove, IL: InterVarsity Academic, 2015.

Wright, Paul H. "The Road from Jerusalem to Damascus." In *Lexham Geographic Commentary on Acts Through Revelations*, edited by Barry J. Weitzel, 222–28. Bellingham, WA: Lexham, 2019.

Yamauchi, Edwin. "Synagogues." In *Dictionary of New Testament Background*, edited by Craig A. Evans and Stanley E. Porter, Jr., 1145–53. Downers Grove, IL: InterVarsity, 2000.

www.ingramcontent.com/pod-product-compliance
Lightning Source LLC
Chambersburg PA
CBHW070233230426
43664CB00014B/2287